P9-DCJ-116

ALSO BY ADAM SMITH

The Money Game

Supermoney

Powers of Mind

Paper Money

THE
ROARING

SUMMIT
BOOKS
NEW YORK
LONDON
TORONTO
SYDNEY
TOKYO

'80s

BY
ADAM SMITH

Summit Books
Simon & Schuster Building
Rockefeller Center
1230 Avenue of the Americas
New York, New York 10020

Designed by Irving Perkins Associates
Manufactured in the United States of America

10 9 8 7 6 5 4 3 2 1

Library of Congress Cataloging in Publication Data

Smith, Adam
  The roaring '80s.

  1. Economic history—1971–   . 2. United States—
Economic conditions—1981–   . I. Title.
HC59.S556   1988   330.973'0927   88-29480
ISBN 0-671-44788-2

Some of the material in this book has previously appeared in different form in
New York Magazine and *Esquire*.

CONTENTS

Preface   11

1. Debt: A System Loosed from Moorings   13
Mr. Volcker Reflects on a Singular Turn in History   20
Was Kwartler a Chump, or Ahead of His Time?   29
The Day They Sold the Navy   35

2. Several Americas   41
"Just Tell Me What I Did Wrong!"   44
Peter Drucker: The Best Opportunity Since 1910   58
William H. Whyte and the Decline of Fear   61
Liz Claiborne's Secret   66
Working Women   70
Newly Blonde Women, Hirsute Men   77

3. Confucian Capitalism: The Rise of the Rim   83
The Rise of the Rim   85
*If Japan Becomes the New America, What Happens to the Old
One?   86*

Ezra Vogel: Japan as No. 1   93
Theory Z: "Don't Be Rikutsupoi"   97
*If the Japanese Made the F-15, Would it Come Out Smaller
and Half the Price?   102*
Significant Signs: Robots, Skis, Saturdays   106
What Did Iacocca Do?   111
Carver Mead: Breakthroughs from Chaos   115
Soichiro Honda: "I Am One of MacArthur's Children"   121
Through Japanese Eyes   126
The Japanese Walter Cronkite   134
From MITI to DARPA   139
The Sneaker on the Table   144
A State Goal in China: Fa Chai! Get Rich!   149
Lee Kuan Yew: Surviving on the Rim   154
Confucian Capitalism   159

4.   What Really Governs?   165
This Idea Is Going to Come Back Under Another Name   167
Million-Dollar Wands   172

5.   Slickems   177
Slickems   179
Is the Game Still Kto Kogo?   185

6.   Fortunes   191
T. Boone: Sail Ho!   193
How to Do an LBO   199
*Henry Kravis Would Make $400 Million! Without Lifting
Anything Heavy!   204*
Cycles: "Greed Is Healthy"   209
Why Did Ilan Do It If He Never Took the Money?   214
Crash!   220
*Warren Buffett: Two Billion Dollars, and He Still
Makes It Look So Easy   227*

7.   The Roaring '80s   237
*Why Is One Master's Degree Worth So Much More
Than All the Others?   240*

But What Do Investment Bankers Do?   *244*
"You Ought to Get Rich"   *248*
John Marquand and Yesterday's Yuppies   *252*
Cigar, Champagne, and Sermonette   *256*
Mr. Phillips and the Seven Laws of Money   *259*
Why Mort's Apartment Is Worth $8.5 Million   *263*
Getting Noticed, the Metropolitan Way   *268*
The Closing of the American Mind   *272*
Serious Money   *277*
A Profound Change in World History   *282*

8.   Bad News, Good News   **289**

PREFACE

Decades, of course, do not start and end neatly with years that end in zero, when we use them as a colloquial phrase for an era. What we think of as the '60s began only midway through the decade. So we don't know where this era of easy debt and easy spending will end, even though the first users of the phrase, the Roaring '80s, meant to recall the good times and easy spending of another era, the Roaring '20s.

This book is a walk through a time, based on hundreds of conversations. Some are with officials of state, some with authors, some with steelworkers, some with bankers and scientists. The goal was to understand the economic complexities of our times. Sometimes these conversations began as a magazine essay, sometimes as a television interview, sometimes as notes, waiting to be written. And some relevant conversations never got set down: Senator William Roth, a seatmate on a flight, saying the Kemp–Roth tax cut will stimulate business, "and even more important, it will give Congress less money to spend, and that's the only way to brake the spending of Congress"; Mrs. Thatcher's subminister in London, saying, "We believe the government cannot be responsible for the national happiness, and we believe that is significant.'' ''National happiness'' seemed such an interesting phrase in a time called the Roaring '80s.

I could not have traveled the distance without the help of my television colleagues, magazine editors, and indeed all those who sent me what to read, who read what I wrote, and who helped guide my steps. I owe them all my thanks.

1 DEBT: A SYSTEM LOOSED FROM MOORINGS

L ess than a month before, the stock market had collapsed, the biggest crash since 1929. But this November night, the market crash receded momentarily in the auction room at Sotheby's, on Manhattan's Upper East Side. Many of the 2,200 people were in black tie. They had sat in fashionable restaurants, leafing through the catalogs. John Marion, the auctioneer, son of an auctioneer, chairman of Sotheby's North America, stood in the rosewood preacher's pulpit that had *Sotheby's founded 1744* on the front in metal. It was clear that Marion had a sense of theater, and that he enjoyed his work.

"Lot twenty-five," he said.

Van Gogh's *Irises* is not an overly large painting. It is twenty-eight inches by thirty-six inches. It had been on display for a week. Van Gogh had painted it in 1889 in the garden of the insane asylum at Saint-Paul-de-Mausole, where he was a patient. Joan Payson Whitney, old Standard Oil money, had bought it for $84,000 in 1947.

"What shall we say to start?" said Marion. "Shall we say fifteen million?" The audience murmured.

"I have fifteen million," he said. "Fifteen five, sixteen. Over here, seventeen, eighteen, nineteen, twenty on my left, twenty-one, the phone in front."

Several of the Sotheby's staff, in black tie, were on the phones to bidders.

"Twenty-one in the center, twenty-two, twenty-four, twenty-eight by the two of you, twenty-nine on the far phone."

15

When the bidding went through $40 million, the crowd applauded. At $42 million, there were gasps.

"Forty-eight million."

"Oooooh, eooowwww," said the crowd.

"Against you, in the back. Shall we say fifty million? Forty-nine million, on the far phone."

There was a pause.

"Forty-nine million," said Marion. "Fair warning. Sold for forty-nine million." Marion banged his hammer. The crowd applauded. The action took less than four minutes.

With Sotheby's commission, the painting had sold for $53.9 million. Marion said it had ended up a duel between two telephone bidders. Tom Wolfe, the writer, said that art certified wealth, it provided spiritual legitimacy. "No one in his right mind," he said, "pays this kind of money for something he simply likes."

The sale of *Irises* was the peak of rapidly escalating prices for blue-chip art. The Yasuda Fire and Marine Insurance Company of Japan had paid $39 million for Van Gogh's *Sunflowers*. A Monet which had sold for $3 million only a few years before sold for $24 million.

Sotheby's catalogs included wines and ceramics and sculpture and real estate. You could find Manhattan apartments for $7 million, an East Hampton summer place on the water for $10.6 million, horse farms in Virginia, even an elaborate ski condo in Aspen listed at $22 million.

Where could so much money come from? It was not as if the Spaniards had suddenly discovered the gold of the Incas. No particular individual had found a Spindletop, an elephant-sized oil field. Of course, the country was prosperous and growing, though the growth was sub-par. There are always new fortunes. But $49 million for a painting, $22 million for a ski condo?

The money certainly did not flow evenly. There were small steel towns in Pennsylvania where half the stores on Main Street were boarded up, and some of the oil service towns of Texas had "For Sale" signs in front of every fourth house. Fifty-five percent of American families had zero or negative net worth. Two percent of American families had 54 percent of the total net financial assets.

Flows of money are hard to measure, even with advanced computers. But there was one thing, it was clear, that the United States was producing in abundance: debt.

Debt is an abstraction, and the eyes tend to glaze over with the size of the numbers. The Reagan years added roughly $1 trillion—$1,000,000,000,000—to the national debt, an amount equal to the debt in the first two hundred years of the Republic. The government was the leader, but only one factor. Debt grew faster than the gross national product, GNP, for more than a decade. Debt grew much

Credit Market Debt Outstanding and Market Value of Outstanding Equities, 1960–87 (Dollars in Billions)

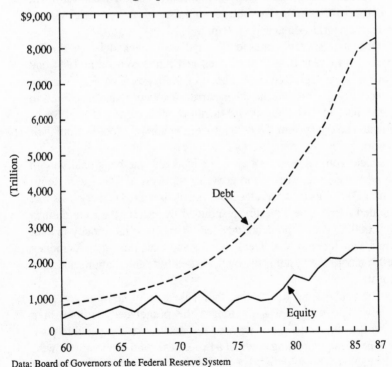

Data: Board of Governors of the Federal Reserve System

faster than corporate profits, debt grew faster than equity. Taking all the households, government, and business, debt rose from $1.2 trillion in 1970 to $8 trillion in 1987.

The attitude toward debt had changed. The inflation of the post-Vietnam years had showed you prospered if you borrowed and could pay back with cheaper dollars. The German word *Schuld,* debt, is the same as guilt, debt as obligation. That sensibility was gone. A new generation grew up that didn't have the fear of debt its grandparents did.

"Willy, we were free and clear, free and clear," said Linda Loman at the gravesite of Willy Loman in Arthur Miller's *Death of a Salesman.* The last mortgage payment had just been made, and they owned the house. The Lomans' grandchildren would have taken debt for granted, and refinanced the house right away.

"It is a system loosed from its moorings," said Henry Kaufman, the former Salomon Brothers economist, of the American—and even the world—financial system.

Once the United States dollar had been backed by gold. The post–World War II system devised at Bretton Woods in 1944 had gold as its centerpiece. One ounce of gold was $35, $35 was one ounce of gold, and all the other currencies were fixed in relation to the dollar. In 1971, faced with a run on dollars, the United States abandoned the system. Not only governments were loosed from their moorings. So were the banks.

Once, you put your money in the bank and the bank paid you up to whatever interest rate the government decreed. That was Regulation Q. But as interest rates rose, people bought Treasury bills that yielded more. The Treasury responded by raising the minimum to $10,000, and entrepreneurs devised an end run: the money market fund, which could pool Treasury bills and bank deposits. As money left the banking system, the banks asked for deregulation, and they got it.

The bankers bid for money, the bankers sold the money aggressively. The banker was no longer the prunefaced Scrooge in a pinstripe suit, thinking of ways to say no. Banks competed to push out the money, creating credit at a faster pace than economic growth. The banker who sold the loan was promoted for creating the fees. If something went wrong, some time later, that would not be on his watch, most probably.

Within a decade, there was a dazzling array of financial innovation. Willy Loman's mortgage was a fixed rate mortgage. Now mortgages floated above the rates of the day, at variable rates. Was money regulated within national borders? The Euromarket sprang up, a wonderful country called Offshore, a big rock candy mountain where there were no rules at all because there was no country. (Ironically, this dynamic tool of capitalism was invented by the Russians. The Moscow Narodny Bank kept its dollars in London, fearful of the political risks of having them on deposit in the United States. Then it began to lend them, and then others lent offshore dollars, especially when, in the '60s, the United States tried to impose cross-border restrictions.)

In the global market, you could buy "shoguns"—U. S.-dollar bonds issued in Japan—and "sushis"—Eurobonds issued by the Japanese. There were "down unders" and "kiwis," the Euro–Australian and Euro–New Zealand bonds. There were dual-currency yen bonds, and ECU-denominated bonds, and zero-coupon convertibles, and options on Eurodollar futures, and range forward contracts that specified a range of exchange rates on expiration dates. Dazzling!

The creative juices of the Elizabethans may have gone into sonnets; the creative juices of the '80s went into thinking up new securities. Guido Carli, the former governor of the Bank of Italy, said the United States had found a wonderful way of living. "It imports machinery and cars, and exports securities, like bonds."

On the domestic scene it became popular to speak of things being "securitized." Go to your dealer and buy a car, go to the bank and get a loan against the car, pay the bank each month. But no longer does the bank sit quietly, checking off the interest payments. The bank sells the auto loan, the auto loans are packed together, pooled, traded, leveraged—the acronym, of course is CARS—new companies spring up, which themselves sell debentures, the proceeds of which go to more CARS.

One man's debt is another man's credit. Put it in the bank, you can write checks against it. Merchants will sell to you as long as you're not bankrupt.

The tax code reflects the process of bargaining in Congress, and some lobbies are more powerful than others, but we assume the tax code reflects the general wishes of the people, or we would board the ships in Boston harbor and throw the tea into the water. The tax code says, in general, that you can deduct the cost of debt. The government will help you borrow. There is no matching reward for investing, for building equity; in fact, you will pay a tax on the appreciation if you trade one form of equity for another.

The people who bought and sold and traded all the paper became prosperous, if not vastly rich. The firm of Drexel Burnham popularized a whole new tier of debt—"junk bonds." A firm that traded government bonds, like Salomon Brothers, had an extra trillion dollars' worth of bonds to trade. As Everett Dirksen once said, a billion here, a billion there, before you know it, it adds up to real money. The chairman of Salomon, John Gutfriend, was featured on two magazine covers the same week, mostly for the style of his wife's parties, the green spun-sugar apples for dessert, the varieties of caviar, the Rothschilds as new friends. Wall Street needed new MBAs to crunch the numbers for all the mergers and acquisitions deals that were now possible with easier debt. The new grads could be in six figures the year after they left school. The Wall Street law firms paid $72,000 the first day out of law school to the best and brightest who could write the twentieth-century sonnets—the M&A agreements, the clauses in the CARS.

The apartments on Central Park West were at least fifty years old. In 1975 some of them sold for $75,000; in 1987, they were between $1 million and $2.5 million. San Francisco, Beverly Hills, Kalorama in Washington, D.C., were not far behind.

Van Gogh was a brilliant artist even when *Irises* sold for $84,000. The denominator had changed.

But *Irises,* and the apartments, did not reflect a runaway inflation, as one might think at first. After 1982, the '80s were a time of declining interest rates, of *disinflation,* even though there was an extra $1 trillion of debt. That wasn't what the economists said would happen. Nor would anyone have thought it possible in 1979, when the inflation rate was 13 percent. The Consumer Price Index, calculated at 100 for 1967, was 217 that year. Never in peacetime had prices gone up so fast. It was hard to remember that in the early '60s, real interest rates—the rate of interest less inflation—were only 1 percent. But the guns-and-butter inflation of the Vietnam years and the oil shocks of the '70s produced a psychology that expected prices to keep rising.

One check on inflation was that manufacturing jobs could be taken overseas. It wasn't just that the Japanese could produce reliable, cheap automobiles. American companies could set up factories in Hong Kong, Taiwan, Singapore, Korea, Malaysia—and that put a lid on labor costs. The slogan in the electronics industry was "automate, emigrate, or evaporate."

But what really cracked the price inflation was the actions of a single institution, the Federal Reserve, and mostly, a single individual.

Mr. Volcker Reflects on a Singular Turn in History

He was called "the second most powerful man in the country" so often it became a kind of cliché. His picture graced the covers of newsmagazines. When he appeared before Congress, he was treated as an oracle who spoke in ambiguities, penumbral phrases rolling toward the bench of congressional inquisitors amid clouds of cigar smoke.

Paul Volcker was the strongest Federal Reserve chairman in a generation—perhaps in half a century. I have known other chairmen. Arthur Burns was a Columbia professor who parted his hair in the middle. G. William Miller was a nice businessman who got lost. But Volcker trained all his life for the job—from research assistant to undersecretary of the Treasury—and when he got it, he was like the eager West Pointer who serves all over the world for forty years and is then handed an army. He even brought a commanding physical presence to bear—a deep baritone voice in a six-foot-seven-inch frame.

The Federal Reserve, it is safe to say, is not well understood. It is our central bank, the "lender of last resort," established in 1913 to avoid panics like the one in 1907, and most Americans take it for granted. It is supposed to make sure the banking system doesn't go down the tube, although in the Depression it almost failed at that. The Fed is supposed to "lean against the wind," curbing excesses in one direction or another. This creates paranoia in some right-wing Americans, who think of the Fed as a focal point of conspiracy, the place where "they"—the Powers or the Illuminati or the Zionist International—hang out.

The usual metaphor given to the operations of the Federal Reserve is hydraulic, as if it were a Bunyanesque plumber, or operations engineer, and the money and credit flowed through a tangle of pipes. Too fast a flow, and the Fed could pull the valves that tightened; not enough, and it could loosen. But the metaphor is necessarily inexact. John Maynard Keynes, writing in *A Treatise on Money*, compared the money supply to water in a reservoir. It was the function of the central bank to maintain the proper level of water. Yet there were many factors that could change the level of the reservoir "besides how much water is poured in—for example, the natural rainfall, evaporation, leakage, and the habits of the users of the system." Even as the Bunyan plumber, the Fed would have some problems, because its gauges measure what happened weeks ago, and the pressures have different intensities, as if part fluid and part gas.

Normally, the Fed can use several actions and several goals. The monetarists said there was no need for such complexity. All that was necessary, said Milton Friedman, the leading monetarist economist, was to keep the money supply constant, humming along at an increase of 3 to 5 percent a year. No hands, no policies, just an oil change every ten thousand miles. In practice, a monetarist policy produces volatile interest rates. You say, "We'll hold the *supply* of money steady, and interest rates can go wherever they are taken by all the factors that play on them—they'll find their own level."

In the financial community, newsletters and consultant services sell their interpretations of the Fed's numbers—even of the phrases used by the chairman—like Roman necromancers reading chicken entrails, or the court physicians sniffing the urine of the emperor of China. Awesome powers are attributed to the Fed, especially the ability to change interest rates. With the leverage now available through futures contracts, even a flicker of movement in Fed policy can produce profit or loss in the hundreds of millions of dollars. A few months after Volcker left the Fed, I had a talk with him. I wanted some insight before his experience of being Fed chairman receded further. In particular, I wanted to know what the Fed's board was thinking back in 1979 when it stopped trying to control interest rates to curb inflation, and instead began to try to control the money supply. Major dissertations have already been written on this shift: Volcker is credited by some with breaking the back of inflation—others accuse him of producing the most severe recession in fifty years. But what is really important is how these decisions are made. I started by asking what it was like when he took office, right after Jimmy Carter appointed him.

"You couldn't get a handle on inflation," he said. (Volcker frequently says "you" when many of us would say "I" or "we.") "Inflation was accelerating, and what prompted the change—certainly in my thinking—is that we were always psychologically behind the curve. Whatever the Federal Reserve did to tighten was determined to be too little and too late, and I'm not sure that was wrong—our process was very reactive."

"The markets were running ahead of the Fed?"

"*Inflation* was running ahead of the Fed. The perception was that we would *never* be able to deal with the problem. Right after I became chairman, we had several discount-rate changes within six weeks—and they were pooh-poohed—too little, too late! And the critics said, look, it's a four-to-three vote"—the Fed has seven governors, including the chairman. "They were saying, next time he loses, next time he doesn't get the vote. They'll never raise the rate again.

"Now, I could see I had four solid votes, but you had to go back and say, how can we get a little more psychological *jolt* here and introduce some *uncertainty* into the situation; to be more convincing that we would take strong enough measures to deal with it. So we resurrected this approach [of controlling the money supply]. My gut feeling was it would be popular at the Federal Reserve.

"We were looking for something new and different to do. We needed to be more credible."

"Something new and different?" I asked. Volcker waved a match under his cigar. It had been smoked about halfway down. We were sitting at a table in the conference room of his office.

I asked what difference this approach made.

"There were a couple of things. One was putting ourselves in a different position. You had to *change* policy. And with all the monetarist talk and so forth, hopefully it was convincing to the public when you began talking about the money supply and inflation and emphasizing that as the money supply did slow down."

"This was a monetarist policy, then?" I asked.

"Oh, sure," Volcker said. "Even if you weren't a full-blooded monetarist—which I wasn't—you were using their techniques and their approaches to make a point, and they had been doing a lot of public education, which helped in the groundwork."

"What did you expect?"

"A better impact on public psychology and economic performance and a prompter effect in lowering interest rates and inflationary expectations. You expected interest rates to go up in the aftermath, but I was so naive as to hope short-term rates alone would go higher. You would have had a great success if long-term rates didn't go up very much, or went up and came down again. But it didn't happen. Rates went up and stayed up all the way along the line."

The inexact nature of managing a central bank came to me with the phrase "I was so naive as to hope." It didn't quite fit the image of the Fed chairman as an infallible Pope.

"Did you expect interest rates to go as high as they did?" I asked.

"No, I certainly didn't expect them to go to twenty-one percent."

"What *did* you expect?"

"That—twenty-one percent—would have been out of the ball park. The other thing that surprised you during that period—1979 and the winter of 1980—was that the assembled economic wisdom said we were on the edge of a recession, if not in one. Instead, with interest rates going up, and things getting tighter, the economy kept expanding. When you were *guessing* what interest rates might be, you wouldn't have assumed that the economy would be as strong as it was."

"Did you feel uneasy as you saw the rates go from twelve to fourteen to sixteen to eighteen percent?"

"Uneasy? The uneasiness over interest rates was moderated by the lack of evidence that the economy was collapsing. Inflation was getting worse—inflation of eighteen percent and interest rates at eighteen percent are in context—you had a higher inflation rate and a stronger economy."

"Did you expect that it would produce the recession?"

"No. Nobody realized it at the time, but the recession was created by credit controls. The recession was severe in terms of sharpness, but not in length."

"If you had it to do over again, what would you do?"

"I wouldn't do credit controls, that's for sure. I went along with it, but it was the administration's idea—Carter's. He wanted to get consumer spending down—but consumer spending wasn't that strong and wasn't the source of inflationary expectations. But Carter said, I've taken all these tough budgetary measures on everything else, we've got inflation going through the roof, how do I send a message to the American people? Carter's budgets were being scoffed at; people said, you call *that* a tough budget? He needed a gesture. Well, he announced credit controls that pushed installment loans from fourteen percent to fifteen and a half or sixteen percent and affected bank credit cards. He announced it one day and the next day the bottom fell out of consumer credit."

When Volcker had announced the shift in Fed policies, in October 1979, there was little reaction. The language was obscure, and only Fed-watchers knew something was different. But when Jimmy Carter went on television in March 1980 to announce credit controls, the effect was immediate and dramatic. VISA lost 500,000 cardholders and Sears's sales were down 15 percent in months. "The darned economy just fell off a cliff," said Fred Schultz, a Fed governor.

But the 1980 recession was like a passing thunderstorm. On the charts it made a quick, sharp V. In two months, interest rates fell by half. By August the recession was over, and interest rates and GNP growth were on their way up again. Interest rates gyrated wildly— from 20 percent in April to 11 percent in July, and back to 21.5

percent—the highest ever—in December. The wild gyrations were very tough on businesses dependent on bank loans.

Ronald Reagan took office, and his program of cutting taxes and increasing defense spending produced expectations of inflation in the bond market. The quick recession of 1980 had produced pain but no relief from inflation. In his speeches, Volcker said the money supply would be gradually reduced, until inflation was squeezed out. Ronald Reagan had been tutored by Milton Friedman and could draw rough charts of the money supply with his hands in the air, so the White House was content, for the moment, with the chairman. By mid-1981, with the prime rate over 20 percent, business was slowing down. The Consumer Price Index dropped from 10 percent to 5 percent in October 1981. The recession hit heavy industries especially. Unemployment in autos, steels, and construction was in the 20 percent range. The Kentucky Home Builders Association printed "wanted for murder" posters of Volcker and the other Fed governors. Volcker reluctantly agreed to a permanent bodyguard after a distraught man entered the Fed with a sawed-off shotgun, intending to hold the governors hostage.

Volcker faced critics in Congress, sometimes on television. It played well in Peoria, the congressman attacking the hardhearted banker for the woes of his constituents. Senator Kennedy said the Fed policy was "scorched earth." Small businessmen especially were suffering, and being picked off by their larger competitors. Volcker addressed the convention of the National Association of Home Builders in Las Vegas. He did not falter. We all want a recovery, he said. "Most crucial," he said, "is that growth be sustainable—we cannot let up now, or the pain we have suffered would have been for naught." He got a standing ovation.

Volcker says we would have had a recession sooner or later, one way or another. By mid-1982, the economy was still sliding. But price inflation was over: it had dropped from 13 percent to 4 percent.

Volcker spoke frequently with Anthony Solomon, the president of the Federal Reserve Bank of New York. Solomon had been Undersecretary of the Treasury under Carter, and had championed Volcker as Federal Reserve Chairman. The New York Fed is the most influential of the Federal Reserve Banks, and Solomon was a pivotal member of the Federal Open Market Committee.

"Paul said he was getting nervous about when to ease," Solomon said. "He said, this is our one chance to break the back of inflation, if we could just stay tight a little longer. I told him I didn't think the country could stand much more. He agreed readily. He was ready to move."

"It was getting to the point where we had to ease, no matter what," Volcker said. "I was becoming antsy about the economy. There was no sign of a turn, so when the time came I jumped."

The time was July 1, 1982. The money supply had finally stayed within its targets for a brief period. The Fed declared the target achieved. The announcement was bland, and only the nuance-watchers could catch it. "Somewhat more rapid money growth would be acceptable," said the Fed policy committee.

There were some moments of tension at the Fed. The valves turned, and the supply of money increased. But would the prospect of easing rekindle the fears of inflation? That had been the Fed's warning—that easy money did not mean easier interest rates, as you might expect; easy money could produce *higher* interest rates, because it produced fears of inflation, and then lenders, the bond buyers, translated their fears into higher rates. As it happened, Wall Street was glad to see the easing. The long-term rates rallied, as well as the short-term rates. The bond markets took off; the stock market took off, too, and was up 50 percent within six months.

Volcker's critics said he had no idea how much destruction the Federal Reserve had caused—he was out of touch, surrounded by technocrats. But to the world at large, it looked like a virtuoso performance. The Fed had stuck to its guns and broken the price inflation. The economy had tottered on the brink, and then recovered. The experiment with monetarism was over. Anyway, the Mexicans had come to Washington, saying they were broke, and major American banks which had lent them $100 billion would follow them right down the tube if the Fed did not help. The Fed settled comfortably into being the "lender of last resort," and dispensed the money.

"What would have happened," I asked Volcker, "if the Fed *hadn't* switched its course in 1979?"

Volcker rumbled a bit, and lit another cigar.

"It would have taken more public aggravation with inflation before the Fed screwed up its courage to act."

It seems strange to me that the Fed has to screw up its courage. Technically, it has to answer to no one. It is so independent that in the period of high interest rates, Volcker was accused of enjoying the sight of small farmers and small businessmen going under. He did not, of course. He had to endure not only criticism from Congress—which was itself responding to distressed constituents—but sometimes face-to-face encounters with those same constituents. But no one faulted his courage.

When inflation broke, it broke like a fever suddenly over. Bonds boomed, and with lower interest rates, the takeover era in American economic history began with a vengeance; "junk bonds" became easier to sell, and that meant no company was too big to take over. Vast fortunes were made in the stock and bond markets, and in the takeover business. The economy went into a gradual climb. The stock market hit record highs.

What had the Fed done? Well, something wasn't working, so it tried something else. And after that, it tried the first thing again. Far from dictating imperially, it always had its moistened finger in the wind. The Fed is made of people—people guessing at the course of interest rates, sometimes surprised at the effects of their own actions, never 100 percent sure. Paul Volcker was ironic about economists— "the perceived wisdom of the community," he kept saying, when they were wrong. The Federal Reserve's prestige is high now, Volcker became a megastar on the world stage, the United States has produced more new jobs than any other country, and the Fed is considered America's bulwark, the only stable economic force when Congress is gridlocked. But in hindsight, Volcker's Fed was much like the abbot in the French Revolution who was asked why he was marching behind the crowds to the barricade. "I must follow them," he said. "I am their leader."

Was Kwartler a Chump,
or Ahead of His Time?

It took the worst recession in fifty years, but the psychology of inflationary fears was broken, that frantic search to get out of the currency and into some other store of value: land, gold, silver, art, baseball cards. But if inflationary fears were tempered, they were not reversed. The savings coffers of the country did not fill. The government borrowed, the consumer borrowed, the corporation borrowed. The government borrowed because spending was up and revenues not as much, the corporation borrowed because such leverage was greeted warmly in the financial markets, and the consumer borrowed because he or she wanted it *now*.

A Manhattan resident named Charles Kwartler wrote a letter to the *New York Times*. The letter was such a clear expression of the attitudes of a generation that I clipped it, knowing I would find the occasion to use its economic significance.

Wrote Mr. Kwartler:

> My wife and I have always considered ourselves "children of the Depression." We were both raised on the principle of saving; we have never spent as much money as we have earned, and have never purchased anything on credit. If we have not had the cash on hand for a car or TV or travel, we did without. For most of my working career, I have been either salaried or self-employed, and some ten years ago, my wife went to work to enable us to continue paying our way while sending two sons through college.

Mr. Kwartler and his wife have been putting "a few dollars a week" into a savings bank. Deposits like theirs enable such banks to offer mortgages to homeowners. Congress further subsidizes homeowners by making the mortgage interest and taxes deductible. The Kwartlers, however, rent an apartment and, like other renters who live frugally and save, are penalized by the taxes on their interest income. In his letter, Mr. Kwartler proposed that savers like himself who never receive the subsidies homeowners get be given, after the age of fifty-five, a tax exemption on savings income up to $125,000.

Kwartler's attitude seems warm and familiar to me, because my own parents were traumatized by the Depression. Thrift is a virtue; hard work is a virtue; if you can't pay for it, don't buy it. It seems almost incomprehensible now, but the value of the dollar *appreciated* during the Depression. As prices fell, the value of savings rose. Those who were in debt were punished by the debt, for they had to work harder and harder to pay it off.

Some time after Mr. Kwartler's letter was published, I presided over an all-day seminar in Denver, sponsored by the Harvard Business School Club of Colorado. The seminar participants, mostly businessmen in oil and real estate, had come to discuss future interest rates, OPEC pricing policies, and prospects for the oil and securities markets. Halfway through the afternoon, to liven things up, I sprang a surprise exam. Blue books and pencils were passed out, as well as a quiz on what we had covered. (Even though there were no grades, the sudden appearance of blue books caused these mature businessmen to blanch, and some of them went into pencil-chewing and forehead-rubbing postures they may not have used for twenty years.) With the quiz came a copy of Kwartler's letter. The final part of the quiz asked: "Do you think Kwartler's proposal is fair, or sensible? Would you tell your children to live as he did? If you would not, what does that say for our society?"

Only one of the sixty-five seminar participants thought Kwartler's proposal was fair and sensible. That one said Kwartler was "a generation ahead of his time" and that an exemption on savings interest such as he had proposed would be a dramatic incentive to capital formation.

The other seminar participants were all annoyed, in varying degrees, by Kwartler. Wrote one:

> Good Lord, if the chump picked an incorrect path because his father was a Quaker minister or something, that's tough. He probably received great psychic return on paying-as-he-went, and continually applauded his conservative judgment. The data was there, and trends should become apparent, certainly within thirty years.

And another:

> Should the government protect the citizenry from its own mistakes? No one forced Kwartler to live in an apartment or to put his money into a savings account.

The other answers followed the Kwartler-is-a-chump line, some with a nod at the lost virtue of thrift.

> Kwartler could read the rules and play the game, which he failed to do. He is going to have to get his satisfaction out of his very conservative life-style and good ethics and leave the profits and benefits to those who play to win rather than to always be safe and secure.

> Kwartler did not change with the times . . . the premise of a free market is the opportunity to react to this.

> Kwartler took no risk, and that expense [should be] factored into the rent schedule.

Most of the seminar participants would not advise their children to follow Kwartler's example. Some advised moderation on personal borrowing, but nearly all of them saw a threat of inflation. Hence they wanted their children to learn to be shrewd and nimble, to borrow for investment. "I hope they will be living in a world of individual choices where people are willing to accept the responsibilities and the results of their actions," wrote one, implying that Kwartler did not.

> Don't do what Charlie did, kids. You've got to take risk, must work hard to invest your money, and you should enjoy where you're at. Lots of things are changing, so you'll have to be patient to find the opportunity, but to wait thirty years as a saver and to ignore what's happening! It's a changing world. You're going to have to take risks, and invest. Follow trends, try to stay ahead, and look for new opportunities.

While almost every participant saw a continuation of inflation, and hence the necessity to borrow to pay back with cheaper dollars, some saw the answer as the development of personal skills:

> Develop the personal skills and education that make you a viable member of society.

> My advice to kids would be to become doctors and make so much money that it won't matter whether they spend it or save it. And

I do not intend this as a facetious answer. The return on effort
spent at career development far exceeds the risk-adjusted return
spent on trying to outguess the future of investments.

One participant—only one—thought he saw a straw in the wind:

Not to follow Kwartler's behavior implies a belief in continued
inflation. . . . Lenders are learning now to charge real interest
rates which reflect their belief in continued inflation. If this continues, Kwartler's behavior will be more appropriate in the future.

The "real" interest rate is one that is set at several percentage
points above the inflation rate. For example, if the inflation rate is 12
percent, a real lending rate may be 16 percent or 17 percent. If
lenders begin taking inflation into account, then the days of hedging
by borrowing are about over. It will pay to borrow at 17 percent only
if the rates are going to 25 percent or if the investment returns more
than the cost of the debt. It is the conventional wisdom now that one
must borrow to beat inflation, but borrowers do not think through to
the ultimate conclusion, as I wrote in *Paper Money:*

How do I beat inflation? How do I stay ahead? Hedging depends
on a continuous supply of gulls, of suckers, of greater fools, of
people who haven't gotten the word. Think a minute: somebody
has to sell you that "inflation hedge." . . . Why should he? . . .
Hedging only works when there is *unanticipated* inflation.

None of my participants got much into what their borrow-
and-hedge advice meant for the society as a whole. (I probably did
not allow enough time. As it was, one of my middle-aged oil
company vice-presidents wrote at the end of his Kwartler essay, "I
am a graduating senior, and am taking this course pass/fail.") Obviously, borrowing has to come from someone. If the Charles
Kwartlers will no longer lend at the passbook-savings rate, where
does the money for investment come from?

We had, earlier in the seminar, considered the needs in two fields
over the next ten years. The oil people in my seminar estimated that
their industry would need a trillion dollars—one *trillion* dollars—to

find, produce, and deliver the energy for the next ten years. And the real estate people were looking at documents that said we would have to generate *two trillion* dollars in the next ten years for development of the kinds of housing we have become accustomed to.

At the same time, we are going to have to renew and refurbish our industrial plant in order to compete with the Japanese, the Germans, and the rest of the world. Against this, we have the savings habits of adolescents who will always be bailed out by their parents. Projecting interest rates and savings rates, the investment banking house Salomon Brothers wrote:

> The maturing baby boom is causing the 25- to 44-year-old age bracket to be both the largest and most rapidly growing. This is the generation that has grown up in an environment where consumption has been stressed and indeed been rewarded by the onset of inflation and the backing of public policy over the past twenty years. *This experience has produced a large group of people who really don't know what it means to save* [italics mine]. The desire for immediate gratification will help sustain the economy at a higher level than might otherwise be the case, yet the required savings needed to restore this country's competitive position will be slow in coming.

We have really had only one kind of saving in recent years on a personal level, the forced saving of making payments on a house. Statistically speaking, the bulk of Americans' savings is the equity in their houses. The problem with this for the economy is that buying a house is not a very efficient form of saving. A house is not like a new machine that enables workers to turn out goods better and cheaper. Nor is a house like a new company that will employ workers. Homeownership is a stabilizing social force, but it really doesn't help us to compete.

The maturing baby-boomers, twenty-five to forty-four years old, don't really know what it means to save. And they have their corporate counterparts. The corporate treasurer who borrowed to the hilt ten years ago at a long-term fixed rate of 8 percent is a hero and probably insured his corporate career. The corporate treasurer who kept the nickels intact is a chump, like Charles Kwartler. Nevertheless, we now have a problem with our corporations: they have piled up so much debt that their balance sheets are askew and they have lost much of the liquidity that comes with savings. This means that they may go to the marketplace to borrow more frequently.

Whom do they meet in the marketplace, bidding for the savings? First of all, the government, which is living beyond its means in twelve figures annually. Second, the millions of individuals who borrow through their banks and with credit cards.

We have borrowed from foreigners, especially the Japanese, to keep our spending running. The Japanese government, like ours, runs a deficit, but it has a huge domestic savings pool to draw upon. The Japanese household runs very much like the Kwartler household—it does not like to buy on credit, and it saves.

Sooner or later, the ant-and-grasshopper story turns out the way it did in Aesop. The optimists say we aren't really grasshoppers, we have international deficits because capital likes to come here, and this is a good thing, as the Marshall Plan was for Europe. And we haven't saved because the baby-boomers are such a large part of the population, and young people don't save, but as the baby-boomers turn forty, you'll see, they will save, older people save.

The pessimists say our international borrowing isn't a Marshall Plan because we consume it, we don't build with it. Grasshoppers keep borrowing until something stops them, and that something will be a real crunch. Burn the trees for firewood and the next generation has no shade.

This is more than a financial problem. There is a very deep-seated instinct in mature people and in productive societies to build things, to leave something for the next generation. A hundred years ago in this country that might have meant leaving a farm in good working order or participating in the development of one's town or community. It takes a generation to grow good trees (even in this country of instant gratification, no one has produced an instant tree). A farm that consumed its seed corn was out of business. Nationally, we have been living on our seed corn.

I would agree with my seminar participants; Charles Kwartler had ample time to stop saving, to get himself some credit cards and a mortgage, and to go into debt. No one forced him to save, and he should not look to the government to bail him out. But if we continue to praise the debtors and think of the savers as chumps, we will in the long run not have a very agreeable society, or even one that survives in the form in which we now know it.

The Day They Sold the Navy

I first heard that the United States Navy was selling some of its ships to investors from a lawyer doing some of the paper work. He happened to mention this to me merely as a point of some intellectual interest, as if it were a problem in constitutional law.

"You probably heard that the Navy is selling ships to investors," he said. "Now, this brings up a curious problem in the insurance—"

"Just a minute," I said. "The *Navy*—our Navy—is *selling* ships?"

"Where have you been?" said my friend.

"To whom does it sell them?"

"To investors, in this case large investors. Then the Navy leases the ships right back again."

"What do the investors get, then?"

"Well, they get the lease payments, and they get terrific tax write-offs from the depreciation of the hulls. The Navy says it's cheaper to lease than to buy—"

"Just what ships is the Navy selling?"

"I'm not up on everything, but most recently the Navy has sold the Rapid Deployment Force."

"The Navy has sold the Rapid Deployment Force," I repeated, just to be sure.

"Actually, the cargo ships of the Rapid Deployment Force. It's a handsome deal, two point three billion dollars' worth of ships."

I thought this was charming. Would the Navy sell an aircraft carrier? Would it sell the *Saratoga?* The *Eisenhower?* The *Independence?*

"In principle, I think it would," said my lawyer friend. "It is already exploring the sale of what they call 'adversary aircraft.' "

"What happens," I said, "if I own some ship that the Navy has leased back and somebody puts a shell through it?"

"Naturally, the Navy takes care of that," said my lawyer friend. "It brings up the problem I keep trying to tell you about. In the normal course of ship charters, the operator of a vessel is required to give thirty days' notice if the ship is sailing anywhere near a war zone. That's just standard insurance coverage, it's been in effect for hundreds of years. But of course, it's in the nature of a *navy* to go *to* a war zone, isn't it? And the way a navy *moves* doesn't permit thirty days' notice mailed to an owner and his insurance company. Theoretically, the Navy should send a registered letter, saying, 'In thirty days, subject vessels will be sailing at such and such latitude, to, to wit, the Strait of Hormuz.' "

I told my lawyer friend I loved the thirty days' notice. It takes all the tensions out of the missile age. The old ICBMs brought the end of the world in thirty minutes, and the Pershings and Russian SS-20s have brought the time between firing and nuclear death to six minutes, and the Navy is mailing out 30-day notices to the people who own its ships.

"Fascinating problem, eh?" said my lawyer friend.

It seemed like a tax scandal to me—legal, but a scandal.

What the Navy has been doing is a version of the "tax leasing" rules added to the 1981 tax code. For example, you bought an airplane, and with it the depreciation—the tax write-off—of the airplane. You could detach the tax write-off from the plane and sell it for cash. A buyer could pay you cash and use the write-off against his own taxes. That was how General Electric—$27.2 billion in revenues, $1.6 billion in net earnings—paid no taxes in 1982. It simply kept building tax write-offs until it had no more tax liability.

To the Navy, of course, it makes sense. It *is* a bit cheaper for the Navy to rent than to buy, but it isn't cheaper for the *taxpayers,* whose taxes will eventually *increase* by the amount of tax that the investors who bought the Navy ships don't pay.

The staff of Congress's Joint Committee on Taxation went to work on this, and they calculated that the *real* cost to the Treasury was 12 percent higher if the Navy sold its ships and leased them back than if it simply bought them outright. The Defense Department hired a consultant to prove its own case, and when that consultant reported that leasing was more costly, it fired that firm and hired another one, and the second one came back with a better answer.

A Texas Democrat, J. J. Pickle, who first blew the whistle on the Navy's caper, said, "If this kind of thing continues, we're going to see E.F. Hutton own the Air Force and Merrill Lynch rule the waves." Congressman Pickle didn't actually mean E.F. Hutton would own the Air Force. He meant E.F. Hutton would *sell* the Air Force—taking a hefty commission on the front end—to doctors and dentists and whoever else wants to buy a tax write-off.

Even though the Navy leasing deal wasn't news—it came some time ago—I decided to do one of my television commentaries on this subject. What does it say about our country when even the Navy is producing tax gimmicks? And why stop with ships? What about individual soldiers and sailors? There was a Peter Arno cartoon I recall in which a rich dowager is leaning over the third-base rail ogling the players and talking to the manager of a ball team, who says, "Yes, we do sell them sometimes, lady, but only to other teams." When I was in the Army, it was common to see the privates and the corporals mowing the lawns of the colonels and generals. Would the Army consider leasing some enlisted men?

My commentary went out to 270 Public Broadcasting stations, and I have to report the American people did not rise in wrath at the injustices of the tax system. The switchboard lit up, all right—rather feebly—and what the callers said was this:

"Say, that fella that was on TV last night? Talked about the Navy selling ships? Get a big tax write-off? How do I get in on that?"

They were told to write to the Pentagon. To get in on *this* particular wrinkle, they had to write quickly, since Congress was working on a law to prevent the sale of Navy and other public properties.

I told Senator Howard Metzenbaum that the American people had not risen in wrath in response to my TV commentary. Senator

Metzenbaum is an Ohio Democrat who has tied a banner to his lance and gone after the inequities of the tax system.

"Maybe you didn't go far enough," said Senator Metzenbaum. "Why shouldn't we sell the Senate building? In fact, why don't we sell the White House?"

I could see the appeal of that. A Texas oil family is sitting on its terrace with friends. The husband says, "Just picked up a dandy piece of real estate in Washington, D.C., sort of a condo deal," and the wife says, "It's rented out, of course, but to a very nice family."

"It is possible," said Senator Metzenbaum, "to keep writing clauses until *nobody* pays *any* taxes. We have a tax policy molded by special-interest lobbyists. We have a rather right-wing crowd that says we must balance the budget, but they are also the ones most adept at avoiding taxes. Congress ducks responsibility, and the leader is a real impediment—"

"The leader?"

"Reagan? Ronald Reagan?"

I had to interrupt the senator because he seemed to have difficulty saying "the President."

"You can't run this country with two-hundred-billion-dollar deficits," said Senator Metzenbaum, "and we have trouble making cuts. If you don't get enough income, you're going to have deficits. We have twenty-two billion dollars of new loopholes. We have special exemptions for the tax treatment of wealthy families like the Hunts of Texas and the Halls of Hallmark—I think we can do what we need to do if we have the courage, but I don't see the courage in this environment."

I asked Senator Metzenbaum whether a simplified tax, a flat tax, would not work better than traditional tax increases. (This was before Bill Bradley introduced the idea into the Senate.)

"We could start with it," he said, "but then people would say, "What about the churches and the charities?—there's no incentive to give. And won't housing be hurt if we limit mortgage interest?' And it will start to provide for exemption and graduation."

"And a VAT—a consumption tax?"

"That hurts poor people the most and wealthy people the least and it's regressive and I'm against it."

Senator Metzenbaum is not one of the poorer members of that body. While not in the class of Senators Heinz or Danforth, he made some money in Ohio parking lots.

I don't want to leave the impression that our tax system is totally corrupt. Every deduction is there to promote something good, and every clause is to promote something that Congress believes is fair. Theoretically. The Reagan administration reduced individual income taxes at least partly to make tax shelters less appealing.

The most recent tax reform acts ended the practice of buying tax credits. So you're too late to buy a piece of the carrier *Saratoga* and get a write-off on your taxes. Only very large contractors got offered the Rapid Deployment Force anyway, as I understand it. I suppose the rationale was—well, we sell post offices, don't we? (I always wanted to own a post office, and you can still buy them.) The whole idea of buying tax relief, like sinners buying indulgences before the Reformation, was an abomination. General Electric has gone back to paying taxes again.

Tax reform was one of the triumphs of the '80s. Lower tax rates did not produce growth enough to make up for the lost revenue, as the supply-siders predicted, but at least ending the purchase of write-offs, together with the lower rates, put the army of lawyers and packagers creating write-offs out of business. No wonder we were heading toward a population of one million lawyers!

They say that abstract documents, like the Budget of the United States and the Tax Code, are mirrors to ourselves. Well, the Tax Code is now so complex that even accountants cannot understand it, but the mirror has a better image to reflect. The tax reform acts were not easy for Congress, but Senator Bradley, a Democrat, started and worked through one of the best pieces of legislation in a Republican administration, mobilizing bipartisan support. Somehow, it was the tenor of the deregulated, every-last-buck times for General Electric not to pay taxes, for wealthy investors to be in partnerships that bought railroad hopper cars and aircraft and textile machinery, even though the partners were not in those businesses at all.

But selling the Navy! That was a real flash of insight! I wish I had been at the table in the Pentagon the day they sold the Navy. Did buyers and sellers shake hands? Were there any used-car jokes—did anybody say you have to race the engine a bit with this baby if you're stuck in a traffic jam?

And as for all my viewers, why didn't they rise in wrath? Maybe they were all fantasizing and bragging to their friends, "I just bought a piece of a boat. Nine-hundred-and-fifty-footer. Sleeps four thousand five hundred. She's called *Saratoga*."

2 SEVERAL AMERICAS

Most Americans could only wonder about shelling out close to $54 million for a painting. They were confused by the Federal Reserve Board, if they thought about it at all. They might have invested in a sliver of the *Saratoga,* if they had heard about it, but few people did, and if they had any spare cash, which was doubtful.

At any one time, it almost goes without saying, there are several Americas. They look different, they feel different, they sound different, and they can be side by side; these are not geographic differences. For example: Buffalo and Rochester, seventy-five miles apart in upper New York State, could be in different countries. Buffalo is an old ore-and-steel, "ethnic" town. People go to work at the sound of factory whistles and get home early enough to read the evening paper; it is the *evening* paper that survived. Rochester is one of the national centers for sophisticated optics, the home of Kodak, Xerox, and the Rochester Institute of Technology. Buffalo's major industries suffered through the '80s; one of the great steel operations shut down. Rochester's unemployment rate was never half that of Buffalo. But the people of Buffalo did not drive to Rochester to work in sophisticated optics.

Drive down Route 280, south of San Francisco, in Santa Clara County, and you come to one of the most stimulating provinces of capitalism, Silicon Valley. Low glass-and-concrete buildings are sprinkled among the brown hills, like some enormous landscaped junior college. No smokestacks, no railroad sidings, no noise, only "the world's most beautiful freeway"—usually jammed—running through what used to be the orchards of "the valley of the heart's delight."

When Bruno Taut and Le Corbusier thought about "workers," they thought about something like Buffalo. Bruno was a German socialist architect of the '20s who designed the *Siedlungen*, the tight little boxes he thought of as workers' paradise. And Le Corbusier designed a Radiant City full of severe little buildings, with muscle-bound figures strolling its byways. What would Bruno and Corbu have thought of the lunchtime scene at Tandem Computer, with the labor force sunning itself at the pool, playing volleyball, and picnicking at the outdoor tables? Down the road at Rolm Corporation, they would have found the labor force in the Jacuzzi. Bruno and Corbu could sketch a worker's utopia, but their imaginations did not come halfway to Silicon Valley even in fantasy.

"This is a *culture*," says Jim Treybig, Tandem's president. He has a faint Texas accent. He is an alumnus of Hewlett-Packard, the model for Silicon Valley, with its laid-back style and its tenets such as "make meaning, as well as money." "This culture is oriented to *risk*," says Treybig, who is known as Jimmy T. and does not have his own specific parking space. "It is not a problem to fail here. If you live in Detroit, you want to be a vice president of General Motors. Here, if you start a company, that's as good as being president of General Motors, and the risk of a start-up is always failure. We have a pool of people willing to take risks, we found risk capital, we found suppliers and vendors who wanted us to succeed, we found people with an attitude that made us succeed. Silicon Valley is an attitude."

Not everyone sounds like Jimmy T. in Santa Clara County, especially in the sectors beleaguered by Japanese competition. But it never sounds like Cambria County, Pennsylvania.

"Just Tell Me What I Did Wrong!"

I am on my way to Johnstown, Pennsylvania, for several reasons. One is a sentence from a conversation I had with Peter Drucker, the management consultant. Drucker looked into the future and said,

"Blue-collar employment is going to follow the same curve as farm employment." An innocuous, abstract statement, you think, containing words like "curve" and "employment." I thought it was astounding. Everybody used to have a cousin on a farm. Agriculture once used 90 percent of the labor force. Now fewer than 4 percent do all the farming—the other farmers all went to the cities. No more jokes about the traveling salesman and the farmer's daughter. The farmer's daughter is working at Intel, or Texas Instruments, or some insurance company.

But now you're telling me that *factory* workers are going to be only 4 percent of the work force? Even if not right away, still, factories *are* America: cities with big shoulders, stamping, forging—tires, jet engines, locomotives, power turbines, big stuff. If blue-collar workers are going to be only 4 percent of the work force, (a) what is this country going to be making, and (b) what happens to all the people who work in the factories: the hard hats, the steelworkers, the deer hunters, the union men? Can that be right? What happens to *America?*

"It's a world economy," Drucker said. "The Mexicans can make steel and the Japanese can make cars. We have to automate industry or lose it."

Another reason that Johnstown is my destination is that it has very high unemployment—it is a depressed steel town—but it has an unusual program led by a psychologist with a strong interest in the theories of Carl Jung, the pioneering Swiss psychiatrist. Jung did not believe you were frozen into some path by childhood trauma; adults have the capacity to change even in midlife. Jung broke with his friend Sigmund Freud, although he acknowledged Freud's brilliant discovery of the unconscious. But the unconscious, said Jung, was larger than the individual—there was a group unconscious, a collective unconscious. The image of unemployed steelworkers and a working psychologist seemed incongruous to me.

It is not so easy to get to Johnstown. From New York, it might be quicker to Los Angeles. "I'm sorry," says the woman at the commuter airline in Pittsburgh. "This is the third day in a row Johnstown has been socked in. Johnstown is always 'in'—rained in, snowed in, fogged in, flooded in—sometimes in the winter we can't get the equipment out. We'll fly you as far as Altoona, and then a cab ride back shouldn't take more than an hour and a half.''

It looks like a scene from *The Deer Hunter*, these rolling wooded mountains of Pennsylvania, old white frame houses, the highway curving around the mountain, mounds of coal at the edge of a mine, the conveyor belts going up at a 45-degree angle. Signs say DEER BUTCHERING.

The Johnstown Flood celebrated by folk singers was in 1936. The word then among the steelworkers was that the Carnegies and the Mellons hadn't maintained the dam properly. Johnstown's 1977 flood was a freak; a thunderstorm came over the mountains and then bounced back and forth from one rim of the valley to the other for ten solid hours.

The coal near Johnstown is excellent metallurgical coal. The Cambria Iron Company started there in 1852, and Bethlehem Steel built a works there, even though Johnstown did not have major water transportation to barge away the finished goods. Bethlehem Works produced forgings, bars, rods, and wires—and railroad cars, coal hoppers, gondolas for carrying logs, flatcars for auto trailers. You come over the rim of the mountain on Highway 271, and there is Johnstown below, the bigger, rich folks' houses on the hillside; the small wooden frame houses on the valley floor, church spires in their midst; and, like an enormous brown metal river moving among them, the roofs of the Bethlehem Works.

As big as it is, Johnstown is not Bethlehem's biggest plant. Johnstown could pour 1.2 million tons of steel a year, but the Lackawanna plant, near Buffalo, could pour six million tons. That is too big, in a depressed industry. Lackawanna closed in 1983. Johnstown is still operating its 30-21–inch primary mill.

Steel has mythic properties of strength. The dictator of Soviet Russia Joseph Dzhugashvili called himself *Stalin*—''man of steel'' in Russian. "Pittsburgh, Youngstown, Gary," wrote Carl Sandburg, "they make their steel with *men*.'' Steelmaking is hard work. The heat can reach 2,900 degrees Fahrenheit, and exposing skin near a melting facility can produce a burn. When steel is being poured, the pourer must wear cobalt-blue goggles or risk eye damage. But new facilities—and federal OSHA regulations—have made steelmaking less dangerous and less strenuous than it was a generation ago.

In 1977 Johnstown had nearly thirteen thousand United Steelworkers employed. Today it has just two thousand.

How did Johnstown—and the steel industry—get into such a
situation? One Bethlehem annual report went through the litany:
"the poor condition of the economy . . . noncompetitive employment costs, an increasing competitive marketplace, changing markets and product mix, and the continuing high level of imports." In
the recession year of 1982, the company operated at 37 percent of
capacity for the last half of the year, and lost almost $500 million.
The chairman, in his letter, uses CIA-abstract language. Bethlehem
is going to close down a number of facilities to "terminate the
operating losses of those facilities." Further, "remaining steelmaking operations will be jeopardized unless hourly employment costs
are reduced substantially." That means the steelworkers. The union
won't budge, says the chairman, even though steelworkers are getting twice the average wage of workers in manufacturing businesses.
That is, those who are still working.

Tony

I tried out the gist of the chairman's report on Tony, a steelworker
who was seeing off a cousin at the airport when I was leaving
Johnstown. The fog had lifted but the winds were so high—fifty-five
knots—that the little twin-engine Otter was an hour late getting in,
so we had some time in the Skyway Lounge. Tony wore a plaid
shirt; his cousin a down vest.

"I'll tell you what I think," said Tony. "I think he should be
arrested. I think they should all be arrested. For forty years they
never put in new machinery. [Bethlehem says, in fact, that it spent
$100 million on modernization of steelmaking facilities at Johns-
town. But even that spending did not save the bulk of the Johnstown
jobs.] They put the new machinery in Burns Harbor [a modern
Bethlehem plant in Indiana]. They took the money and put it in coal
mines. I don't know where they put it, but this was a good plant."

Tony worked in the wire mill until a year and a half ago and hopes
to go back.

"He says we got too much? I say we put in a good day's work.

I say the American worker is better than any worker in Korea or China or whatever, and we don't eat dog food and we don't work for dog food. We put in a good day's work and we're *worth* it. I think they should stop those shipments coming in from overseas.''

I asked if many of the steelworkers were learning other trades.

"So what should I do?" said Tony. "Learn bookkeeping? Sit in a *cubicle?*"

Tony made the word *bookkeeping* into a sneer.

"Whose money would I count? I don't see any money around here. Go to Texas? The only state I've been in except this one is Ohio, except for the Army. I'm not so sure it's better anyplace else.''

"That's right," said Tony's cousin. "It's not so great in Texas, I heard.''

"I went to work at the mill the day I got out of the service," Tony said. "I gave 'em thirteen years, and now they're gonna take my *truck* away because I got too far behind in the payments. My *wife* is working, and now *you* tell me . . . *What the hell did I do wrong?* I'd like to know, what did I do wrong?''

I asked Tony what his friends were doing. Tony didn't want to talk anymore.

"They're drinkin' depth charges at the Franklin," said Tony's cousin. A depth charge is a shot glass of whiskey dropped into a glass of beer. You down the whiskey and beer at the same time and end up with the shot glass in your teeth. If you get three steelworkers at a bar, it can become a competitive sport. "They're drivin' their old ladies crazy, and waitin' for the mill to call them back.''

"It might be a long wait," I suggested.

Then Tony's cousin didn't want to talk to me anymore either, and they began to talk to each other about the Steelers.

Skip

Skip Paolini is management. He wears his thick, dark hair short, has a firm jawline, a ready smile, and an intense, assured manner. His office is in a red brick building on Walnut Street. He came to Johnstown from Lackawanna and is now the general manager of operations of the bar, rod, and wire division of the Johnstown Works. "My son is the fourth generation of our family at Bethlehem Steel," Skip said. "My father and his brothers and our cousins—our whole family—we span the seventy-five years of Bethlehem Steel. We have a car works here that's down—the rail business is zero. I could show you miles of stacked-up hopper cars in the valley. Trucks made a dent in the railroads, foreign steel made a dent. I've been to Japan. I've seen that Oita plant of Nippon Steel. It cost two *billion* dollars. An American plant can borrow thirty percent of the *original* value to build more, a Japanese plant can borrow eighty percent of the *current* value. We play by different rules. I've never seen a Chevrolet in Japan.

"I'm not an isolationist, but if you're going to get kicked in the balls you should at least put your hands down. We're in a steel glut—Korea, China, Brazil, Mexico, South Africa; new modern mills, all making steel, all looking to dump their steel here. We have mini-mills in this country that spring up. They pay fifteen dollars an hour to our twenty-three dollars, plus a piece of the profits. They're nonunion, electric furnaces—they steal the bottom end of our business. We can compete in the mid-quality and high-quality. But if the Japs and Koreans *target* your industry, they'll tear your ass up. *You count* the American plants left that still make a TV set.

"So everybody wants to dump their steel here. But how long will we be the market? What are we gonna make? We can't just take in each other's washing. Anyway, Bethlehem has a plan. We can't carry the big, old plants. So we're shrinking into something viable. And we break up into smaller units. It's risky—breaking away from the home plant—but right here, we're responsible for what we do, we can't blame the home office. We go over every item—the fuel, the power costs, the oxygen—we deal with our own suppliers. We rip ourselves from conformity, from business as usual; we go to the customer and let him know we're going to give him cost, quality, and service at a reasonable price. We try not to hurt people in this restructuring. We've gone over every job—crane operator, heater helper, we want them to accept responsibility for quality, not to work eleven hours in eight. We have a labor-management approach, we get to the operating people and make them part of the planning."

Fran

Fran Audi is the chairman of the seniority committee of the local
United Steelworkers of America. He has a brown mustache, and
in the office where I met him—he had some business there—he
was wearing a brown leather jacket, faded jeans, and cowboy
boots. Like most of the men at the steelworks, he was born in
Johnstown and came back to work here as soon as he got out of
the service.

"I'm a wire drawer. You draw the wire through these machines—
I'm in the mill about two days a month. The rest of the time I work
on Union Grievance. It took about six weeks to learn my job, and I
been doing it nineteen years. Right now the union is working on
what we call the Brown Book Concession Package—the company
wants to eliminate jobs, so we're working on a package that gives a
guy a special pension for retiring early."

What was the problem? "I'd say bad management. We've seen a
lot of money wasted—four secretaries instead of one secretary, jobs
for their friends. I think the union is more concerned about the future
of the company than some of the management. We were good
working people—give us the equipment and we'll outproduce anybody; we'll be worth twenty-three dollars an hour—but the company
didn't like to spend on maintenance and keeping up. These things
can really handicap you.

"Maybe we did get a little spoiled. Maybe we did have some
sloppy work. We know it's a new way of life now. They say they
have to cut the fat off us. Well, what about cutting the fat off them?
Our international looked at Bethlehem's books. They said they got
problems, all right.

"So we're hinging our future on labor-management
participation—otherwise we don't have much of a future."

I asked Audi how this went over when he tried to sell it to the
members of his local.

"Not so good. A lot of guys get excited, and they try to get
physical with you."

"What do you mean, 'physical'?"

"I mean, a guy will get abusive, he will walk up to you, he might
shove you, he will scream at you, *Don't give them nothing, just shut*

it down! He thinks the company isn't being straight with us; he wants to know why the union isn't doing something.''

"And what do you do?"

"I try to keep cool, because we have to work with what we got. The guys are depressed when they are laid off. First maybe they went hunting or fishing if it was the right season. Then they fixed up their house. Then their wife got a part-time job, and now they are watching the kids, maybe they are even fixing dinner; they feel they're not the breadwinner, they're not a *man,* and their tempers are short when they come to the local. First they thought, 'Bethlehem's gonna call me back anytime.' Then they think, 'Why isn't Bethlehem calling me back?' Then they come down to the local and say, 'Why isn't the union doing something about it?' They depend on us too much. The guy thinks if he doesn't have a job, you take his pride away, he's not a *man.*

"The guy thinks, 'I'm not not working for no three dollars an hour—I'm used to a quality of life.' It gets depressing, because you don't know where to go. You're in a rut, you may be a productive person but you don't know how to get out of the rut, you just don't know how to get to something else, and there's thousands of guys doing what you're doing. Leave town? This is a family town, everybody's parents are here, and their brothers and cousins and nephews. Everybody was born and raised here, so it's tough when you're out of work, you try to stay out of sight for a while. But it's a good town, a friendly town, you're recognized everywhere—it's the *people* here. A lot of towns would ignore you. Here people care.''

"Do you think the company cares about you?"

"In my mind, I think they're responsible for us, they took so much money out of this town. Sometimes we think they're just taking away from us. But they could have broke us, so I think they've got a heart. So that's why the union is working on optional layoffs and early pensions. In 1977 we had eleven thousand working here in steel, and today we've got two thousand, and a lot of those jobs aren't coming back. That's real hard, but that's reality.''

The critics of the steel industry grant that some of the industry was bound to go overseas, but they say that the industry could have preserved more of its business than it did. The American steel industry has not been on the cutting edge of technological change. The Basic Oxygen Process, for example, was introduced in Austria in 1949 and in many other industrial nations soon after; but it was not widespread in the United States until the mid-1960s. By that time Japan had almost completely switched to the process and the Soviet Union was producing more steel than the United States. In the 1970s American steel was a low-margin business. The Japanese made large investments in finishing facilities in developing countries as a market for their semifinished goods, and they were prepared to take a very long-term payback. The efficient Japanese mills were sited at oceanside, the steel ready to go for export, not back in some landlocked valley.

The response of American steel was to edge out of the business. Armco Steel Corporation dropped "Steel" from its name. U.S. Steel chairman David Roderick said, "We are not in business to make steel, we are in business to make money." By 1980 nearly half of U.S. Steel's assets were out of the business, and that was before Big Steel bought Marathon Oil for $6.2 billion. In 1983 Big Steel reported that more than half its revenues were from oil and gas, and that it was getting rid of 15,436 steelworkers. National Steel did get out of the steel business; it sold its tinplate plant in Weirton, West Virginia, to the employees, and its steel operations to Big Steel. "The steel operations of National were probably the most productive," said one steel analyst, "but even so, it is a tough way to make a living."

Steel jobs dropped 40 percent during the recession that began in 1980, and even when the economy turned up, steel jobs continued to be eliminated.

Walter F. Williams is president of Bethlehem Steel. An engineer, he directed the construction of the Burns Harbor plant. In 1981 his total compensation was $239,954. In 1982 it rose to $416,931. Williams's compensation increased so sharply, says the company, because his responsibilities increased. In 1987, it was $458,750. Observers of Smokestack America note that in 1979 Lee Iacocca of Chrysler pursued a different tactic. He also headed a company losing hundreds of millions of dollars a year. Iacocca took a *cut* of several hundred thousand dollars—in fact, to $1 per year until the company turned around.

Critics of the steelworkers say that their wage gains far outdistanced productivity, that their work practices and compensation made the industry vulnerable to foreign competition. In 1980 a Japanese steelworker was almost a third more productive than his American counterpart. By 1983 so many American jobs had been cut that the Americans were about even with the Japanese. More recently, with the dollar weak, American productivity measured even higher.

Even a casual observer of this part of Smokestack America cannot help but feel the pulses of the *adversarial* energy. Steel is an old technology; it used immigrant labor frequently, paid it well for the time, and the immigrant labor used it as the path to a degree of middle-class comfort. But this is not IBM, where if you last one year you supposedly never get fired. And it is certainly not Hewlett-Packard, where they want to know—at least in theory—what is the best in you, bring it out, and use it, where you might do five different jobs in a career. Steel is something else—it is butting heads. It is a class society, not a small-town, dissenting-Protestant, all-equal-here society.

And even a casual observer can see the coming trade-offs: the shrinking industry will try to get more productivity and more quality, and the work force will try to get job security through lifetime agreements, rather than by building fences around the jobs to protect them.

Whether the steel industry might have done more to avoid losing its share of market is by now academic. The facilities were built abroad, and it was not merely that they produced steel more cheaply, more efficiently; the steel industry charged that the foreign producers *dumped* their steel onto American markets, that they sold it—from subsidized mills at that—*below cost*. The *New York Times* had written a liberal, free-trade editorial saying let the cheapest steelmaker win; Donald Trautlein, Bethlehem's former chairman, wrote to the editor that even the efficient Japanese mills, and even the low-wage Brazilian mills, were losing money, according to independent trade information. "There is absolutely no free trade in steel anywhere in the world," said Trautlein, "and the American steel industry is being held hostage to problems and conditions in other parts of the world." Trautlein called for the restriction of imports. Imports have been restricted by a patchwork of quotas and "voluntary restrictions." That was not enough for Trautlein. He filed a complaint with the United States International Trade Commission, asking it to limit imports of all carbon steel.

The problems of the blue-collar work force are not limited to the steel industry. All manufacturing industries are going through a convulsion of redesigning and retooling, pressured by worldwide competition. "Downsizing" is becoming the buzzword of the 1980s, just as "synergy" was the buzzword of the conglomerates of the 1960s. John Deere, the farm-equipment company, survived the recession and came out well because it had built a new $1.5 billion facility in Waterloo, Iowa, that could operate at less than 50 percent capacity—but the new facility also meant one-third fewer workers. General Electric shut down more than one hundred different businesses in the name of "rationalizing." The 1980s were to be "lean and mean." And that meant the jobs disappeared from many towns like Johnstown.

Jack

"The jobs aren't coming back," said Jack Crichton, the chairman of the Johnstown Area Economic Development Corporation, a civic organization charged with doing something about that. "Not into smokestack industry. We have to get our forces lined up so we can survive without Bethlehem Steel. Last year we had twenty-five percent unemployment and we got national attention—and that twenty-five percent may have been low. But we don't look like Detroit or East St. Louis because we have solid family structures, so we don't have unemployment, we have well-educated people who just happen to be out of work. We don't want to be like Youngstown or Lackawanna—when you slip too far, it's hard to arrest. So business leadership is crucial. We're going to have small industry—no, not high-tech, that's Route 128 and Silicon Valley—we're *low*-tech. Somebody's going to have to build the cabinets for the computers. We have the Johnstown spirit. We're not about to die."

Bill

Johnstown has an unusual program for its steelworkers called Mainstream Access, run by William Pilder, an ex-seminarian with a doctorate in educational theory. Pilder is a slim, mustached man of forty-five.

"The social glue of this town still works," he says. "The families and the churches are very strong. But there's another side to it. The men are macho, but they're also dependent and passive. The Catholic Church has been very strong. Bethlehem Steel has been a nurturing company—if a roof of a school needed repairing, Bethlehem would send a crew to fix it. And the unions have said, follow our lead. The masculine spirit only moves when it comes to terms with the feminine—you have to get past the need for the maternal. It has to find its own way."

Mainstream's office is right in the center of town; it is decorated in bright colors, with contemporary furniture. The high cost of rent has come under criticism from state politicians because Mainstream has a state grant. "Some people think we should have rented a little hole at the edge of town, but it's important to project authority and confidence." On the walls of the Mainstream office are bulletin boards with notes from people who have gotten jobs. There is a space for advice to those who are still unemployed: MESSAGE TO PEOPLE STILL LOOKING. "Get out of town," says one. "Don't be afraid to wait in line (and know what to say when you get your chance)." "Take all the interviews you can get, even if it's a position you're not particularly interested in. The contact experience is well worth the trouble."

Rather than retraining, Mainstream teaches job-hunting skills. It administers some standard tests to the unemployed; most of them on what's called the Myers-Briggs test emerge as "sensation" types who "see the trees, not the forest." The steelworkers at Mainstream have formed clubs of twelve to fifteen men that meet once a week as support groups. Mainstream pipes in job leads.

Pilder comes from a strongly Roman Catholic family in Cincinnati. After high school he entered the Marianist order, which sent him to the Marianist University of Dayton; then, as a monk, he taught high school for five years. He left the Marianists after nine years, got a Ph.D. at Ohio State in curriculum development, and began to study Carl Jung. He went on to Indiana University, where he directed a master's program in adult education. "Universities are pedagogues, spoon-feeding children," says Pilder. "We had to design a learning environment for adults—we had, for example, a program to upgrade the skills of government managers."

Mainstream had been founded in 1969 to assist and counsel people leaving the churches, and Pilder used its counseling. In 1977 and 1978 he and his brother, also a psychologist, bought Mainstream and converted it to a sophisticated outplacement service. "It is continuing education for the dislocated worker," Pilder says. The Pilders began with professional people who were making career changes, and then started publishing small books on various industries, such as *The Data Processing Job Finder*. Mainstream is now the fourth-largest national outplacement service. Bethlehem Steel was looking for help in 1983 as it implemented a program to shrink from eighty to forty locations, and incidentally to cut its Johnstown work force in half. Funds for such programs come from the state, which gets them under the Federal Job Training Partnership Act, passed by Congress in 1983. Title III of the act is for workers who will never again return to the same work. Only 40 percent of the participants in the Johnstown Mainstream are from Bethlehem, but the others are victims of the "ripple effect" of Bethlehem cutbacks.

The first session of a Mainstream program in Johnstown tells the worker how the job market works. Then there is a course for four half-days designed to start a transformation. It is uncomfortable for many steelworkers to ask: Who am I? What are my strengths? What do I really like to do? What would I do if I had the chance? They take a workbook home and fill out very specifically the details of hobbies, skills, an inventory of how they express themselves. Then they graduate into Job Search Action Clubs—groups of about fifteen whose members meet weekly to discuss what they are doing to find jobs and what the reactions have been. They continue to meet until everyone has a job. Mainstream pipes the job leads into the smaller groups.

"We get two reactions," Pilder says. "About seven percent just walk out. They say, 'The mill is gonna call me back, the hell with this.' A more common reaction is 'I'll take anything.' You don't want that—that's energy lacking a direction. In order to make this work, you have to get a gut commitment and a personal dream.''

Counseling steelworkers is only half the battle; the community has to develop a positive attitude toward new businesses, banks have to welcome them with loans. The Pennsylvania hills and valleys have always had tension between the "hill people" and the "mill people," between "pork chop" and "fatback.'' It is a long way from the halls of union locals to the Sunnehanna Country Club and the downtown Bachelors Club of Johnstown, where business deals are mulled over, and where women still are not normally allowed.

New jobs are likely to be in much smaller companies, and in buildings that do not have the industrial majesty of a steelworks. They may pay less than $23 an hour. But they may offer an eventual piece of the action. It is a whole other way of life.

''What we have to do is to get people to see themselves in another way—we say put a new frame on yourself,'' says Pilder. ''A man may see himself as a millwright, an unemployed millwright, but he has a lot of other skills.

''Our work is really healing serious depression, healing depressed energies and getting them going. Carl Jung said you don't choose change, life steps up and challenges you and either you have the capacity to respond or not. So we're talking about a transformation of the psyche; individuals have to believe they can transform themselves in midlife—then the collective will move when the individual energy is freed.''

Pilder hopes that if Mainstream works at Johnstown, it can work other places, it can become a process that will ease America's structural unemployment. It is intriguing to think of depression as being something in the psyche as well as something in the economy. Can released energies create two hundred small businesses in Johnstown to replace just part of Bethlehem Steel? It is true, of course, that the Fortune 500 has added no new jobs in the last ten years, that all the jobs have come from newer, smaller enterprises. Talking about releasing depressed energies seems ''soft'' and indeterminate to some state legislators, and probably also to the designers of an "industrial policy" that would orchestrate the decline of America's "sunset industries."

The United States *will* have a steel industry—with any luck a livelier, more responsive, smaller one. But the jobs that went to Korea and Brazil will not come back. And the people who once held those steelworking jobs face a traumatic change.

Can they "reframe" themselves? It is a wonderfully American idea—pragmatism truly tested; if you have a funny face, learn to sing. We have always had, in this country, the idea that you should make something of yourself; now we have a generation of industrial workers who will be called on to make something *else* of themselves. A century ago, facing change of such magnitude, they might have lit out for the Territory; now the Territory is another state of mind. What we know is this: in an era of rapid change, many other Americans who now think themselves in secure and stable jobs may find themselves as lost and stunned as the steelworkers. And it may be the capacity of the spirit to respond that makes the difference.

Peter Drucker: The Best Opportunity Since 1910

What kind of time do we live in now? I asked this question of Peter Drucker, who has been an astute observer of business arts and practices for many years. A professor of social science and business administration at Claremont Graduate School, Drucker has written twenty books and has been an adviser to governments and management around the world.

"The next wave," he said, "is entrepreneurship. People think of Silicon Valley and high tech when they think of entrepreneurs, but high tech is the smallest part of the picture. Entrepreneurs have created more jobs in this country in the last ten years than have been created in the country's history. All of the new jobs have come from new companies—the Fortune 500 didn't add one job."

I asked what distinguished an entrepreneur from a manager.

"An entrepreneur is an innovator. He sees a gap. And, more recently, he has been doing what they said couldn't be done: applying management techniques to small and mundane businesses—restaurants, barbershops, new magazines. Today's entrepreneurs seem to learn management by osmosis. The younger generation have a laid-back life-style, but they are willing to work twenty hours a day, to risk their marriages—"

"Why are we seeing this burst of entrepreneurship now?" I asked.

"Partly demography. The people born in the baby boom go to work at big companies—General Electric, IBM, the Bank of America—and they find the pipelines are filled by people ahead of them who are only a couple of years older. The previous generation at the same age found a vacuum ahead of it—at twenty-eight, they might have had a boss who was forty-five. Now you might be thirty and have a boss who is thirty-three. So they strike out on their own, this current generation. And then, money—capital for investment—is easier to get, because investors have seen the results of successful entrepreneurship.

"Entrepreneurship can be learned but it can't be taught, so schools are not much good. You need a college degree because everybody has one and you need one to get started. You need some fifth-grade skills, like accounting and computer. The important lessons for entrepreneurs are how to build a team and how to have enough cash. Cash flow is what matters, watching your cash, projecting your cash needs so you don't have to go to the bank."

I asked Drucker what kind of economy he thought we would have in 1995; what kind of a time we are living in.

"I think we are now going to see in production what we have already seen in farming. You know that agriculture once used ninety percent of the labor force, and now it only uses four percent. I think manufacturing will go down to the same level—perhaps we will have four percent of the work force in blue-collar jobs in twenty years. We can automate four-fifths of what remains of America's industry."

"Does this mean the management end of production is a good place to be?"

"I think we have the best opportunity in manufacturing since 1910. Look, these things go in waves, in cycles. Before 1914 all the engineering schools sent their best people to the railroads. After World War I even dumb engineers didn't want to work for the railroads, and the railroads went steadily downhill. Now the railroads are coming back, they are highly automated, highly concentrated, and they are going to be well managed and they are going to attract able young people.

"People with a background in a combination of engineering and management are going to be in high demand, because the labor force is going to diminish. If we require a million workers to produce eight million cars, in ten or fifteen years we may require only one hundred fifty thousand workers for the same eight million cars."

"Do you think entrepreneurship could be applied to the public sector, to government, as well?"

"Government has been the great success story and the great failure story of our time. When I was a boy, governments were really not expected to do much. Then in the '30s and '40s we began to have the dream that governments could do a great deal—until we finally began to believe they could do everything. And now we are beginning to believe they do nothing well—that all they know how to do is wage war and to debase the currency, and now they do not even wage war.

"If this idea gathers momentum, we will see a split between government the provider and government the supplier—that is, the government may still deliver the service, but it will hire an outside contractor. It's not such a radical idea. The government does not build all its own missiles."

Well, here are some major ideas to mull over—and some unresolved problems. If blue-collar workers drop to 4 percent of the work force, what happens to the workers who have been automated out? Placing and counseling those workers is obviously a boom business. So is creating the businesses that people need and that the government will deliver but will have to buy from the outside sector.

Will entrepreneurship stay a favored occupation, or will it fade, like being a *pro bono* lawyer? I think it may have a long run, because it is becoming intellectually fashionable, and that means that the establishments in government and education will create an institutional framework that supports it.

The idea that the entrepreneur is a noble and necessary animal in society is only recently fashionable. The economist who celebrated the entrepreneur, Joseph Schumpeter, is now getting renewed attention; he is, it is said in some circles, as great as Keynes.

Why is this important? Economic theories give justification to the actions we are in the process of taking. In the '30s the government was increasing its role out of sheer desperation in an economic crisis; it was already in the process when Keynes's *General Theory* was published in 1936 and had so much impact. To Keynes, innovation came from "outside"—it was not really part of economics, even though it had an influence. But to Schumpeter, innovation was the essence of capitalism; he called it creative destruction. New products, new processes, new jobs. This dynamism, this constant change, requires new investment, and the new investment requires profit—profit is a cost of doing business. This idea is profoundly different from the view that saw a profit as surplus, something that had been taken out of the hides of exploited workers.

What kind of a time are we living in? We know that business is now fashionable, as it was not fifteen years ago. We don't know how long this particular wave or cycle will last, but right now we believe that markets work and governments do not; that profits are not without honor, and neither are the people who earn them. At some later time these ideas may be reversed, as they have been before, but this is the age of Joseph Schumpeter and the entrepreneur.

William H. Whyte and the Decline of Fear

It is the age of the entrepreneur, says Peter Drucker. Entrepreneurs view the workplace in a different way than the organization men of major companies, and they mobilize their energies in a different way.

I think that the attitude toward work varies directly with the distance from the Great Depression. It's almost impossible to convey the fear endemic in that decade to any present generation.

Imagine a situation like this: There are almost no women working in offices; the only women working have low-paying jobs in factories like textile mills. So few women contribute to household income. One out of every four men is unemployed and has no prospects for employment—even men with good degrees from top universities. There is no unemployment insurance. In many places there are pay *cuts* every year, which make a home mortgage an intolerable burden. And intellectuals are writing that capitalism is dead.

The college graduates of the 1950s had sat at their parents' dinner tables when they were growing up, and heard of uncles and cousins whose firms had folded, or who had been let go, and who had never worked again. William H. Whyte is the author of *The Organization Man,* the classic work of sociological reporting of the 1950s, and in its way the nonfiction companion to Sloan Wilson's novel *The Man in the Gray Flannel Suit.* Whyte camped out with the young businessmen who were so eager to get ahead, who were moved by their companies all around the country, and whose wives moved with them from suburb to suburb.

"It was easy for me to understand them," Whyte says. "In my hometown, near Philadelphia, I remember people who were destitute in the Depression. These weren't alcoholics or incompetents— they were the upper crust at the golf club, the John O'Hara heroes and heroines who had danced the night away in the 1920s, people who had gone to Smith and Vassar and Yale and Penn. And they would literally and gratefully take an old sport coat that wasn't too worn, things like that."

Whyte was an editor of *Fortune* in the 1950s, and he wrote a major article titled "The Class of '49." "People expected another Depression," Whyte says. "The jobs at big companies like AT&T were prized—the guys would say, 'It may not be exciting, but there will always be an AT&T.'

"One of the sad things was that many of these men really believed that the companies were out to nourish them and develop them, that they were being moved from post to post and suburb to suburb for their own development. They would tell each other, 'The company has a plan for you.' Of course, the company didn't reveal the plan, and the shock of a lifetime years later would be to find that there was no plan.

"Big business was deified. The Harvard Business School taught the theology, and if you read the popular fiction of the time—which I did—you read that the boss was gruff and temperamental but underneath was a wise father figure, and his wife was just a wonderful woman. Gradually the generation that had gone to work so gratefully for big business realized the problems. I remember vividly a research director at General Electric, wrestling with one of the big decisions of his life. He said, 'In a company like this, all the major decisions are made for you by other people. Every once in a while, circumstances come together that permit you to make a decision yourself. I hope I don't muff it.' So intelligent people became suspicious of their own large organizations.

"The harsh fact is that big business didn't really want the best people, if by best we mean the most creative, the most innovative, the most intelligent. They didn't want a creative person who would rock the boat. The administrators would say, 'His loyalty isn't to the company, it's to his profession.' I think it's in the nature of bureaucracies to bear down on the individuals. I know—you see a lot of companies trying now to reward innovation, trying to keep the creative people—but the basic thrust of a bureaucracy works against that. The administrators are always in charge, so there is always some paranoia in the big companies, even at the top. Look at the 'golden parachutes' top executives write for themselves now, against the day someone may toss *them* out. And below the top ranks, even paternalistic companies can be cruel. Just this year I've seen people at places like CBS and Time Inc. fired after decades of service, and told to clean out their desks on Friday and not come back.

"We have a mythology of individualism in this country, but basically we are a nation of large organizations. Have things changed since *The Organization Man?* Some of the *style* of business has changed. The organization man worked very hard—and I think the current generation works hard. I talked to college students and I have a certain sense of *déjà vu*—they are conservative, they want to get ahead, and many of them will end up in large organizations. There are trends in motion leading to bigger and bigger companies; RCA was a multibillion-dollar company, yet it was taken over by General Electric. Megamergers seem to be the order of the day, and each merger brings its own wave of truncated careers. That isn't to say that it isn't possible to get ahead, to make a lot of money, to have a good career; it's just to say that the individual is always going to be secondary to the organization.''

One is struck, reading about the man in the gray flannel suit, and the organization man, not by how the businessmen were influenced by money, but by how little money it took. Tom Rath, the hero of *The Organization Man,* thought a raise of $1,000 was large. Now you would have to adjust for the price inflation of thirty years to remember that the first houses in Levittown sold for less than $9,000—the whole house, even though a small house—and that room, board, and the tuition at the most expensive Ivy League institution was probably $2,000 a year. Today I'm not sure that someone would change jobs for a raise of $5,000, if only the money was at stake.

I'm still struck—remembering the distant echoes of the survivors of the Depression—when I hear people say they quit a job because they were bored, or because they had done it long enough, and now they are going to look around. What strikes me is that *confidence* that there will be something there when they are ready to go back to work—something more interesting and better-paying.

In at least two ways we are a far different country than we were in the days of the organization man. We are a far richer country, of course. The parents of today's generation own their houses—we have had thirty years of houses being paid off—and merely to have that much housing *owned* by the people who live in it creates a hugely different psychological state. The banker is not going to twist his mustache and throw the family out on Friday, because the family has a lot of equity. And incidentally, children know that that equity is there, to be inherited someday.

And there is one other aspect of the American economy that I think has made a huge difference in how we perceive work. We still have a Fortune 500—giant companies doing billions of dollars in business—and for the most part, I am sure they are bureaucracies much as Whyte described them. But for the past twenty years, all the incremental jobs have been created by smaller companies. And in new companies, the nature of work changes.

The large corporation grew with the Industrial Revolution. It was characteristic of the large industrial company to have huge assets and require a lot of capital. It took a lot of money and a lot of iron to build a coast-to-coast railroad. To build an aluminum company like Alcoa you need enormous sums of money; producing aluminum requires massive amounts of power and huge plants. No one splits off from Aloca and starts another multibillion-dollar aluminum company. Thirty years ago, the United States was dominated by large manufacturing companies. They had theif own style and corporate culture. Even today, many of the biggest companies in the country are much as they were—the major oil and automobile companies.

But many manufacturing jobs have moved overseas, while the jobs that have grown up here are in the service sector: marketing, data processing, consulting, design—"knowledge" industries. These are industries where the assets are not huge turbines churning out hydroelectric power to produce aluminum—the assets are people. They go down in the elevator every night. If enough of them leave, the company is hurt. If a group of them form a splinter and then start their own company, they may well compete with the parent company. We have heard about the "information society"; one of the aspects of the information society is that the corporations have to be more agreeable places in which to work because the *people* produce the work—not a machine tool or a turbine.

The information society is worldwide, but the culture of the information society sprang up first in this country. We also have something that is unique—the cult of the entrepreneur. Every country has entrepreneurs, but we are now in the process of creating a national entrepreneurial culture. To be a good entrepreneur, you have to take the risk of failing. Entrepreneurs do fail—they count it as growing pains—and start again. The idea that you can take risks—fail—and start again would have seemed as foreign as Saturn to the old organization man. What is most impressive in the changing attitude toward work is the decline of fear.

Business schools now give courses in entrepreneurship. They cite cases like Rod Canion and Jim Harris and Bill Murto, who started Compaq Computer and achieved sales of a *billion* dollars within five years, a spectacular success. But most start-ups do not involve sophisticated computers. Some of them are traditional businesses with new niches, like Liz Claiborne.

Liz Claiborne's Secret

There *is* a Liz Claiborne. I do not travel in designer circles, and I know very little about fashion. Sometimes these names are made up: there certainly is a Gloria Vanderbilt, whose name goes on the jeans, and there is a Calvin Klein and a Ralph Lauren, but there isn't a Sasson, not designing clothes anyway.

I got curious about Liz Claiborne because not only is she the name on the lines of clothes, but she is also an entrepreneur, and it was in that capacity that she came to my attention.

Thirteen years ago Claiborne started a small sportswear company with her husband, Art Ortenberg. Liz had been a designer since she was twenty-one. The Ortenbergs picked up a production man, Leonard Boxer, and a marketing man, Jerry Chazen, and they started the business with $50,000 of their own savings and another $200,000 from family and friends.

Liz Claiborne Inc.'s sales revenues in 1987 were $1 billion. Stock in the company, which went public in 1981, had gone up fifteenfold from the original offering; the market value of the company topped $1 billion. All this in a business known for its cutthroat competition, in which companies start up, streak like shooting stars through the night sky, and disappear. I thought, Liz Claiborne must know something about American women.

I have walked *through* the fashion district in New York countless times—you can't help it if you walk in New York—but I had never been *in* it. I met Jerry Chazen, the senior vice-president for marketing, at breakfast time one morning in the company's headquarters. The streets and elevators were full of men and women—mostly women—going to work, and the atmosphere was acutely different from what lay only a few blocks away.

In the world of television or magazines, the women often look casual; some of them might even go to work in jeans and sneakers. Here around Seventh Avenue each outfit was an event; getting dressed in the morning was preparing to go onstage. On the street corner, a woman in purple stockings and a purple dress with a paisleylike pattern (my primitive fashion vocabulary inhibits me) waited for the stoplight to change. The woman standing next to her nodded, said, "That's pretty." The woman in purple nodded in return, reached over, felt the lapel of the jacket of her commentator, traced the line of a buttonhole with her thumb, and said, "Nice." Then the women walked off in opposite directions.

"What made it happen?" said Chazen over breakfast as he talked about the company's growth. "Two things. One is that the women went to work. The schools are pumping out a half million of these ladies a year. Some of them used to marry early and stay home. If you stay home, all you need is jeans or a cotton dress. But the difference in women going to work—especially now that women have gone into the professions—is billions of dollars a year in clothes. Billions. And the second reason is Liz herself. She has an eye as finely tuned as a musician with absolute pitch.

"I think of one particular incident that told me what was going on. We shipped this twill skirt around the country and waited for the reception. A retailer in Houston called me and said he had sold six in one day. I said, that's great, do me a favor—find out who bought them and why. The retailer called back and said, get this, all six were bought by the same woman. She came in with her mother; her mother said, 'She's just graduated law school, and now she's going to work.' "

"I'm Liz," said Liz. Liz has close-cropped black hair, oversize tinted tortoiseshell glasses, a handsome smile. She wore a checkered shirt, cowboy boots, and stirrup pants. (Stirrup pants, for males whose fashion vocabularies are also limited, have loops to put your feet through, which anchor the pants and give them a taut silhouette.) Liz's office is very white—white walls, white surfaces everywhere. Flowers. No chairs. We sat on two stools at a white table.

Liz Claiborne is from an old New Orleans family. Her father worked for Morgan Guaranty in Brussels, so Liz grew up in both the United States and Europe and went to art schools in Brussels and Paris.

"I've always loved clothes. My mother liked sewing. I studied painting, and I think growing up in Europe was a help to the eye. Europeans have a more careful sense of the visual than Americans. Americans might put a paper carton of milk on the table; Europeans would pour the milk into a pitcher and put the pitcher on the table. I told my family I wanted to work in fashion, and they were dead set against it. It was—well, too New York, too rough. But at twenty-one I won a *Harper's Bazaar* design contest and headed for New York with a sketchbook. I was a designer at Jonathan Logan for sixteen years before we started this company."

I asked Claiborne if her family had ever changed their mind about the rough New York business.

"It took a long time. It's not as rough now."

I said building one of America's fastest-growing companies must have helped—and also the idea that she owned stock in her own company worth hundreds of millions.

"It did," said Claiborne.

She has a son in his thirties, from her first marriage. Both husbands have been in the apparel business.

I asked Claiborne what she could tell about corporate society from its clothes.

"When the women first went to work, they had no sense of themselves," Claiborne said. "The clothes were all designed to make them look like mini-men. The designers took the man's pin-stripe business suit and just changed it a bit so it would fit a woman. White blouse, floppy bow tie, sometimes even a four-in-hand tie. It was as if all the men were in the boardroom and all the women would be in the boardroom, too—as if everybody started at the top. But the women weren't *in* the boardroom.

"You can still see that style in very high-powered New York law firms, or financial firms. Where money is real money and power is power, you'd better be in hose and high heels—but even there you don't have to be in a man's suit.

"I think the clothes women wear to work are getting more feminine, as women become more secure in business. Also, corporations themselves are getting looser, more oriented to people—they've heard so much about the Japanese. The Japanese have quality circles and they ask for all the workers' opinions—at least, that's what you hear.

"I walk to work. I get a kick out of seeing how women dress—women are busy, they don't want to bother as much with clothes, and they need reassurance, they have to be told it's okay. I've had a woman ask me, 'Can I wear your shirt with an Anne Klein pant?'

"Fashion can flow from the street up. Paris is a great laboratory, because European women get a sense of their own individuality more quickly than Americans do. California women have great confidence in casual wear. We started in sportswear, and we still produce a more casual look."

I asked Claiborne what was the most surprising thing about American women that could be learned from the clothes that they bought.

"Well, you hear a lot about fitness. You sell sports clothes and jogging clothes, and the general feeling is that women are much more fit than they used to be, but the clothing sales tell us that 30 percent of them are overweight.

"I'll tell you a secret. The *image* of American women that's out there is a slim, trim California blonde. That's the TV commercial. She runs along the beach in a bathing suit and she opens a Pepsi and laughs. She brushes her hair, she has perfect teeth, she sells you toothpaste. In the pantyhose commercials she comes down the stairs and walks along the street and men turn around.

"That's the Madison Avenue image. But we know. We know, because we see what sizes sell, and we hear what sizes the women *want* the sizes to be. I know who buys my clothes. I *like* these women, I know them. The fact is, the American woman is, well, *pear-shaped*. But you don't see pear-shaped women on TV. We make clothing for women shaped the way they are, and they look good, and they feel good about themselves in them, and that's the secret."

Unlike some of the older American apparel firms, Liz Claiborne Inc. has few factories. Most of its production is contracted out to independent manufacturers who produce the finished clothes—and most of their factories are in the Orient.

"We don't do a design and then add the cost of producing and selling. We do a sample, and then we think—*I* think—if I was going to wear this to my job, how much would I pay for it? Then we try to keep the cost to that.

"I go to Hong Kong, Taiwan, Korea," said Claiborne. "We have contracts in Sri Lanka and the Philippines."

Isn't this tough on American jobs?

"It is. When we started, we manufactured here. We were a union shop. But you can't match these developing countries. Let's face it, in the developing countries, working in an apparel factory is a good job. But no American mother wants to see her daughter sitting in front of a sewing machine in a factory."

What happens to American jobs, then?

"Well, we worry about that, just like we worry about the legislation that would put on tariffs or quotas to protect those jobs. Americans can produce clothes at the high end, the luxury end, but even Japan exports jobs to India and China. We just can't be labor-intensive."

Except, I suggested, on the design end.

"Well, that's right. When I started, design was a glamour trade for women. Come in, sketch, long lunch, worry about parties and whether you're going to them, leave at five. Now the designers fill their heads with research, and they work twelve hours a day. You have to be involved all the way—the business is changing. We have megaretailers, buying megabatches of clothes. It's not just Lord & Taylor, it's *forty-five branches* of Lord & Taylor, and the product has to be there."

Stock-market lore tells us that when the hemlines rise, so does the market. In the Depression the hemlines dropped to the ankles— where to now?

"Hemlines are all over the place, both up and down," said Liz Claiborne. "All I can tell you about the trend is that things are moving faster and faster and faster."

Working Women

"What made it happen?" asked Liz Claiborne's partner. Women went to work. Of course, women have always worked, but now they are going *to* work, to offices, in Liz Claiborne's clothes. F. Scott Fitzgerald described a character in *The Great Gatsby* as having a fine, solid stripe—"as if she had first learned to walk upon golf courses on clean sharp mornings." In cities where people walk to work, like New York, you can now see that stride everywhere. The women that don't wear Liz Claiborne may still wear suits—a modification of the man's pinstripe that is the uniform of serious purpose. They wear white Brooks Brothers blouses, floppy bow ties, white athletic socks, and running shoes. Handbag over the shoulder, or leather Dunhill briefcase in hand, they cover block after block. Where are the high heels, the Pappagallos and the Garolinis? In the closet at the office, or in the filing cabinet. High heels are not made for the Scott Fitzgerald stride. One only wonders why it took so long to arrive at this point. Adaptation is how the species survives.

The working woman is not new, even though there is a real revolution in the kind of work women are doing. The Pill gave women sexual freedom and more control of their bodies; the economy is giving them opportunities far beyond the Gold Card from American Express. Economists report dryly that women are entering the work force, as if previously they were all somebody's mother playing Mah-Jongg in a Philip Roth story. Women have always been in the work force, and not just in the uncounted work force of domestics. We know of the horrendous factory work in the early industrial age, but sometimes work was collegial and not unpleasant.

There is a column called "A Hundred Years Ago Today" in my town's weekly newspaper. Some of the columns go back further. Two hundred years ago, a hundred years ago, the town was a college town and a farming community. What is surprising—at least in the microprocessor age—is how much work was done in the evening and collegially. You had quilting bees and shucking sessions, you had weaving and canning, and church in midweek was also a social occasion. It was still work, but without the isolation that suburbia brought a hundred years later.

So what is new is not women working, but women working in what used to be a man's world.

Some of the pioneering women were, with the first stage of feminist consciousness, quite bold. I sat on a visiting committee sometime ago at Harvard. Our chairwoman brought her infant to the annual meeting, nursed it while crisply going down the agenda, and conducted the meeting with the baby still at her breast. When the infant was sated, she wrapped it up, patted it, and put it into the opened file drawer of a desk. Some of the older members of the committee struggled to keep their eyebrows from arching. I'm not sure women put infants in file drawers anymore; that seems more like a first-stage phenomenon. Children are the stress point of the current revolution in the workplace. You can see the anguish prototypically in magazines: "I want to use all my abilities and talents," say the young women. "I want to have children. How can I compete in the working world and still have children? How can I try a case at nine A.M. if I have a two A.M. feeding? Do I have to be Superwoman?"

This is a lament that does not arouse much sympathy from the women who missed the first stage. I mentioned it—the problem of the competitive job and the demanding infant—to a woman novelist whose children are now teenagers. "I've heard it a lot," she said. "I'm tired of the whining. That whining is making its way into a lot of women's fiction. I wish I'd had the *chance* to go to law school or business school—I might have been terrible at either—but when I went to college I was also cooking for my husband, who was in graduate school. Children don't stay infants forever—they're out the door and at least on their way to school in a surprisingly short time, and they adjust rapidly. The hard part is to be in the men's world on men's terms." The first-stage women were highly mobilized; hence *Superwoman* did not seem so farfetched.

I once worked with a very bright, extremely attractive woman named Kristin who was perhaps three years out of the Harvard Business School. She was a first-wave Nikes-and-stockings, and she was also a demon for work. If I went to the office in the evening, she was there. What was she doing till midnight? "Just crunching some numbers," she said. "Something I want to get done." When, then, did she see her friends? Her male friends? "When the guys call, I tell them to pick me up at midnight," she said. "I'm serious about work, and if they understand that, they do, and if they don't, there are others."

Kristin used to pass along to me prospectuses of magazines that were for sale. "You want to own them, not work for them," she wrote across the top of one. "We could turn this dog around, what think?" Kristin set up a meeting for me one night with seven of her women friends from the Harvard Business School. They were in finance, broadcasting, advertising, politics. They all intended to have families, and they were confident they could keep the family priorities in line with their ambitions. I took notes. Each of them said, "My mother told me I *could,* and my father encouraged me." Kristin went off to Hong Kong, but I have no doubt that her high-energy group managed both career and family. All it takes is the kind of discipline that gets the men to pick you up at midnight, the sense of organization that knows the file drawer is empty when you want to put the baby in it, and the energy to arrive for work at nine-thirty the day after a day that began at midnight. It isn't really fair; it's like noting social phenomena from the vitae of class presidents.

Superwoman is not every woman, and every woman should not have to be Superwoman. But the *image* of Superwoman is much older than the Harvard Business School. Some of these images are very deep in the unconscious. Consider, for example, the "virtuous woman" in Proverbs. (The version quoted here is from *The Bible Designed to Be Read as Living Literature,* published by Simon & Schuster.) She has a family because "her children rise up, and call her blessed." She is a very efficient homemaker:

> She riseth also while it is yet night
> And giveth meat to her household,
> And their task to her maidens.

So she is up before dawn, delegating tasks. And while Proverbs says, "Her clothing is fine linen and purple," she is very much at home in the pinstripe power suit. She is in real estate—

> She considereth a field, and buyeth it;

in agriculture—

> With the fruit of her hands she planteth a vineyard.

in manufacturing and selling—

> She perceiveth that her merchandise is profitable:
> Her lamp goeth not out by night. . . .
>
> She is not afraid of the snow for her household;
> For all her household are clothed with scarlet. . . .
>
> She seeketh wool and flax,
> And worketh willingly with her hands. . . .
>
> She maketh linen garments and selleth them;
> And delivereth girdles unto the merchant.
> Strength and dignity are her clothing;
> And she laugheth at the time to come.

So the virtuous woman is buying fields, negotiating the mortgage, planting the vineyards, determining the state of the textile market, dealing with merchants as to linen garments and girdles—and don't forget, not all the maidens to whom she delegated could be expected to do their tasks perfectly; some of them must have showed up late, or loitered with the local louts. What, you might ask, did the virtuous woman's *husband* do?

> Her husband is known in the gates,
> When he sitteth among the elders of the land.

That's what he does, he sitteth. And praiseth her, saying:

> "Many daughters have done virtuously,
> But thou excellest them all."

Well, I would, too. Praiseth, that is, Superwoman! I think the virtuous woman was invented by a man.

Something happened to the image of the working woman between the virtuous woman of the Hebrews, 300 B.C. or so, and nineteenth-century England. Perhaps work was considered brutish in England, and hence with the first fruits of the industrial age it was thought that no genteel woman *ought* to work. Virginia Woolf has a lovely little book, a kind of tone poem, called *A Room of One's Own*. The book is the text of two addresses delivered in 1928 and 1929, and in it she muses about what an upper-middle-class girl could do:

> I had made my living by cadging odd jobs from newspapers, by reporting a donkey show here or a wedding there; I had earned a few pounds by addressing envelopes, reading to old ladies, teaching the alphabet to small children in a kindergarten.

Now, that is really sad, but, I suppose, very much the proper English upper-middle-class lady. What a limited environment! No delivering girdles to the merchant, no making linen garments and selling them, no buying fields and planting vineyards. The English lady of 1910 was no match for the virtuous woman of Judea, 300 B.C. The English lady had learned some French, enough perhaps to travel across the Channel in genteel circumstances. She might be able to paint a watercolor. It's possible that she might have had a whiff of household accounting. But—at least according to Virginia Woolf—she could not go out alone after dark; she was always waiting upon men or for them, waiting for brothers to bring home their friends, or for husbands to return from wherever, waiting with pale skin—to have a sunburn meant to be a farm girl—behind closed drapes. Progress is not always continuous.

But while Virginia Woolf lamented the constraints of her own middle-class education, she could see that that of men was limited as well:

> It had bred in them defects as great. . . . The instinct for possession, the rage for acquisition which drives them to desire other people's fields and goods perpetually; to make frontiers and flags; battleships and poison gas; to offer up their own lives and their children's lives.

This has become a common theme among feminist writers—that women are *different*, more nurturing, more tuned in to relationships, more caring. But women are still "cats in a dog's world," as one lecturer recently put it. "They have to learn to bark." Women have, writes Frances Wickes, a Jungian psychologist, some qualities men do not have, whether thinking or feeling, intuition or sensation. But their education is geared to suit the man's world. "From kindergarten to college, the curriculum is often a hand-me-down, patterned on what was formerly considered the proper training for the masculine intellect only. In this world the young woman finds herself competing with men and measuring herself by masculine standards."

I have brought up these different images—the virtuous wife and poor, constricted Virginia Woolf—to arrive at two seemingly obvious but rather dynamic conclusions.

The first is that the United States is different from Europe, and that what is going on with women and work is on the cutting edge. The Japanese, British, and Germans will follow in five or ten years. Virginia Woolf lamented how little university education was open to women in Great Britain, but in the United States the state universities, at least, had admitted them since right after the Civil War. (True, they could not attend many of the classes, sometimes merely on the grounds that it distracted the men.) Recently I attended a conference on folk tales and fairy tales, since these stories often reflect the attitudes of society. You want quiet, passive women? Look at Sleeping Beauty and poor old Snow White. Talkative, clever women must be witches. It takes a handsome prince to wake up Snow White. But while the German Cinderella of the Brothers Grimm is quite passive, the American Cinderella develops a spunkiness of her own. Told she has no clothes to go to the ball, she says, "I'll make them"; told she is dirty, she says, "I'll wash." That is why I have always liked James Thurber's version of Little Red Riding Hood. Told to approach a little closer to the wicked wolf, the wise little girl pulls out an automatic and shoots the wolf dead, and the moral of the story is, *It is not so easy to fool little girls nowadays as it used to be.* So my first conclusion is that what is happening to women in the workplace is happening fastest in the United States.

My second conclusion goes back to my first image—the young woman in the pinstripe power suit, striding along in her stockings and her Nikes. She is happy because life is not charity, roses, and niceness—in fact, it is quite exciting. But she is still in a power suit, educated in a masculine curriculum, competing with men in a masculine world. What would that world be like if there were a critical mass of women operating with *women's* sensibilities? It might experience the most startling turn in its history since the invention of the wheel.

Newly Blonde Women, Hirsute Men

The Virtuous Woman of our time may well be working in an office, and certainly has more in common with the Hebrew woman of 300 B.C. than post-Victorian Virginia Woolf. Did Virginia Woolf ever considereth a field and buyeth it? She had a marvelous sensibility, but I'm not sure she had a checking account. Like Jane Austen, she thought luxury was to have a room of one's own.

The contemporary Virtuous Woman may well be blonde, or partially blonde, even if she was not born so. This is a fashion, taken for granted. It was not always so. In the courts of the Catherines of Russia, women dyed their hair black. To be blonde, in fact to be tan or sunburned, was the mark of a peasant. No one else was out in the sun; ladies of breeding and class strolled with parasols (para sol, guarding against sun).

This particular revolution—blondeness—was triggered by an advertising copywriter named Shirley Polykoff, who was working on the Clairol account. Before Shirley Polykoff, "bleached blonde" was a derogatory term, and most women were *not* blondes. Shirley Polykoff asked, do blondes have more fun? The idea was that you could *be* a blonde—try out your blonde self—and retreat if you didn't like it. It worked brilliantly, the Clairol colors suggested California, beach, summer. Clairol and its competitors had a new multibillion-dollar market. Women became Summer blondes, California blondes, Sunbeam blondes, Topaz blondes, no more mouse-brown hair. Other shades were not neglected—there was Moonlit Brown, Honey Red, Silvery Pearl—but blonde was the revolution, blonde was what you changed to, and now we have Summer blondes even in darkest winter and Clairol is one of the engines of a great worldwide company, Bristol-Myers.

There is some evidence that men may be about to have a hair revolution of their own, but it doesn't involve hair color. It's the hair itself. We are on the cusp of another revolution, this one somewhere between blondeness and the Pill. The Food and Drug Administration is evaluating the topical application of an existing high-blood-pressure prescription drug, minoxidil. Minoxidil, it seems, grows hair.

Like many scientific breakthroughs, the minoxidil story hinges on serendipity. The story begins with the Upjohn company of Kalamazoo, Michigan. Upjohn has been in the drug business for a century, since William Upjohn, a country doctor, devised what he called a "friable" pill. Pills in the 1880s were so hard that they frequently passed right through the patient without dissolving; the friable pill could be mashed with a thumb. Like many nineteenth-century drug companies, Upjohn began with ointments, elixirs, and syrups, but in the early twentieth century a distinguished Yale-educated scientist named Frederick Heyl led the company into organized medical research. Within a few decades, Upjohn was selling products that are still around: Kaopectate for diarrhea, cod-liver oil, Unicap vitamins. In the 1950s, Upjohn became a leader in the sale of steroids as anti-inflammatory drugs and expanded into veterinary medicine; in the 1960s, it branched out into health-care services as well. Today Upjohn is a worldwide company with annual sales of $2 billion.

In the 1970s, some Upjohn researchers tested a white, crystalline solid called minoxidil, a generic compound whose patents had already expired. Technically, the substance was called a pyridine; its formula was 2, 4-pyrimidinediamin, 6-(1 piperidinyl)-, 3 oxide. Its molecular weight was 209.25. Upjohn thought that minoxidil would improve cases of high blood pressure, and it was tested on groups of volunteers. The compound was successful in the treatment of high blood pressure. The test data were submitted to the FDA, the drug was approved, and minoxidil became the Upjohn prescription drug Loniten.

Some of the volunteers reported a curious side effect. They were *growing hair*—chest hair, leg hair, and scalp hair. Not all the volunteers reported this, and among those who did, not all the hair was "terminal," or normal; some of it was "vellus," or fine and downy. The hair growth didn't seem to affect minoxidil's properties in the primary area of blood-pressure control, and since the side effect wasn't harmful, the original Upjohn researchers ignored it.

The Upjohn researchers did ask themselves *why* minoxidil had this effect. It was a peripheral vasodilator—that is, it dilated blood vessels that would otherwise have been too constricted to allow hair growth. Perhaps the increased supply of blood was good for the scalp. But there are other vasodilators that don't grow hair. Standing on your head can also increase the flow of blood, and headstands have not been known to cure baldness in anyone. What happens at the cellular level when minoxidil is applied to the scalp is still obscure, but Upjohn filed a report with the Securities and Exchange Commission in April 1986 that detailed the testing of Rogaine. It said that 65 percent of the 1,833 men tested reported "a smaller-diameter bald spot."

Male-pattern baldness is called alopecia androgenetica: *alopecia* meaning hair loss, *andro* referring to the male hormone, and *genetica* meaning inherited. In some genetic patterns, the hairline recedes as male hormones diminish, a bald spot develops on the crown of the head, and finally the male is left with a horseshoe-shaped band of hair around his skull. In most instances hair stops falling out when it has reached the horseshoe shape.

Baldness cures have been sold for thousands of years, and while bald heads may be considered virile by some, most men would rather have hair. So it was not surprising that word of the minoxidil tests got out. Dermatologists began mashing up Upjohn's Loniten tablets to a powder (the "friable" quality of Dr. Upjohn's pills remained), then mixing them with a base solution, sometimes cold cream. Some charged hefty fees for this, and very soon the minoxidil-mixers were not limited to dermatologists.

Upjohn heard of this in 1985 and warned there might be side effects—the FDA had approved minoxidil as a prescription drug only in specific dosage, taken internally, for high blood pressure. But a kind of gray market in minoxidil began to grow.

Meanwhile, the attention spread far beyond the usual bands of security analysts who follow drug companies, to the rest of Wall Street, which certainly has its share of bald heads. In August 1984, Upjohn sold on the New York Stock Exchange at less than ten times its anticipated annual earnings. Upjohn's competitors, Merck, Pfizer, Lilly, and Squibb—other major pharmaceutical companies—sold slightly higher in relation to their earnings. Analysts worried at the time that Upjohn's biggest earner, Motrin, an antiarthritis drug, was losing ground.

But in less than two years, Upjohn quadrupled. The market value of Upjohn stock went from $1.5 billion in 1984 to $6 billion in 1986. Many of Upjohn's drugs are doing well; it has an antianxiety drug, Xanax, and a sleep inducer, Halcion, that have been well accepted. But at least some of the incremental billions in market value have sprung from *perception,* and anticipation. It isn't minoxidil, the high-blood-pressure drug, that has caused the excitement. Loniten is doing only about $40 million a year. It has been the prospect of the baldness cure Upjohn is calling Rogaine. (It tried *Re*gain, but for some reason that didn't work.)

In one report to the SEC, the Upjohn researchers were counting hairs to the inch. And Wall Street has been counting bald heads—heads with receding hairlines, heads with bald spots on the crown, heads with only a horseshoe left. How many of those are there? How many in the world? No one knows, but the idea provides the same kind of exciting fantasy the Boston textile merchants entertained when they considered the possibilities of trade with China in the nineteenth century: if only each Chinese wore a robe one inch longer. . .

Wall Street loves these factors:
- Rogaine doesn't work on everybody—but nobody knows whether he is in the chosen group until he tries it.
- Rogaine will be a prescription drug. Thus it will have the authority of the medical profession behind it. Some of the doctors might use it themselves, and—
- You have to keep taking it! If Rogaine does grow some hair for you—and you stop applying it—the new hair falls out!
- Rogaine will be expensive—and very profitable.

And finally, the Upjohn company will be able to start up a whole array of over-the-counter, nonprescription products to go along with Rogaine—shampoos, conditioners, and so on. They have already begun work on shampoo.

So here is what I foresee:

I see gentlemen on commuter trains and in locker rooms comparing the patches on their scalps.

I see a lot of anxious peering into bathroom mirrors early in the morning. Did it work? Didn't it work? Was that hair there before? Is that terminal or vellus?

I see medical researchers, fascinated with biochemistry, trying to figure out *why* a vasodilator will *grow hair*.

I see disgruntled alumni of Rogaine—those who tried it unsuccessfully, or those who tried it and decided it was too expensive, or too much trouble for the visible results.

And I see every *other* major pharmaceutical house furiously reassembling chemical nuclei like pyridine and piperidine, trying for a formula that will have the same effect, yet safely skirt Upjohn's new patents. Sooner or later, Rogaine will have a competitor.

And after a few years, society will take it for granted. Some men will have some new hair, many more will still be bald, and some will be defiantly bald, or balding, just as some women today have never been any shade of blonde in spite of Shirley Polykoff.

3 CONFUCIAN CAPITALISM: THE RISE OF THE RIM

The jobs that left Johnstown and Toledo and Peoria did not disappear altogether, they migrated. Occasionally, they went to Brazil, or to the *maquiladores,* the custom-free zones in Mexico. But the migration was chiefly to the Far East, to the countries of East Asia, anchored by Japan, that became known as the Rim of Asia.

The Rise of the Rim

A system loosed from moorings meant that actions were no longer contained neatly and hermetically within national boundaries. Once you had to fill out a form to move money across borders. Now you could move literally trillions in foreign exchange with computer keyboards. Factories were no more anchored than foreign exchange. It was a bit more cumbersome, but if the costs were really cheaper, you could move the plant from Illinois to Taiwan or Singapore, and with jet freight aircraft, have the product back again quickly, especially if it was labor-intensive, like garments, or small, like electronic parts.

The sociologist Max Weber wrote in *The Protestant Ethic and the Spirit of Capitalism* that the Protestant countries of northern Europe, and the United States, by extension, treated work as a positive good. Material prosperity was blessed by heaven, and one way to see whether you were in a state of grace was to work hard and try to win success. In *Tokagawa Religion,* Robert Bellah pointed out that the same strains existed in Japan. Certainly Japan, although it had no natural resources such as oil and coal, became the fastest-rising major power of the post–World War II period.

The essay below—an antique now—appeared in the July 27, 1970, issue of *New York Magazine.* The article followed a trip to Japan to arrange a conference. I was lucky. The translator of my book *The Money Game* was a director of the Bank of Japan. He had done the translation for fun. The Bank of Japan already had its plan to pass the Soviet Union in economic output. The experience of visiting Japan as an author is agreeable. The Japanese are such *readers*; the literacy rate is far higher than that in the United States. (In 1987, they printed a billion books.) My Japanese publisher even produced a TV commercial to promote the book, a rare event in this country.

Since July 27, 1970, Lee Iacocca has switched jobs. The Japanese are waiting in the wings, he said then. To beat out General Motors and Ford? asks the naive author. How impossible that seemed! The gap in the savings rates has actually increased. Otherwise, things are the same to an amazing degree—only the sense of naive wonder at Japanese plans for growth has been replaced by a feeling of floating discomfort. The sociologist quoted here is Noritake Kobayashi.

If Japan Becomes the New America, What Happens to the Old One?

I am sitting with this friend of mine, a British merchant banker, in his muted mahogany chambers, getting depressed in the pleasant— and legal—haze of our after-lunch Havanas. My friend is spinning this globe like a character in one of those Sydney Greenstreet movies and telling me how he used to go to New York three times a year, but this year he is only going once. I am depressed because we have just finished lunch in the dining room, and the urbane merchant bankers have been ever so urbanely writing down the United States, quite detached, quite cool, the same way they must have coolly written off the Shanghai Street Railway Debentures and the Moscow Power and Light 6½s of 1909, when the time came.

"We used to have most of our money invested in New York," says my friend, the globe spinning beneath his fingertips, "but we took it out about a year ago. For the first time in a hundred years, America looks like a place to avoid, confused, purposeless, not master of its own fate."

My friend is responsible for, say, a hundred million pounds, and that money can go anywhere in the world it will bring a maximum return. In the City, in London, they're quite used to looking at the whole world.

"I cut my New York trips from three to one," he says. "And substituted a trip east. You have to go where the action is." The globe has stopped spinning; the fingertips are over Japan.

The international money went to Tokyo, and, a bit later, so did I, with two good reasons. One was that my book *The Money Game* had been translated into Japanese, and became a best-seller in that language. That meant the local editors and economists and reporters and bankers and professors all wanted to talk to the *gaijin* author. The second reason was that the Japanese stock market had gone straight up, while the stock markets in London and New York and even Zurich and Amsterdam went down. The Japanese economy was growing faster by far than anything else on the planet Earth, and the Japanese market seemed immune to the worldwide blahs. A couple of months ago it did crack, but the Japanese explained there was nothing wrong, no Japanese were selling, it was only the *gaijin* acting crazy and selling. *Gaijin* means "foreigner"; more, it has an emotional shade: "them," like *goyim*.

I could see two Trends right in the waiting lounge for the flight from the United States to Tokyo. Trends: Lee Iacocca is worried, and the tourists on this package tour to the U.S. are carrying these boxes that say—wait a minute—Barbie? The tourists are Japanese, a whole 747-ful of them, each with a camera over his shoulder. The men are wearing slim, conservative three-button suits, and two-thirds of them have souvenirs to show the cousins in Osaka where they've been: *a Barbie doll? Toys* to Japan?

If that carries no irony for you, then you never listened to Captain Midnight and the Green Hornet and you never had a toy with the legend "Made in Japan" on the bottom. You got the toy, you played with it, and it fell apart. Those were the old bad-guy, black-hat Japanese, Marine you die, to hell with Babe Ruth, all thumbs. Copycats. The old battleship story: they sent some naval architects and copied the plans of some battleship, they built the battleship, launched it, it slid down the ways and turned bottom up. They read the plans upside down or left to right or something. The black-hat Japanese couldn't even build the Bridge over the River Kwai. They'd get the bridge about a quarter of the way out into the Kwai and it would fall down. Alec Guinness and the good old pukka British prisoners had to build the bridge.

So why is Lee Iacocca upset? He is the president of Ford, and the morning I left for Tokyo he was asked whether he thought the 1971 small cars coming out of Detroit would be successful. "They better be," he was reported as saying, "because the Japanese are waiting in the wings." To beat out Ford and General Motors? The Japanese in Detroit, camera-laden, three-button-suited, toting Barbie dolls back to Osaka! The Greater East Co-Prosperity Sphere, all the way to Lake Erie! The transistor may have been invented in New Jersey, but that tide of minicomputers, minicars, mini-TV sets, and mini-motorcycles is coming the other way, not to mention jumbo tankers and cameras that still have the Germans blinking.

The twenty-first century, says futurist Herman Kahn, is the Japanese century. Japan is the fastest-growing major industrial power, the second-biggest in the non-Communist world and the third-biggest in the world. From a standing start it has passed Italy and France and England and even the industrious Germans. No wonder they are thoughtfully spinning globes in the London merchant banks. Can this really be? How come? And where will it all end?

We are sitting in an elegant restaurant in a parklike setting in Tokyo, three of us, the distinguished director of the Bank of Japan, his research assistant, and myself. Through the open door is a garden scene seemingly measured to the size of the door. We are cross-legged on the floor, and the distinguished director is pausing, a

delicate sliver of raw fish between his chopsticks, to make a point.
"In the 1960s, Japan surpassed Italy, France, Germany, England,"
says the director. "If our total output, our gross national product,
continues to grow at this rate, we will pass the USSR in . . ."

The chopsticks pause momentarily. "Nineteen seventy-nine,"
says the research assistant, his eyes downcast.

"Nineteen seventy-nine. Of course we would not pass the U.S.
until . . ."

Now both men pause; it may not be truly courteous to speak of
passing the United States.

"Sometime in the 1990s," says the research assistant. "That is,
of course, a long way off, and many things could happen."

"How did we do this?" says the distinguished director. "First,
we received generous help from the U.S. after the war, and in
procurements during the Korean War. But since? Look. Our people
save *twenty percent* of their wages. No other country saves so much.
In the U.S. it is closer to six percent. Our work force is highly
educated; our literacy is higher than that in the U.S. now. In the
U.S., businesses invest about half of their gross profits in new
technology, new plant and equipment. Ours are investing *one hundred and fifty percent* of their gross profits in new plant."

"How do you invest more money than you make?" I asked.

"You borrow. You see, the savings of the people are channeled
into the banks, and the banks loan the money to the corporations."

"So the people are indirectly loaning the expansion money to
their own employers. Why do they save so much?"

"Well, we don't have such elaborate social security as you do. So
one saves to take care of one's parents. And to educate one's
children."

There are a lot of people here, and they are all in a hurry. That is
the first idea that comes across in Tokyo, and the second is how
much sleekness has appeared in the last ten years. Freeways criss-
crossing the city through the smog, just as in Los Angeles, filled
with sleek little cars. And the sleek new office buildings with their
sleek new noiseless computer-controlled elevators have sleek executives zipping up to plan some sleek TV commercials amid all the

carpeting and paneling that looks like Manhattan and Century City when the market is roaring. Somewhere out there the ladies are clip-clopping along in their traditional *geta*, small little steps, and colorful kimonos. The old ladies. The new ones are working at Matsushita in nice uniform smocks, and Madame Butterfly is long gone.

"Why does everybody work so hard?" I asked the university sociologist. Another cross-legged session on the floor, another sliver of raw fish between the chopsticks.

"You see, when someone finishes school in Japan," said the sociologist, "and goes to work for a large company, it is generally for life. You will never be fired, and the company provides many fringe benefits. There are very few strikes, and this harmonious spirit leads to harder work."

"No one is ever fired?"

"No. It is very hard for a Japanese even to understand what 'fired' means. That particular emotional anxiety isn't there. On the other hand, the employees are willing to settle for less individualism than in Western countries. For example, you would certainly ask your boss's approval of your fiancée, and you would work where the company thought best."

"And what do people do with the money they earn?"

"Well, appliances first, I suppose. The first item is an electric rice cooker. That saves the labor of building a stove fire. Then a washing machine and dryer. That saves more labor. Then a television set—almost every household has a TV set—and then perhaps a motorcycle or small car."

So, as I understood it, the housewife who used to have to labor from dawn to dusk washing and drying and cooking rice now has a lot more time on her hands. What does she do with it?

"Perhaps watch soap operas on TV . . ."

That can't be helping this roaring gross national product very much.

"Perhaps devoting more time to the children. There is more and more pressure on getting into good schools. So you might say the lady of the house is encouraging her children to study."

You mean nagging the children to study harder, to get ahead, to get into a better school, a better college, like Mrs. Portnoy?

"You could certainly say the mothers were nagging the children to study harder."

Good heavens, *fifty million Jewish mothers!* I said it out loud. Maybe they will pass the Russians. . . .

"Fifty million Jewish mothers?" The sociologist's chopsticks paused in midair flight. "Japanese Jewish mothers? Well, yes, you could say that."

Something else occurred to me. What else do the wives do, when all the children are in school?

"Some of them," said the sociologist, "use the time to meet other men. But it's very difficult. First, the other men are also working very hard, and second, we have an acute housing shortage. We really do not have that much living space per person. One's mother-in-law may still be around."

We are at a major television network, still on the local weight-watcher's diet of delicate uncooked fish, and we are talking with a documentary maker and social critic. The social critic isn't sure all this rapid growth is a good thing.

"Sure," he says. "We are building ships in Singapore, we are assembling motorcycles in Belgium, we are making cars an hour from Mexico City, and do you know what they call us everywhere? *The Yellow Yankees. The Yellow Americans.* That's how the world sees Japan. The foreign minister of Pakistan says the Japanese is *an economic animal.* Who needs that? We are the third-biggest industrial power in the world, we are the fastest-growing; at this rate we will pass the Russians by . . ."

"Nineteen seventy-five?" I suggested.

"That sounds about right. But we look across the Pacific at the U.S., and we can see that prosperity doesn't bring happiness. We are such a collective country, our people are still used to working together, so in each plant the workers start out each morning singing the company song, they play baseball on the company team, but we read about Detroit, the industrial psychologists say the workers can't stand their jobs, they sabotage cars sometimes and have no pride in the product. Maybe that lies ahead of us, but it's hard for people from American cities to realize you can go almost anywhere in Tokyo without getting mugged. Anyway, by the time we catch up with the Russians, we will have polluted ourselves to death.''

''Is that what the students are protesting about?''

''No, you shouldn't get the wrong idea about our student protest from your TV news film clips. Much of it was about university policies, and it has died down. Then the radicals are always protesting about the American presence. But protest is very well defined, it takes place at a specific place and a specific time, and it's very well contained. The Tokyo riot police are not armed, and no one has ever been shot—in fact, there has been only one riot fatality, and that was a girl who was trampled in a stampede, ten years ago. The radical student will graduate and go right to work for Mitsubishi.''

''How do you feel, personally, about the U.S.?'' I asked.

''I spent a year there. I think it's a great place. But vis-à-vis Japan, the American attitude is very ambiguous. First, the Americans were so afraid of Japanese militarism that they wrote Article 9 into our constitution; it says we must never arm again. Then American generals come and complain that we aren't carrying our share of the load, that we have a 'free ride' because the Americans are protecting us. You can't have it both ways. It has helped our economy enormously not to carry all the unproductive arms spending that you and the Russians do.''

By the end of the visit, I am convinced that all the characteristics of the Protestant ethic are endemic in Japan: hard work is salvation. I have conducted a very minor poll based on a single question: how much vacation do you take a year? The answers come back: two days, one day, three days, two days. Officially, say my pollees, we get two weeks, but Japan is a small country, the beaches are too crowded, the ski slopes are too crowded, and besides, if you work the two weeks of your vacation you get paid for it.

Will Japan really pass the United States by the year 2000? Will the rest of the world call us the white Japanese?

My friends the senior economists doubted it. For one thing, even with a hundred million people, labor is scarce in Japan, and the cost of labor is rising. In the realm of cheap labor, the Koreans and the Chinese cut into the Japanese superiority. And if the Japanese continue their terrific spending on automation, then there will be problems of getting enough capital to finance that expenditure. All that investment has gone into the private competitive sector, leaving big gaps in the public sector: schools, housing, roads, pollution. Japan is still quite dependent on its trade with the United States, and if the United States leaves Vietnam and cuts down its spending in the Pacific Basin, that will let some air out of the balloon. Besides, will everyone continue to work so hard when there is a TV set and an electric rice cooker and a washing machine in every household?

We need a souvenir, everybody needs a souvenir. We already have a Japanese doll, and now we have picked a little car, a police car with the Japanese characters for "Police" on the side. The doors open, the red light on top lights, it's really cute. Of course, these things break so quickly. . . . We turn the car over. On the bottom it says *Made in USA*.

Ezra Vogel: Japan as No. 1

Where will it all end? asked the naive author of 1970. The trade deficit with Japan would grow to $60 billion—about a third of it in the Japanese cars American dealers and their customers signed up for so eagerly. American governors trooped to Japan, offering concessions for the Japanese to build plants in their states. Business theorists discovered just-in-time delivery, consensus-building, and quality control—though the highest Japanese prize for quality was named after an American, W. Edwards Deming. And the sociologists began to write about Japanese society as if it were the city on a hill: the streets were safe, drugs were not a problem, children obeyed their parents and studied, everybody saved money. Were there really lessons for us?

"Do you remember," said my visitor, "the stories about Usa?" My visitor was an old friend, an American who lives in the Far

East, where he drums up business for his American firm. As for Usa, it is a town on the main southernmost Japanese island, Kyushu.

"The story used to be," said my visitor, "that because Japanese goods were so cheap and shoddy, they were all sent to Usa before they were exported to be stamped MADE IN USA, so that people would think they had been made in the United States.

"But you haven't heard stories like that for twenty-five years. Detroit is reeling from Japanese imports, and you see joggers wearing earphones and carrying little Japanese tape decks not much larger than cigarette packs. I have to go meet some of my Japanese associates in New York now. They think New York is charming—and so *cheap,* they keep saying. Such *bargains.*"

The Far East hand left with me a book that is a huge best-seller in Japan. It was written by a Harvard professor, Ezra Vogel, and its English-language edition has sold a respectable 25,000 copies. But in Japan it is a runaway success: 455,000 copies sold. The title is *Japan as Number One: Lessons for America.* "The very title," said Edwin Reischauer, a former ambassador to Japan, "will blow the minds of many Americans. Japan today has a more smoothly functioning society [than ours] and an economy that is running rings around ours." One Japanese official has said that the United States has now taken the place of Japan's prewar colonies. The United States supplies the raw materials—the coal, the grain and soybeans, the timber—to this superior modern industrial machine, and it gets back the machine's superior industrial products.

Japan's economic performance has been well documented in Vogel's book. In 1952, Japan's gross national product was one third that of France. By the late 1970s, it was larger than those of France and Britain combined, and half as large as that of the United States. Japan is the leading automobile manufacturer. Of the world's twenty-two largest and most modern steel plants, fourteen are in Japan and *none* are in the United States.

Health? Japan has the world's lowest infant mortality rate. In 1967 the life expectancy of the average Japanese passed that of the average American, and in 1977 Japan's life expectancy rate passed Sweden's to become the highest in the world.

Education? About 90 percent of all Japanese graduate from high school, and they generally spend sixty more days a year in high school than do their American counterparts.

Crime? In Japan the cities are safe, and the Japanese carry large amounts of cash and don't even worry about it. Americans are accustomed to annual increases in the crime rate; in Japan, the crime rate is going *down*.

Labor? The Japanese visitors are shocked again. Professor Vogel says that the American factory seems almost like an armed camp to them: "Foremen stand guard to make sure workers do not slack off. Workers grumble at foremen, and foremen are cross with workers. In the Japanese factory, employees seem to work even without the foreman watching."

What are the Japanese doing right? And how have they done it on a crowded group of islands, without enough coal and oil, without significant natural resources, without adequate farmland?

The rather chilling answer is that they have done it by a social process—by a kind of group behavior modification. An average Japanese who goes to work for a company is there for life. He works throughout the day in an atmosphere in which consensus is always the goal. If, as his career progresses, he needs retraining, the company will retrain him, so he need not get involved in the protection of rights that American unions strive for. The company's goals are his. The people he sees socially are from the company.

The government works the same way, striving for consensus within itself and for consensus with business. Elite bureaucrats, their ties reinforced by social contacts in the geisha houses and on the golf course, form an elaborate old-boy network and move in lockstep through the age ranks.

And all this starts very early. Children are taught the value of cooperation, says Vogel, "however annoying they may find group pressures." The group pressure helps to explain the low crime rate. The policeman is part of the group: his little kiosk also contains the neighborhood bulletin board. The criminal, in fact, is encouraged to turn himself in. Even Japanese gangs exist in a consensus with the police.

The whole design of group activity is a conscious one. After World War II, the Japanese decided what they needed to survive, and they followed their decision. They even learned golf and baseball with the same sense of purpose that they applied to business and government. Americans win arguments; the Japanese win agreements. Americans try for victory; the Japanese try for consensus.

Nobody can deny Japan its success. What is so chilling is the implication of that success: Japan works and America doesn't. The Japanese leaped from feudalism to a modern corporate society without the intervening four hundred years of individualism that have characterized Western Europe and the United States. Our individualism was all very well in its time, but that was when energy was plentiful and the world was agricultural. But now we live in a postagrarian world, and individualism doesn't work anymore: "Our institutional practices promote adversary relations and litigation, divisiveness threatens our society," warns Vogel.

What we ought to do, he argues, is to borrow some of the models that have worked for the Japanese: more group direction, more "central leadership oriented to a modern economic order," more cooperation between business and government.

You can see why this is at once so provocative and so chilling. Should we all gather behind the banners of IBM and General Motors? When William H. Whyte, Jr., wrote *The Organization Man*, the phenomenon he documented was considered alarming. Do we really want five hundred highly trained bureaucrats, a close-knit group from elite universities, to establish our goals and run our government? Our experience with the best and the brightest was not totally happy. Should we teach youngsters not to win, just to tie?

Japanophiles point out that America, too, had groups: New England town meetings, farmers' granges, professional guilds. But in our mobile society, group solidarity has become attenuated. We have lost a sense of community.

This is not the direction we are going in. Americans complain that their government is too big and directs them too much. They are more and more suspicious of big business. They distrust, the polls show, all of their institutions.

There isn't any doubt that we are losing ground in the world, and that we have forgotten what safe cities and a sense of community feel like. Is the group model what it takes to survive? Could we adopt it? More to the point, is it the way we want to live?

Theory Z: "Don't Be *Rikutsupoi*"

There is an old market axiom that says: Sell on the news. It exists even in French: *Achetez aux canons, vendez aux clairons.* Buy on the cannons, sell on the trumpets, that is, buy when the enemy artillery is pounding your city and everyone is gloomy, sell when you hear the cavalry charge that will drive out the enemy. The corollary in journalism is: The cover of *Time* is the kiss of death. Whoever is being profiled has just peaked. When John Keynes published his *General Theory* in 1936, it *was* controversial. In 1965 Keynes was on the cover; by 1971 Richard Nixon said, "I am now a Keynesian," and Keynesian policies have been in trouble ever since. Or consider American management techniques, which were once considered the model for the world. In 1968, French journalist Jean-Jacques Servan-Schreiber published the best-seller *The American Challenge.* Servan-Schreiber said that Americans were taking over the world with their spiffy techniques—and American management has been considered decadent virtually ever since. (W. Edwards Deming, whose name is carried on the highest Japanese award for quality, says America's problems are 85 percent management.)

If these rules hold, and I think they may, Japan has just about peaked. Japan has been on the newsmagazine covers, and now there are two books on Japanese management, both of which received handsome attention in the press and even more handsome paperback sales. The first is *The Art of Japanese Management,* by Richard Tanner Pascale and Anthony G. Athos; the second is *Theory Z: How American Business Can Meet the Japanese Challenge,* by William Ouchi. Japan, say these authorities, does it right.

The stories of Japanese attention to detail and quality are now taking on mythic overtones. For example, a team of engineers visited the Buick dealership in Tokyo. It seemed to have a very large repair facility. With some embarrassment, the Japanese Buick dealer told his visitors it wasn't a repair facility; the Buicks entering Japan were all taken apart and reassembled according to stricter standards, because Japanese buyers, while they liked Buicks, would never accept the low quality coming out of Detroit.

Now the Japanese *Wirtschaftswunder* has terrified even the Germans; the Reagan administration has asked Japan to please not sell so many cars here, and conventional wisdom says we must learn from the Japanese genius. What is it that we Americans do so wrong in business?

We concentrate on the short term. Companies worry about this quarter, about year-to-year comparisons. The boss doesn't worry about the company ten years down the road: he will be retired by then; he wants to look good now. The image admired by American business is *macho*. Who are the ten toughest bosses in the United States, *Fortune* asked. "One has only to pick up an issue of *Fortune, Business Week,* or the *Wall Street Journal,*" say professors Pascale and Athos, "to read about some CEO slashing here, firing there, acquiring, divesting, or otherwise acting like a hack surgeon. One would be hard pressed to find similar episodes in Japan. They surely would not be honored."

The Japanese technique is cooperation. Takeo Fujisawa was the early partner of Soichiro Honda in founding the Honda Motor Company. He once observed that Japanese and American managements were 95 percent the same and yet "differ in all important aspects." The Japanese corporation is not simply a moneymaking device, according to this observation, it is a social instrument, it seeks to answer the individual's "social, psychological, and spiritual needs" as well. In the United States we leave those objectives to the family, the community, the church, the various governments, from local to national. In Japan, employment is for life, and feelings are never bruised.

Or so say the authors of these Japanese management books. My more limited experience is that feelings do get bruised in Japanese companies but not suppressed. Tell Takeo he's getting sent to oversee the plant in Hokkaido when he just got engaged, he will say yes sir, but he will bite his lower lip.

And the authors have concentrated on the major Japanese companies. But each Japanese giant is surrounded by a ring of vendors, companies that feed it and supply it and make the famous just-in-time inventory systems work. Those are much smaller companies, and they are the buffers for the big ones. In small companies, employment is not so secure. If Toyota or Mitsubishi or any of the dozen companies named Dai Nippon wants to cut back, it cuts back on its suppliers. It's the suppliers who then have to absorb the contraction, and fire people.

But employment in the major companies is still for life. And having joined the company for life, the Japanese employee is rotated through various jobs, which makes him, say the Japanophiles, more versatile than the American specialist. The Japanese spend a lot of time on each employee and, since they will have him for life, make a greater investment in him. They build *interdependence* much as we build competition and independence. Then, too, Americans are used to winning and losing, to seeing things in black and white. "The Japanese accept ambiguity, uncertainty, and imperfection as much more of a given in organizational life," say Pascale and Athos. A Japanese employee may serve on several company committees, play on a company baseball team, live in a company apartment. The oft-quoted example is that of Matsushita. "It seems silly to Westerners," says a Matsushita executive, "but every morning at eight A.M., all across Japan, there are eighty-seven thousand workers reciting the code of values and singing together."

Since the avoidance of conflict is a cultural and corporate goal, the Japanese cultivate vague language. "There is too much American trust in increasing the clarity in communication between people, especially when their disagreements are substantive. Getting a currently hopeless impasse clear is often unwise and likely to make things worse. Second, vagueness in *intention* legitimizes the loose rein permitted in certain organizational situations in which further insight is needed before corrective action can be taken." Thus, say Pascale and Athos, the Japanese "conduct their dialogues in circles, widening and narrowing them to correspond to the other's sensitivity to feedback." In the Japanese language the verbs come at the end of a sentence, so the listener doesn't know where the speaker is headed until he gets there. If you are too bright, too logical, you are *rikutsupoi*, pushy. Americans *decide*, Japanese *flow*. Water wears down stone, says the Zen aphorism.

The Japanese corporation makes its decisions by *ringi*, in which each document passes from hand to hand, with each manager affixing his seal to it. Thus one document may have sixty-four *ringi* seals attached to it, and the neophyte is taught the value of cooperation. What is the American process? It is, say Pascale and Athos, for the manager to say, "We need to kick some ass down in the mill," or "I'm going to fire the s.o.b." The American technique is derived from the lone pioneering spirit, the Japanese from villages that had to work together.

Of course, there is a price to all this homogeneity. "Probably no form of organization is more sexist or racist than the Japanese corporation," writes professor Ouchi. "They do not intentionally shut out those who are different, nor do they consider male Japanese to be superior. Their organizations simply operate as culturally homogeneous social systems that have very weak explicit or hierarchical monitoring properties and thus can withstand no internal cultural diversity."

Still another drawback is that the Japanese meritocracy closes off options at an early age. Scholarships are given to the best universities, and the graduates of those universities get the best jobs. Naturally competition is intense. The competition is not only for the best high schools, whose graduates have the edge in getting into Tokyo University, Japan's most prestigious college. Ouchi reports that a Japanese friend was preoccupied one day because his four-year-old son was taking the entrance examinations for a special kindergarten. The special kindergarten was the fast track into a leading primary school, whose graduates went to the leading high school, whose graduates had another fast track into Tokyo U., and thence to the Daiwa Bank, Sony, and Matsushita. Ouchi said that the four-year-old was very bright and thus was assured of a spot in the kindergarten. No, said the friend. "In this special kindergarten there are only thirty openings for more than five hundred applications. Of those five hundred, more than half have been going to a special summer school that does nothing but drill those children for eight hours a day, six days a week, in how to take that entrance exam for that one specific kindergarten." Although his father earned a good wage, the Japanese four-year-old had not gone to the cram school, because the tuition was a thousand dollars a week, which was too stiff. Life was over at five: a minor university, a secondary firm, the slow track to a noodle shop at fifty-five.

All the professors of business administration cite successful American firms that have some of the characteristics of what they admire in Japanese firms. Delta Air Lines, for example, is an industry leader admired for its management style. "You don't just join a company," it is said at Delta, "you join an objective." The Delta "family feeling" has made it hard for unions to gain a foothold; when the airlines suffered from the oil price hikes, Delta did not lay off employees as did some other airlines. "Now the time has come for the stockholders to pay a little penalty for keeping the team together," said the chairman.

IBM is the firm most often cited, and IBM's successes are too well known to cite here. But at IBM, as at Japanese companies, the "family feeling" does not come without a family price. The first year I worked on Wall Street, I rode downtown with a friend who was an IBM salesman with an office in my building. At nine every morning he and the other salesmen stood inspection; they wore identical charcoal-gray suits, white shirts, conservative ties. I watched the inspection once or twice, and so help me, the division manager inspected everybody's fingernails. But it was unheard of to get fired. At least, at that time.

Recently on a cross-country flight, I had a seatmate who was a very interesting dissident, a Kim Kurosawa of Motortronics of Kent, Ohio. Kurosawa was born and schooled in Japan, but after one year at the University of Pennsylvania he elected to stay here, and now he is a very successful salesman of elevator motors in a booming business that supplies new construction in oil rigs and apartment buildings. Why did he elect to live in Ohio?

"I like it a lot better here. In Japan, you move with your age group, layer by layer, up the levels. If you get ahead too fast, they don't like you. I could never make this much money in Japan so fast."

Kurosawa is making $65,000 a year. He is twenty-nine years old. His background is in electronic engineering.

"I had pretty good grades in high school, but not great. So I got into the third-best university. I could have had a good job, but not as good as I'm doing now. I travel a lot, and now I'm friends with a lot of my customers. It gets a bit lonely, because most of my business is in Texas and Florida, and they don't have big Japanese communities."

Kurosawa is engaged and has bought a house in Kent, Ohio. "In Japan, housing is so expensive that the only thing young people can get is company condominiums.

"What's good about American business," he said, "is the flexibility. You see a market, you go after it. You make decisions fast, you don't need the approval of sixty-four guys to make a decision."

"In moving from Japan to America, didn't you join the losing team?"

"I think America can come back. My Japanese friends I went to college with are no smarter than my American friends. They just target their opportunities, and then they work six days a week."

"And you don't mind working for an American company?"

"No, it's just great. Of course, when my American company ran low on capital, it was sold."

"Was that good for you or bad for you?"

"It was just fine. The parent is now Watanabe Electric Motors of Osaka."

If the Japanese Made the F-15, Would It Come Out Smaller and Half the Price?

It is not the vested interests that rule the world, said Lord Keynes. It is ideas: "indeed the world is ruled by little else. . . . Madmen in authority, who hear voices in the air, are distilling their frenzy from some academic scribbler of a few years back." Keynes, of course, was a man of ideas, and it was natural for him to end his *General Theory* with a tribute to the influence of ideas. However, ideas can be flawed sometimes not because they lack internal symmetry but because they contain an implicit notion of how human beings behave that turns out to be wrong.

I recently attended a conference on Japanese-American relations that was not about behavior per se, yet all the discussions there were based on some unspoken suppositions about it. We were in a pleasant, airy room, sitting around a square table, a nameplate in front of each of us. Half of the participants had come from Japan. They included a labor union leader, a retired vice-admiral, and a number of government officials, academics, and corporate executives. The Americans were also heavy on the government and academic side. The Americans spoke in English, the Japanese spoke in Japanese, and some marvelous interpreters gave us simultaneous interpretation into our earphones. Outside the conference room, the sponsors made every effort to get the Japanese and the Americans together at social gatherings. Nothing in particular depended on this conference; the point was to "increase understanding."

An underlying irritation surfaced first when an American, a former congressman, told how he had been defeated after twenty-two years in Congress because his district was heavily dependent on auto-parts manufacturing and much of the business has been lost to the Japanese. "I believe in free trade," he said, "but it hurt me. I don't believe that it's in our best interest to keep out Japanese cars if Americans want them, but unemployment was high in my district, and if you're an unemployed American auto worker, it's not so easy to be for a theory that puts a lot of Japanese cars on the streets. My opponent was able to hurt me with that." The Japanese auto-union leader said he hadn't known that unemployment was almost 15 percent in some of our auto-producing areas; 2 percent is a problem in Japan.

The trade discussion went on. The Americans protested that it is easy for the Japanese to sell in the United States and hard for Americans to sell in Japan. The Japanese replied that one of the reasons the Americans are having a hard time selling in Japan is cultural. For example, not many Americans learn to speak Japanese, but it is standard practice for Japanese businessmen to learn to speak English.

I began to get a bit uneasy when I heard the American government

representatives move from the subject of trade problems to an in-
sistence that the Japanese rearm. Rearm? Only if you are very young
will names like Pearl Harbor, Midway, Guadalcanal, Iwo Jima, and
Tarawa have no emotional impact. But that is history and the American officials were worried about the present.

We are spending 5.9 percent of our GNP on defense; the Japanese
are spending only 0.93 percent. Yet here we are, a security umbrella
over Japan. No wonder the Japanese can keep clobbering us
commercially—they have more resources available for commerce.
Our best engineers are busy figuring out how to track Russian
missiles and satellites while the Japanese engineers can spend their
time on videotape recorders and television sets and figuring out how
to make Toyotas and Datsuns take corners better.

The Japanese said politely that Article 9 of their constitution
forbid rearmament and that, after all, their constitution was written
by General Douglas MacArthur and his staff.

The Americans said the Japanese are getting a "free ride."

The Japanese said that they already have the world's fifth-largest
defense budget, that they can't recruit enough people into the army
and the navy, and that, anyway, they have more destroyers in the
Pacific than we have in our Seventh Fleet and the rest of Asia is
getting nervous.

The Americans asked, what if the Russians attacked?

The Japanese said, well, if the Russians attacked Japan, no force
they could muster would be enough, and, besides, the Americans
would have to defend the American bases in Japan and attack the
Russians.

The Americans said that since Japan is dependent on imports and
exports and is a maritime nation, shouldn't it have a bigger navy?
Who would defend the sea lanes?

There followed a half-hour discussion about where the sea lanes
are and who is likely to attack them. The Japanese said nobody could
defend all the sea lanes and they didn't think the Russians would
attack. The Americans said the Russians took over in Afghanistan
and there are Russians and Cubans in Angola and Ethiopia—who
knows where they might turn up next? The Japanese vice-admiral
said he would like to build F-15s in Japan.

I began to get restless. It seemed to me that the American assumption was that future Japanese would be just like present Japanese: polite, agreeable, golf-loving baseball fans. At home they put on white lab coats and make tape cassette players the size of your thumbnail. In international relations they know who their friends are, so they are good guys, on our side. It is true that in 1979 we asked everybody to boycott Iranian oil while our hostages were under the gun and the Japanese raced in and bought our share of the oil, but when we got mad, they backed down and said they were sorry.

But if you really warmed up the Japanese arms industry, maybe there would be a different crowd in Tokyo. Money and economic activity have their own momentum, and if the glory is coming from missile frigates, that's not the same mentality that makes microwave ovens. The missile-frigate crowd probably has shinier shoes and stands up straighter. It seems to me that the American assumption was that you can change the mix and have the Japanese character stand still. But maybe future Japanese will be more independent and less agreeable.

I am not sure the Japanese should make F-15s, either. Everybody wants our F-15s, and we dangle them before our allies as rewards for proper behavior. If the Japanese start making F-15s, the F-15 may come out lighter, smaller, and half the price—then where do our customers go?

No, it seems to me that we run a risk in asking the Japanese to change. What the Japanese should do is stay out of the missile and warship business and send us a very large annual check. We will be good mercenaries; we will take it as a fee for keeping the peace and we will let the Japanese be the mercantilists. Do we really want to promote a more militant Japan?

Keynes was certainly right; everybody now takes the power of ideas for granted. The Russian army and missile force are directed at us because of the writings of an exiled nineteenth-century German scribbling in the British Museum. But while ideas are powerful, the implicit assumptions about people contained in them may not work out to be true. "From each according to his abilities, to each according to his needs," said Mr. Marx, and while the symmetry of *that* seemed quite beautiful from the British Museum, it turns out that a certain amount of coercion is needed to implement it in this less than idealistic world. Japanese rearmament and supply side economics are natural reactions to imbalances that have grown up, but even their most ardent advocates cannot predict what changes in behavior those policies might bring about.

Significant Signs: Robots, Skis, Saturdays

I can remember—dimly now—that when I first visited Tokyo a generation ago, it seemed Oriental. That is, there were twisted, winding streets just wide enough for one ox, and the sound of *geta* (wooden clogs) clip-clopping along, and the smell of smoke, wood, and charcoal. The numbers on the houses reflected the date they were built, not their relative position on a street; so if you were looking for an address and you did not speak Japanese, you had someone write out in Japanese characters a series of directions on several sheets of paper. You pinned the first to your lapel, like a small child being sent to his grandmother, and someone would put you off the subway at the right stop. You then replaced the first sheet of directions with a second sheet and a passerby would send you to the noodle shop, from which the third set of directions would get you to the house. A sweet-potato vendor with a basket of roast sweet potatoes slung around his neck wandered the narrow streets, crying a distinctive sweet-potato call, much as Molly Malone wheeled her wheelbarrow through the streets of Dublin crying, "Cockles and mussels."

On a recent visit to the Shinjuku section of Tokyo, I found that the twisted streets, the *geta,* and the smell of charcoal had all disappeared, replaced by gleaming skyscrapers indistinguishable from those in Houston. Between the skyscrapers were cement and brown lawn. The shops had moved to a kind of underground mall. Surprisingly, the sweet-potato man was still there. His basket was now on an electric cart, and the sweet-potato song came from a cassette he played through a loudspeaker, barely audible over the roar of traffic.

Some stories that affect us profoundly run for years along a common theme. One such story is how the oil-producing states seized control of the oil and raised its price, dampening the growth of the world economy. Another is the industrial success of Japan. One by one the Japanese went after each area and conquered it. Recently the Japanese targeted information—that is, computers, telecommunications, and so on—as the field of the 1980s. The semiconductor may have been developed at Bell Labs, but it flowered into Sony Walkmans and Casio calculators. At any time in the last twenty-five years, you could find, as a theme, that the Japanese were gaining dominance in some new market and piling up money from exports.

I asked a Tokyo banker what was most dynamic in Japan. "Robots," said my host. "Japan is leading the world in robots. The robot symbolizes the final age of the industrialized society. Industry is machinery. The original industrial age gave industry its muscle; now it is getting brains. The sensor and the microprocessor will complete the age of machinery." So many people have applied to visit the Fujitsu Fanuc factory where robots manufacture other robots that the company can no longer allow visitors. I went with my banker friend to visit a couple of robot-manufacturing firms. One was in the fountain pen business. Said its managing director, "The fountain pen business is mature, very flat. Then we thought, we could convert the machines we use to make the fountain pens into machines that could assemble consumer appliances. So we did."

"Who else can make a machine like yours?" I asked—a standard question—expecting to hear the Germans, or perhaps the Americans.

"There is one other firm," said the managing director, "in Nagoya."

Another robot-making firm also leads the world in making the works for music boxes. "If you can make a machine that makes parts delicate enough for music boxes, you can make a fairly sensitive robot," said the company's vice-president.

When we think of robots, we are likely to think of R2D2 and other characters from *Star Wars*. But no robot has yet reached the anthropomorphic stage of R2D2. Today's robot is just a machine that can perform a repetitive task; with sensors and a microprocessor, it can adjust to the results of what it is doing, count, and, in a clumsy way, even get itself around.

Robots are, of course, very nice for productivity. They do not take coffee breaks or summer vacations, they do not go on strike, and they are happy to work twenty-four hours a day. There is no turning back from the robot revolution. Factories will buy robots; they will have to, or a factory somewhere else, perhaps in some other country, will simply get all the business. Workers ought to welcome robots, because any job that a robot can do is a pretty boring job. Statistically speaking, robots need not drastically reduce the total work force, because there will be more jobs that require programming, sales, maintenance, and other skills we think of as mental rather than physical.

I could see that the Japanese were going to be adept at making the cheapest robots, but I told my host that robot technology did not seem as sophisticated as, for example, that of high-speed computers.

"I don't think the technology is as sophisticated," he said. "The difference is, which society is going to *adapt* most quickly to robots? Here in Japan we think we have an advantage, not just because we are producing the robots but because our corporations have a tradition of lifetime employment. We do not have a worker in one job and then lay him off if we do not need him. We move him around from job to job, and he is conditioned to cooperation. The robot is going to change the nature of work and the idea of a factory. Who knows more about that than the workers? So the workers must cooperate in inviting the robots in; they must help with the preparation of software, with ideas on the work process and on how to use the robots.

"Japan is leading the world in robots," he continued, "because our industry has a high demand for them and our workers are not threatened by them. Our unions are company unions. But we believe there will be more trouble in Europe and in the United States, because you have more of a history of antagonism between labor and management and the workers will feel threatened by the robots."

Computers, microprocessors, sensors, robots, a work force that goes six days a week—it sounded like the 1980s version of the

Japanese success story of previous decades. "Tell me, Adam Smith," said the popular TV talk show host Kenichi Takemura, on Channel 8 in Tokyo, "don't you think we Japanese work too hard? Maybe we don't know how to live."

"I think you're doing just fine," I said, and I hope that was what Takemura relayed to his audience.

But I see some clouds in the blue skies of the miracle economy. The first I picked up almost subliminally, watching television commercials. A handsome young husband in a white cashmere sweater sits puzzling before a Go board, and his pretty, pink-cashmered wife dumps some frozen veal stew in a pan and stirs it; she serves it; he dips his chopsticks in, tastes, smiles; she rejoices. A dazzling young couple load up their car and go skiing; sometimes the commercial is for the car, sometimes for the skis. (American ski manufacturers, by the way, have a hard time even getting permission to sell in Japan, because, they are told, "Japanese snow is different.") Various TV actors play the dazzling young couple, and they do not look especially Japanese—or what we used to think of as Japanese. (Somehow, they look vaguely Italian.)

If we can take the TV commercials as a social indicator—and I think we can—then something has also happened to the Japanese spatial sensibility. The old Japanese room was bare; the sleeping mats were unrolled at night and taken away in the morning. The meals were served on a table so low and so portable it could be brought in with the dishes. We associate that austerity with concentration upon a single beautiful object—the single vase, for example, in the bare room. We know from pop Zen that one could not appreciate the doughnut without the hole.

It must have looked strange, a telephone resting alone on the floor. And then a TV set resting on the floor. Before long, the low table was permanently in the room. Then the sleeping mats became beds, and soon the rooms were filled with furniture. The mother-in-law who shows up at the door (quick, open another package of frozen veal stew!) is shown to a chair. The single beautiful object now has competition, and austerity is no longer seen as the virtue it once was.

It suddenly occurred to me, very faintly, like the first bat squeak reaching the radar antenna, that if the handsome young couple were loading up their car to go skiing, the chances were that they weren't in the office on Saturday. Given the cost of land, houses and apartments are very expensive. Those ski trips are not cheap either, nor are the popular winter vacations on the beaches of Saipan, Luzon, and the Pacific Islands (ironically, the very beaches the Japanese landed on during World War II). Sounded like somebody wasn't saving 20 percent of his income anymore or working twelve hours a day. I asked the investment bankers for the name of a finance company.

Ah, yes, said the officer from Orient Finance, we are growing as fast as any robot company. The folks over thirty-five still have a thing about saving—but the young generation don't mind borrowing, and more of them do every day. They don't want to save up for a car, they want it now, and friendly Orient Finance will help them.

There is a bigger problem than the erosion of the old Japanese work ethic. The Japanese heavy industries—steel, chemicals, shipbuilding—are soft. Only exports have kept up with growth. The Japanese have been prospering by shipping out the cameras and the copiers and the cars. Japanese financial surpluses have piled up.

The central bankers and commerce secretaries of the West grow moody and dark: the Japanese, they say, pay no share of their defense, do not contribute enough to international organizations, do not help the underdeveloped world enough. (Recently, the Japanese have begun to work on loans for Latin America.) For the most part, they are content to be twentieth-century mercantilists, piling up money in the bank, the big winners in the zero-sum game. So when Western union leaders and trade associations ask for relief and protection, governments give it to them; then the free trade that has made the world so prosperous for a generation disappears. The Toyotas and the Canons begin to meet walls of tariffs and quotas.

The robots and the new microprocessors are well on their way, and I certainly wouldn't bet against the Japanese. But that commercial is beginning to have an effect, the one where the handsome young couple go skiing, skipping work on Saturday. The Japanese real estate and hotel interests have bought the entire beachfront in

Waikiki, and richer Japanese have bought so many "second homes" in Hawaii that they have doubled the price of residential homes in some sections of Honolulu. Genshiro Kawamoto, of Tokyo, bought 170 houses on Oahu, for $100 million. He made the papers because of his procedure: he drove around in a Rolls-Royce limousine and, when he saw a house he liked, rang the doorbell and made the surprised owner an offer he couldn't refuse.

Furthermore, the Japanese *domestic* economy is booming. The demand for housing is growing, and if the Liberal Democratic Party could ever get free of the influence of the rice farmers, who hold so much near-urban land, then housing would explode.

But most of the country still works six days a week. When it slows down, the trading patterns may finally level off. Anyway, the Japanese have provided their own answers to our problem of competing with a country that works weekends. We could buy Japanese robots. Robots not only work Saturdays, they work Sundays and nights, too. Just point them in the right direction and keep them oiled.

What Did Iacocca *Do*?

The year is 1993, and Mr. and Mrs. Yamamoto, from Tokyo, have just run into their friends the Takemuras on Fifth Avenue. They compare notes about all of the terrific bargains the four of them have found in the United States.

"But the clerks are so rude," says Mrs. Yamamoto, "and they don't know the merchandise."

"Americans are so dumb," says Mrs. Takemura. "We had a taxi driver who didn't even know where the airport was. He barely spoke English."

"Not all Americans are dumb," says Mr. Yamamoto. "They used to be very good in business, you know."

"Really!" says Mrs. Takemura. "How can you say that, when everything they make falls apart so quickly?"

"Americans actually invented the transistor," says Mr. Takemura. "Look, it's getting dark, we'd better get back. You know it's not safe after dark. Did you notice that even our nice American friends have burglar alarms?"

"They used to be number one," says Mr. Yamamoto. "Hard to believe, but they blew it. Poor motivation, self-delusion, no acting for the common good. All the energy into litigation, paper shuffling, takeovers. You know, in the nineteenth century the British were *ichiban*. Pax Britannica. Then the Americans came—Pax Americana. And now we have to look out for Japan in the world—Pax Nipponica."

"We deserve it, we worked very hard. And Americans are such a dirty people," says Mrs. Yamamoto.

"Maybe we should have an aid program for them," Mrs. Takemura says.

In other words, the Yamamotos and the Takemuras are behaving, this day in 1993, just as Americans would have ten years before in some Third World city: Manila, Lagos, or Nairobi—or Calcutta.

This little scene does not exist in *Comeback: Charting America's Strategies for Responding to Japan's Economic Challenges*, by Professor Ezra Vogel, but it well might. It is my dramatization of the scenario laid out for the future in Vogel's book, which compares Japanese and American styles and strategies.

Vogel is the Harvard sociologist who kicked off the Japanese book boom with *Japan as Number One: Lessons for America*.

Vogel is back to say: you saw what they did in steel and autos and television sets, now watch what they do with high tech—computers, telecommunications, biotechnology, ceramics, lasers, fiber optics, pharmaceuticals. When you talk about supercomputers (very fast computers with extremely sophisticated scientific applications) and "fifth generation" computers (computers that can work through inference—that almost do their own thinking), then you are really talking about the industrial leadership of the world. With only half the population of the United States, Japan already produces more college graduates in engineering, and it produces 50 percent more electrical engineers. The Japanese take out more patents worldwide than Americans, and Japan is now surpassing America in the proportion of gross national product spent on research. (Much of our R&D is spent on defense, which has little commercial payoff.) One might say, taking the Japanese view, that the United States is like Rome in the late days: a big army, a big defense budget, but crumbling at the edges, the heyday over.

In order to continue with the lessons-for-America approach, Vogel now discusses several Japanese success stories that emerged from what began as difficult problems. The island of Kyushu, for example, was the coal-mining area, hardscrabble enough that many of its citizens went overseas to Taiwan or Korea. When coal mining became uneconomic, the government stepped in with programs to retrain workers, or resettle them, and then with a combination of local and national efforts that brought Kyushu good airports. With good air service and low labor costs, Kyushu became a semiconductor center, "Silicon Island."

The Japanese successes in computers and telecommunications and machine tools are perhaps better known. They all have the same ingredients: some form of consensus-building, followed by government action that helps focus the industrial (and postindustrial) energies.

The United States has had its share of consensus-building, targeting actions that worked, and Vogel touches on these as well. With the New Deal we had a national consensus that we wanted housing. Hard to remember, but before the creation of federal agencies for housing, a mortage down payment could be 50 percent of the purchase price, and many mortgages were due in five years, which put most housing beyond the reach of many people. Nearly half the housing units in the country, during the Depression, had no private bath or shower. In the last fifty years, through Fannie Mae and Ginnie Mae and all the agencies whose names came from housing-industry acronyms, the middle class was able to realize its dream of a home for every family. But it took a consensus, then federal action.

Agriculture is a similar American success story. But we had land-grant universities to support agricultural subsidies and all the other interactions between the government and agriculture.

It sounded to me as if Vogel was heading in the direction of industrial policy. With industrial policy, a national board in Washington would decide—much as the Ministry of International Trade and Industry in Tokyo does—what the national directions and targets are, and how we should go about focusing on them.

"I do think we are going to have to do more than we are doing, or our standard of living will decline," Vogel said, when I spoke to him recently.

I suggested that the national mood seemed to be for less government direction, while "industrial policy" seemed like a mandate for bureaucrats.

"We have an industrial policy," Vogel said. "It's an ad hoc policy. We give aid to defense-related industries and housing and agriculture. We support the price of tobacco. We give relief to industries that suffer from targeting by foreign exporters. We support a lot of R&D, but not with an eye to our international competitiveness."

There are, to my mind, at least two telling arguments against industrial policy.

The first is: Look what happened to defense. Our defense program is only theoretically based on deciding what we need and letting it be built exactly by who can build it best. But everyone who has ever dealt with Congress knows that, in fact, congressmen are sent by their constituents to wheedle money from the government. The process is as old as the Republic. Army bases are found in southern states because southern congressmen were the chairmen of the appropriate committees when it came time to hand out the contracts. Wouldn't an industrial policy quickly be warped if it were subject to our regular political processes?

"It probably would," Vogel said. "But much of what goes on in defense is secret. If you had industry councils, operating sector by sector, in which everyone could speak freely and openly, I think we could get to a consensus."

The second argument is: What bunch of bureaucrats knows which are future industries? Mightn't they pick the wrong ones?

"NASA worked well, and NASA was a small government group," Vogel said. "I'm not for an outright, comprehensive industrial policy like Japan's, because we aren't homogeneous as the Japanese are. We have to build the consensus before we can build the policy."

*   *   *

We have made a hero out of Lee Iacocca in this country. But think about it—what did Lee Iacocca do? He got government support to bail out Chrysler and helped get the restraints that kept Japanese imports down. That is an industrial policy of sorts; I doubt that Chrysler would have survived without a bailout, and I agree that if Nissan and Toyota had been able to send all the cars they could make, without a quota, even Ford and GM would have been sent reeling. But an ad hoc, crisis-by-crisis string of cases does not really add up to policy.

Without granting future superiority to the Japanese, I think we are going to need some new priorities to recover our international competitiveness. And at the top of that list would come education. Our blue-collar workers don't have the mathematical or engineering background to operate sophisticated machines. On the university level, we are churning out lawyers and M.B.A.s, but theirs are not the skills that will be most in demand in a technological age, as the planners in Tokyo know.

Carver Mead: Breakthroughs from Chaos

Not everybody believes that you need the government out front in dealing with the Japanese. Carver Mead doesn't, and George Gilder doesn't. Gilder is the author who celebrates markets and Carver Mead is Mr. Chip.

If they still made movies about scientists the way they made the old black-and-white ones, about Alexander Graham Bell, Thomas Edison, Madame Curie, they might make one about Carver Mead. He is not exactly a household word, but as Gilder has written, "No single individual has exerted a more profound influence on modern human productivity than [this] visionary physicist." Mead is a controversial Caltech professor who is a renowned architect of semiconductor design. He is also a superb teacher whose textbook *Introduction to* VLSI *Systems* (VLSI means very-large-scale integration), has trained a generation of students.

The transistor was invented at Bell Labs in New Jersey in 1947. Some twenty years later Mead predicted the million-transistor chip. At the time, this was thought to be a design task akin to creating a street map of California that would include each stoplight and list its timing. Today that vision is a reality.

Mead's contributions to semiconductor technology are acknowledged everywhere, but he now finds himself at the center of a controversy about how best to encourage American technology and how the future technology ought to be shaped. Not surprisingly, Ronald Reagan is one of Mead's fans.

I might have gone unaware of Mead but for Ronald Reagan's appearance at a broadcasters' convention where I was to moderate a panel. Addressing the convention, the President spoke warmly of his own days in broadcasting. He said he was going to talk to Gorbachev about missiles—and he quoted Carver Mead. The Industrial Revolution had enhanced productivity by a factor of a hundred, Reagan said, microelectronics had enhanced it by a million—and this was just the beginning. Carver Mead had said of the future, "We're not going to need the federal government to come in and bail out all our electronics. We're going to do just fine, thank you."

In fact, that message is a subject of debate. Silicon Valley has become part of American mythology, but much of it is now beleaguered by Japanese competition. A while back, the semiconductor industry went to Washington to make a pact with the Japanese that would stop "dumping"—the sale of Japanese chips in the U.S. below cost—which resulted in restricted sales. American computer makers have done well, American software writers lead the world, and Americans innovate brilliantly in microprocessors. But the Japanese completely dominate the world market for memory chips. When there is a shortage of chips—as there is at the moment—the fear grows that Japanese chip producers deliver to their classmates from Keio and Tokyo rather than to the *gaijin* in Santa Clara. Even beyond the chip business, there is growing national concern about the Japanese and technology; we seem to come up with inventions and major innovations like the videotape recorder or the integrated circuit, and they cash in on them by bringing their superior manufacturing technology to bear on the market. According to the prophets of Western decline, the Japanese target our technological industries, undercut them, outsell them, and destroy them. In the end we will become a farming colony that sends beef, citrus, and soybeans, while the Japanese send us the products of advanced civilization—robots and superconductors and computers with artificial intelligence. Mead, however, believes new developments will soon produce a creative explosion in the United States that will reverse this tide.

So I went to Caltech to meet Carver Mead. Mead, fifty-four, has a mustache and goatee. He describes himself as a "backwoods Californian," a native of Big Creek who came to Caltech for an undergraduate degree, and stayed. He built the first commercially successful gallium arsenide transistor in 1965. Later he learned computer theory and envisioned the advances possible in chips. Today megachips are commonplace, and many have been designed by Mead's former students. I asked Mead why he was suddenly attracting so much attention.

"I think people are tired of hearing gloom and doom," Mead said. "There are a group of us who have been doing something positive to innovate our way out of the problem."

Mead believes new design tools called silicon compilers will transform the semiconductor industry. Like the templates on a printing press, silicon compilers will permit the makers of telephones, computers, autos—practically anything—to design their own chips. A semiconductor factory designed for the mass production of general-purpose chips currently costs $100 million or more. In Mead's analogy these chips are the paper, not the book. The book is the information written by the author. Who cares who manufactures the paper? Silicon compilers, in effect, give each author the ability to produce his own book.

In Mead's scenario, if you had a specific application for a chip, you would sit down and design it. If you were building an automobile engine, for example, you could design a chip to control the fuel mixture in the piston. Then you would send the design out to a silicon foundry, and your personal chips would come back in weeks the way your film and prints come back from the photofinishers. Soon, Mead says, there will even be desktop foundries where you can make the chips yourself. The result will be an explosion of creativity—and an atmosphere especially suited to Americans.

"Americans have a frontier mentality," Mead explains. "We always feel that around the next bend is something startling. We work well as individuals. I would hate to see us adopt the Japanese methods of government help, big bureaucracy, and teams of people."

"But the Japanese have succeeded," I said.

"They have succeeded at manufacturing our ideas. I don't deny them what they're good at. But I'm talking about breakthrough innovations. Our system is chaotic, built for surprise. Innovations always come from a place you're not expecting," Mead said.

"It takes so much money to set up in this business; are you saying you can't plan?"

"You can plan the predictable innovations, those along the same curve. But you can't plan the jumps. From the vacuum tube to the transistor was a jump no one saw. From the transistor to the integrated circuit. From random logic to the microprocessor."

"How does a jump come about? With the national future at stake, I would think governments would try to create the atmosphere for just such a jump."

"First, you have to realize that the establishment—whatever establishment there is, science, government—wants things to keep going the same way, because it understands that way. But the jumps come because somebody looks at the problem a different way. A new paradigm, a new model. You need the vision to start something new.

"Research breakthroughs take place in little places and are done by individuals or small groups of individuals. Technology will find the places where it wants out."

Mead's vision very much fits what we like to believe. Two guys in a garage start Apple Computer and it grows up to be a multibillion-dollar company. But critics say Apple was an aberration. A more common scenario runs like this. Tom, Dick, and Susie work at Hewlett-Packard, an enormous company that has parented many start-ups. They have an idea for a new widget. They form a new company, get some money from venture capitalists on Sand Hill Road in Silicon Valley, and produce Model 001 of the widget. It is successful. But at a sales level of $50 million or so—when Model 002 is necessary because competition has already produced a *cheaper* Model 001—the money runs low, some of the staff peels off, and troubles abound.

Critics call these start-ups "vulture capitalism." The entrepreneurs have used their Hewlett-Packard experience and the potential of the stock market to capitalize a company, but it isn't yet a real company. After they have skimmed off some of the best ideas from a major company, Tom, Dick, and Susie sell to the Japanese or the Japanese appropriate the technology, improve the manufacturing, and take over the field.

"The U.S. semiconductor industry," writes MIT's Charles Ferguson in the *Harvard Business Review*, "often functions as a public service organization for its foreign competitors. Many companies have licensed technologies to the Japanese giants, disinvested, and exited. Then downstream industries [like computer makers] switched to Japanese suppliers while the U.S. semiconductor industry lobbied for protectionism." Ferguson sees chaos and ferment in the industry as a problem. It is chronically entrepreneurial, he says. "Big Japanese companies license—or steal—the intellectual property of little U.S. ones."

Ferguson is one of the first to say that entrepreneurs are not the answer to everything. In fact, he says, they are destructive. He's certainly swimming against the tide on that point. He thinks the government ought to be involved. Carver Mead says it doesn't need to be, and that it will get in the way of the yeasty chaos and surprise. But it ought to do better at protecting patents and software in the United States. "We do need intellectual property protection," Mead says. "The government doesn't do a good job protecting software and chip design. We need to be able to copyright designs. You need to protect the information, not, as in a press, the actual template that makes the impression."

Carver Mead sits down at a machine in his cluttered lab. He picks up an electronic stylus and begins to sketch with a light beam. On the computer screen, stacks of multicolored cubes appear, changing positions and patterns. "Let's try it this way," Mead says, wrist and fingers moving like a Sunday-in-the-park artist, but the computer screen looks more like *Star Wars* than Seurat. Jimmy Stewart could have played this role in the old black-and-white movie, the favorite student with the nervous Adam's apple standing by, saying, "Gosh, professor, this will change everything!"

Will it? The skeptics say it will take fifteen years to get good desktop foundries, for one thing because you need an inspection system that makes sure you get what you designed. And they say that niche markets like those of the new Mead chips would only be 20 percent of the business. But even skeptics say that chips specific to a given application will have an impact. It's stimulating to be at a place like Caltech, with everyone—faculty members, graduate students, and undergraduates—working on projects that are the frontiers of science. But Mead has been at Caltech for thirty-six years, and I think his vision of America is patterned by it. Caltech has no varsity football team, no prom queen; the entering freshmen have math SATs of 760. Everyone is desperate to learn.

If the United States generally was more like Caltech, if we had eighty Caltechs and hundreds of thousands of students clamoring to work in them, I wouldn't fret about Hitachi and Fujitsu. But the Japanese engineers are very literate, and I have no doubt they read Mead's papers as quickly as the students in Pasadena. The energies of American entrepreneurs may be superior, but the Defense Science Board says that of twenty-five microelectronics technologies surveyed last year, the United States led in only three, and was gaining in only one. As of 1985, Japan accounted for twice as many integrated-circuit patents as the United States.

So I'm sure Carver Mead's custom chips and desktop foundries will create another revolution. His students will be in the next wave of chip design. With as much venture capital as there is floating around today, I bet the first half-dozen of them who know how to write a business plan will get financed in some aspect of the business. There will be a dozen public companies in the desktop design-your-own-chip business. There will be a bust of Carver Mead somewhere, and he will deserve it. I just don't know whether the bust will be in Pasadena, Santa Clara, or Tskuba, outside Tokyo.

Soichiro Honda: "I Am One of MacArthur's Children"

"I have never met Mr. Honda, and I've never even seen an interview with him," said my Japanese translator. We were waiting with a camera crew in the conference room of an office building. I wanted to talk to Mr. Honda about Japanese technology, and whether the Japanese would be able to innovate as well as to adapt other people's technology. Soichiro Honda started with nothing and created a worldwide enterprise and his name is on the product, just like Chevrolet, only this is the original Mr. Honda, and everybody has forgotten there was a Louie Chevrolet. I had been to see Mr. Morita and Mr. Ibuka, the founders of Sony. Mr. Ibuka had told me how they were scratching around for a way to survive, in the 1950s, and they went to AT&T, because Bell Labs, that great research organization, had come through with a magnificent breakthrough, the transistor. They got the license for the transistor for $25,000. AT&T asked what they would do with it. They said they thought about making a small portable radio. The AT&T people said they'd never make any money from that, you couldn't charge enough for a portable radio, they should make hearing aids, you could charge hundreds of dollars for a hearing aid. I said $25,000 for the license to make the transistor was as big a bargain as Peter Minuit's purchase of Manhattan Island for $24. Mr. Ibuka didn't know the story.

The translator said he had heard Mr. Honda was a character. "He has an accent," the translator said. "You won't be able to tell, but in Japanese it makes some people smile, this is what I'm told."

I wanted to know what kind of accent.

"Maybe like Arkansas, or Oklahoma, in American," the translator said.

Mr. Honda came in, a small man with iron-gray hair and a lined face. He looked uncomfortable with the knot of his tie against his throat.

"I wasn't sure about this tie," he said. "My wife said, you're going on Yankee television in *that* tie?"

I said the tie was fine. I told Mr. Honda I had bought two of his cars. Mr. Honda brightened. Which two? Preludes, the same car. Why? Predecessors from Detroit were always in the shop.

"Cars don't break if the people who build them make them right the first time," said Mr. Honda. He looked over to an aide, as if to ask how he was doing.

"Let's go back to the beginning," I said. "When you started this company, did you have a plan? Did you ever think it would be the huge worldwide company that it is?"

"I don't think anyone can make predictions about his own destiny," said Mr. Honda.

"When you founded the company, was the technology Western or Japanese?"

"We had both, but basically it was Western. Until my father's time, my family was in the sword business, making samurai swords. That takes a lot of precision."

I hadn't known that the original Honda business was samurai swords.

I asked what Honda had made first.

"It was after World War II. You have to remember that the country was devastated. Everyone was poor. What public transportation was left was impossibly crowded. And the means of transportation was the bicycle. So the first thing I did was to clip engines onto ordinary bicycles."

Mr. Honda began to relax, thinking about the beginnings.

"Japanese engines?"

"Western engines."

"But now Japanese leads the world in these engines. Do you think the Japanese can be innovators across a whole spectrum of technology?"

"I think we can be. Because of our long history of isolation, we lagged behind, but now we've caught up."

I was still trying to get Mr. Honda to loosen up, and he was still polite and correct. But I really wanted to know how to go from samurai swords to cars.

"You're a remarkable person, an entrepreneur who started a great worldwide enterprise. Was that easy to do in Japan? Would it be easier today?" I asked.

Mr. Honda thought for a moment.

"Looked at in one way, you might have thought it was a difficult time. We didn't have enough materials, we barely had enough food. But—do you know the phrase 'MacArthur's children'? Up until World War II—until the end of World War II—most of industry, most of the economy, was monopolized by powerful figures, by a group of families and companies, the *zaibatsu,* and the military was tied in. But we lost the war. And as a result of losing the war, our freedom was restored. And General MacArthur came and wrote a constitution. The old combinations were broken up, or diminished. And new people could get started, people like me. I am a person who worked in shirtsleeves, and the people like me who came up with this new freedom were 'MacArthur's children.' So I am very proud to be one of MacArthur's children. I admired General Mac-Arthur, and when I was a kid reading about America there were other Americans I admired, Henry Ford, Thomas Edison, Alexander Graham Bell.

"So you ask, was it easy to do then. It was not easy, but everything depends on circumstances in which the individual is placed, and the circumstances under which I started the company were favorable to me." Mr. Honda now seemed happier, and more eager to talk.

"Would it be easy for someone to be an entrepreneur today?" I asked.

"I don't think the comparison between then and now is very relevant. Whenever anyone wants to start an enterprise he will meet some degree of resistance or some set of problems and it is his way of thinking which will make his job easy or difficult. It is not totally a matter of time and circumstances."

"Well, what was the Honda way of thinking?"

"The first thing I had in mind was to create a very friendly and cooperative atmosphere to overcome the difficulties. I thought everyone would be happy if he could earn enough money to eat three times a day and if he could lead a happy life. At the same time there were competitors, other companies doing the same thing I was. The last thing I wanted to do was to be defeated by them. I just didn't want to lose to the competition. So I had my shirtsleeves up, and if I criticized my workers with my hands in the grease, I asked my workers to criticize me. Otherwise we would not survive.''

"Americans have become fascinated with Japanese management techniques, with lessons we could learn to apply," I said.

"I don't know about management techniques as such," Mr. Honda said. "I only know about engineering and people. The most important thing is the respect for people within the corporation and so it's incumbent on the managers to create an environment within a corporation in which all the employees are encouraged to take initiatives in carrying out the work, and doing the work with pleasure. It's important to have an atmosphere of equality. So in the early days, my hands were always greasy, and you can see that one of my fingers got shorter from tinkering with the machines. The burden on me—and my partner, Mr. Fujisawa—was to rack our brains to pay more to our employees and figure out the next product that would sell.''

That seemed much like the small-town factory in Illinois or Tennessee, if the factory was owned by a local family.

"You were adapting existing technology. Do you think the Japanese will be innovators as well?"

"Yes," Mr. Honda said, "and let me give you one example. When a German company developed a rotary engine, every automobile company in the world, including General Motors and Chrysler and the other Japanese companies, put it under license. There was one exception, and that was our company. Because we took that engine apart until after midnight every night. And we didn't like the combustion system—the shape of that combustion chamber is guaranteed to get the worst fuel consumption. So we started over, and we developed our own system, CVCC. The minute you develop an innovative system you need money and manpower, but again, what is most important is to have motivated employees; a respect for people.

"Many corporate managers place emphasis on hardware, money, profit, but I think that is wrong. I am told some American companies think 'assets' means buildings and machinery. The 'assets' are permanent, but the people can be fired when you don't want them. But I think the assets are the people, because without the right people you end up building the wrong engine.

"So we encourage employees to submit to their managers whatever they want to say. We say, you are working in your own workshop. We say, we recognize the worth of your work. Of course, that doesn't mean there aren't complaints. I complain about my wife because she scolds me every now and then but despite that, I recognize the value of my wife, and that applies to relationships in work. The job is to keep the complaints from being serious.

"I went to our plant in Marysville, Ohio," Mr. Honda continued. "I think the majority of the workers are happy workers. I may feel self-satisfied, but that's the way I feel. There were three thousand employees at that plant. I shook hands with every one of them. My hand was sore and swollen but it made me happy and I am sure that the employees were happy as well. Their hands are a whole lot bigger than mine and their grips hurt but the feeling of hurt was not something that would rush me to a doctor. It was a very pleasant pain in my hand because of the warmth of the employees.

"Sure there is trouble from time to time. When I left home this morning I said I was going to be interviewed by an important American television program and my wife started saying—with your *accent?* And your manners? Now don't do this, and don't do that. So I shouted back at her—I know these things—and so on. This is a little fight but it enhances the relationship of a husband and wife as you grow older, and you could have a similar analogy between managers and employees within a corporation. When they fight they can gain understanding from each other. Without that, there would be no husband-wife relationship and no manager-employee relationship."

The Japanese educational system provides a high degree of training but does not encourage individuality. So I asked Mr. Honda whether the Japanese educational system would match the need for innovation.

"I think it's the individual, rather than the system. Remember, I told you, my family were sword blacksmiths. I never dreamed of manufacturing automobiles, and I never sought school training of that sort. So even if the government imposes certain things in the educational field, it doesn't mean that every citizen is going to agree, or support that. Not every child listens to its father.

"Now we operate globally—we are in fifty-four countries—and we buy and sell globally. But I still admire the United States. I think about Bell and Edison, and I hope that spirit hasn't died out, and will come up again. We are now the third-largest *American* automobile producer. When we decided to set up a plant in the United States, part of my motivation was to set up an operation in that great country I still respect and admire. There is no Japanese flag on our plant in Ohio. So if you go there, you will see our company flag, and the Stars and Stripes, and you can remember, this was one of MacArthur's children."

A sociologist who specializes in Japan read the account of this conversation with Mr. Honda for me. She said that, since Commodore Perry's black ships first entered the harbor of Tokyo, there have been only three brief "windows" in Japanese history where someone like Mr. Honda could break through the class structure, and the widest of these was when General MacArthur presided over Japan.

Through Japanese Eyes

Honda prospered through the '70s and early '80s; Chrysler did not. In 1970, Iacocca saw the Japanese waiting in the wings, but in his autobiography he told how the Chrysler Aspen and Volare series had been sold without adequate engineering or testing, guaranteeing that the owners would make interminable trips for repairs. The Japanese took the entire low end of the market away from Detroit, and would have taken more, except that, under heavy pressures from Washington, Japanese automakers "voluntarily" limited their exports.

Here is the way it looked through Japanese eyes, in an adult Japanese comic book. Japanese adult comics are a large and a serious business. They have as sharp a point of view as "Doonesbury," and use the close-ups, varied angles, and stop-frame techniques more common to movies than comic strips. These panels are from *Japan Inc.*—*Manga Nihon keizai nyūmon*—published by the Japanese equivalent of the *Wall Street Journal,* the *Nihon keizai shimbun.* It is a best-seller.

You probably remember the image of American workers smashing Japanese cars. It played well on television—in fact, the smashing didn't start until the TV cameras were in place. Car-smashing does lend itself to television far better than experts and statistics. The car-smashing scenes (and, some years later, the smashing of a Toshiba radio on the steps of the Capitol) made a deep impression on Japanese television viewers. You can see, in these panels from *Japan Inc.,* that "President Ironcoke" of "Chrysky Motors" looks like Lee Iacocca.

The success of the Japanese automobile makers was one of the coups of industrial history. The initial American response was to bail out Chrysler and to "suggest" quotas to Tokyo, lest something worse be passed through Congress. Congress also began to consider "local content" laws, requiring manufacturers selling more than a specific number of cars in the United States to use American-made parts. Japan has few lawyers for its population, but the money certainly flowed from Japan to those American law firms in Washington, D.C., that could lobby in the halls of Congress. I wouldn't be surprised if the total funds spent on legal services by the Japanese was as great in Washington as in Tokyo. The Japanese automobile and truck makers began to put up plants in the United States. A Honda made in Marysville, Ohio, wasn't subject to quotas.

In a decade, the Japanese won a huge slug of the world automobile market. The panels of *Japan Inc.* suggest the Americans were paying attention to the stock market instead of investing in plant and equipment. The ranks of American state governors flying to Japan swelled, and as they appeared with their inducements, financing plans, and tax exemptions, word would go around the "industrial castle-town" that maybe the new plant would be built in Smyrna, Tennessee, or Marysville, or Georgetown, Kentucky, or Flat Rock, Michigan. There is a streak of woe-is-me breast-beating in the Japanese, as well as the pride in Dai Nippon, Great Japan.

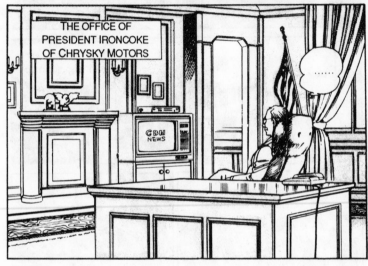

CITY P, PREFECTURE F — TOYOSAN FACTORIES STAND IN A ROW. NEARBY, THE SUBCONTRACTORS WHO MAKE THEIR PARTS ASSEMBLE. THIS IS AN INDUSTRIAL CASTLE-TOWN, WHERE OVER 50% OF THE PEOPLE ARE CONNECTED WITH TOYOSAN OR ITS SUBCONTRACTORS.

Since self-restriction began, production has stopped growing

Things are tough because the yen is so high

The future looks pretty dark too

Woe is me, says the Japanese subcontractor, I'm going to be left behind.

The automobile workers who smashed the Japanese cars were expressing a frustration, but frustrations existed on many levels. The Japanese sold us cars and VCRs, we sold them bonds. Congressmen made speeches, so did the members of the Diet in Tokyo. It was not a stable situation. NHK, the Japanese Broadcasting Corporation, proposed that we do a joint venture on the crisis in U.S.–Japanese trade relations. I would do a one-hour special on PBS, our public stations, and that hour would become part of a larger series in Japan, anchored by Hisanori Isomura.

It was an American magazine, *Consumer Reports,* that helped call the attention to Japanese quality. (It was also *Consumer Reports* that destroyed the U.S. sales of the Suzuki Samurai by reporting that it tipped over.) For its automobile issues, *Consumer Reports* constructs a chart rating the components of the cars it has tested— transmission, brakes, lights, and so on. A red dot is superior, a black dot is inferior. I went to Detroit to see Harold Poling, the president of Ford, and I took the latest auto issue of *Consumer Reports.* The Japanese cars were a sea of red dots—superior. The pages on American cars looked smallpoxed with *black* dots. Just for a second, Poling winced when I folded the page of black dots in the Ford section.

"Well, that's the way it was," he said. "It didn't happen to be on my watch. But we're going to fix it." And in fact Ford led the recovery of American automakers.

We may have seen the last of the automobile smashing, anyway. All of the worldwide auto companies have partnerships and ventures with companies in other countries, and parts are made all over the world. Fords don't just come from Michigan, and you wouldn't smash a Honda made in Marysville, Ohio.

The Japanese Walter Cronkite

The leading anchorman of Japanese television became my colleague for a week. NHK, translated as the Japan Broadcasting Corporation, had proposed that we do a joint venture on the crisis in U.S.–Japanese trade relations. I would do a one-hour special on PBS, the U.S. public station, and that hour would become part of a larger series in Japan, anchored by Hisanori Isomura.

Isomura was described to me as the Walter Cronkite of Japan. Indeed, when he first turned up for dinner, he seemed to exude that same air of solid authority and poise that we remember in Cronkite. When I told him how he had been described, he said, in colloquial and barely accented English, "I would rather think of myself as Ed Murrow than Cronkite. I was a reporter in Vietnam when the French were there, before the American Vietnam War. Then I was in Paris for seven years, and a bureau chief in Washington for five." Isomura went back to Tokyo and in 1974 became an anchorman. He quickly proved one benefit of his stay in Paris in a lengthy discussion in French with the captain at our restaurant.

I asked Isomura what inspired the Japan Broadcasting Corporation to propose our venture. Trade problems aren't exactly what you'd expect to find on prime-time television.

"That the trade imbalance has gotten so big so fast," Isomura said. "Even though we have put a voluntary quota on cars and do not send all the Toyotas and Hondas that could be sold, the trade surplus will be sixty billion dollars this year. Your Congress now has more than three hundred [trade] bills awaiting action. But the trigger for us was an article we read in the *New York Times Magazine* by Theodore H. White."

Teddy White, who was a friend of mine, is best remembered for his books on American presidential elections, but he reported on Asia almost all his life. He wrote his *Times* blast the year before he died. Isomura said, "Theodore White was a reporter in China in World War II; he spoke Chinese; he was shaped by his war experience in China. That is why he attacked Japan."

White's article was indeed an attack. He began with the surrender of the Japanese on the deck of the U.S.S. *Missouri* in Tokyo Bay. He described how, in 1945, we had fed the burned-out and desolate Japanese, how we helped them set up the institutions that enabled them to become a major commercial power—and how the Japanese had succeeded so brilliantly that they were now destroying American industry, sector by sector. "Today, forty years after the end of World War II," White wrote, "the Japanese are on the move again in one of history's most brilliant commercial offensives, as they go about dismantling American industry. Whether they are still only smart, or have finally learned to be wiser than we, will be tested in the next ten years. Only then will we know who finally won the war fifty years before." The Japanese, White wrote, first kept us out of their markets, then targeted ours. We invented television, they produced the TV sets. We invented the videocassette recorder, but they made them better, cheaper, and so swiftly that almost all VCRs are made in Japan. From their success grew a further threat from the Japanese: their cash surplus from exporting has accumulated so fast that the Japanese can buy into and own businesses everywhere—they have fifteen hundred firms in Los Angeles alone. White quoted Secretary of Commerce Malcolm Baldrige: "Japanese export policy has as its objective not participation in, but dominance of, world markets."

"This article," Isomura said, "really got noticed in Japan. It was Theodore H. White and the *New York Times.*" The senior news staff of NHK had a meeting, passed White's article around, said the Japanese equivalent of "Wow!" and decided to air some special shows that would explore the trade-based tensions between Japan and the United States. Trade tensions are nothing new in Japan's relationships. Japan cut itself off from the outside world for hundreds of years. It took Commodore Perry's black ships—and a threat to lob a few cannonballs into the emperor's garden—to open trade in 1854.

White's points were raised in our television show. The Americans said the Japanese markets were closed; it took twelve years just to get the paperwork done to sell baseball bats. The Japanese said the markets were open, the Americans just didn't try—they didn't speak Japanese, they didn't adapt products to the Japanese market. Senator Lloyd Bentsen of Texas listed the nontariff barriers—the red tape and paperwork—that stopped ships from unloading American goods in the first place. A Japanese professor and adviser to Prime Minister Nakasone said he thought tensions would increase because the Japanese only respond to pressure, to hard negotiating. It took that outside pressure to get them to form a consensus, and Japan only moves by consensus.

Later I asked Isomura how he felt personally; he had lived in the United States.

"I think many Americans are so used to looking at Japan as a nephew or younger brother that they will have trouble treating the Japanese as equals. I am cautiously optimistic, because I don't think we have anywhere else to go—not the Soviet Union, not China. We like America: we play baseball; we eat McDonald's hamburgers. But time may change this.

"I belong to the generation that grew up right after the war. As children we saw Japan in ruins. We call ourselves MacArthur's children. We recognize what the Americans did for us. But now a generation is growing up in Japan that has known only prosperity. Of course, they do not remember the war. They resent criticism—and I think they might get more nationalistic. In the 1930s the Japanese military regime wanted to produce what it called the Greater East Asia Co-Prosperity Sphere. It led to the disaster of World War II. Now we like to think of ourselves as a peaceful, almost Quaker nation. It would be ironic if the next generation took us back to militancy, even if that militancy is in trade."

I suggested that maybe the Japanese would not always be as they are. As the Japanese yen gets more expensive, it might get harder to sell the Toyotas and Hondas. And perhaps the Japanese wouldn't always work as hard.

"Well, we do have some yuppies now," said Isomura. "The next generation in Japan says it doesn't want to work on Saturday—remember, their elders worked a six-day week. But it takes a long time to change habits, and we are a pessimistic people. We have few resources, not enough farmland, and we have always had typhoons and earthquakes, so we work for the best and expect the worst. Americans are optimistic people. They have an open country, and respond to criticism."

If the Japanese grew disillusioned with the United States, where would they turn?

"Back to Asia," Isomura said. "There is no substitute for the United States, but we already hear we should perhaps pay more attention to the rest of Asia. Just what the old military regime wanted to do in the Co-Prosperity Sphere. But Asia cannot totally replace the United States.''

Japanese Prime Minister Nakasone, well aware of his American trade problem, urged his countrymen to buy American. Every Japanese family, he said, ought to buy $100 worth of something American, anything American. Pretty girls stood in Japanese department stores, giving away California oranges. But the Japanese didn't buy, and the trade imbalance grew bigger. When Nakasone visited Washington, he said a commission had recommended to him that Japan concentrate more on its domestic markets and less on its exports.

Doing the television show with the Japanese left me with an uneasy feeling, even though the Japanese broadcasters were eager to get at the problem of trade relations, and reported that their own show was a success. I know that we lose manufacturing jobs not only to Japan, but to South Korea and Taiwan and the rest of Asia. The Asians work harder, they get paid less; they can do the engineering we used to think we were so skilled at.

But my uneasiness comes not only from the current problems—they are already with us—but from what the relative states of the education systems bode for the future. For example, the Japanese are said to overdrill their children. There are coaching schools for nursery-school applicants. The Japanese debate whether so much effort spent on exam scores and passing to the next level doesn't stifle creativity.

Yet we have a larger problem. If labor is going to be skilled, Asian, and cheap, we will have to keep innovating; the society that hopes to keep raising the standard of living must pioneer in knowledge and technology. The Japanese have nearly 100 percent literacy; we do not, by a long shot. They graduate more students from high school than we do (90 versus 75 percent), and theirs are in many ways far better prepared—they have had several years more of math and science and foreign languages. Japanese teachers are more highly paid than ours; it is the extracurricular programs and physical plants that are inferior. American students have long vacations, teaching is less of a prestige profession, and American families, being less coherent than Japanese families at the moment, are not as demanding of their schools. In the opinion of some educators, the average Japanese eighteen-year-old is on a par with the average American college graduate.

The trading practices will be in the headlines. American companies will open plants in Taiwan and South Korea; the Japanese will open plants here. Trade war will be with us until the next television special. But the gap in education and training will give us even more severe problems in decades to come.

From MITI to DARPA

Teddy White's charges continue to echo. The Japanese Ministry of Trade and Industry, MITI, it is said, determines what it thinks best for Japan. Infant industries are protected; more mature industries are encouraged to cartelize. But it isn't the consumer—the marketplace—that is the guide, as in the West. It is the industrial future of the country, as determined by MITI in Tokyo, that wins out. This goes against the prevailing theory in the West, which says that each country should pursue its "comparative advantage." If you have a large unskilled labor force, you concentrate on labor-intensive activities, like textiles; you sell the textiles to the countries that make aircraft, and buy the aircraft.

But that model is static; it assumes that you stay where you are. Nations change, economies change, new technology and organizational systems can overcome a paucity of resources. If new technology comes from research and development, and if there is severe price competition, then profits may not be great enough to support the research and development. If interest rates are too high, debt service can eat into R&D.

Naohiro Amaya is the former vice-minister of MITI. He is white-haired, cordial, polite, and MITI's favorite delegate to international conferences, so I met him half a dozen times in those forums. "Businessmen are risk-averse," he told Clyde Prestowitz, one of our trade negotiators. "Therefore if the invisible hand cannot drive the enterprise to R&D, then the visible hand must." By "visible hand'' he meant central direction, economic policies that serve the industrial policy, such as encouraging industries with high technology content, in which costs decline as production increases and there is a ripple effect—for example, semiconductors determine the capabilities of computers.

In MITI's logic, industries get low interest rates so they can have an advantage competing with the *gaijin*. Consumers pay high interest rates. Energy prices are high for the consumer, low for industry. The individual Japanese has a per capita income that is now greater than an American's, but he or she does not live better. To a generation that didn't have them, consumer applicances made a huge difference. First the rice cooker, then the television set and the refrigerator. Nearly 100 percent of households have them all. Because of improving technology, prices of appliances scarcely moved. Comfort—except in the amount of living space—arrived in Japan.

The cost of services went up much more sharply. In nearly twenty years, the cost of telephone service actually went down. But a bottle of beer doubled, a haircut went from 160 to 2,700 yen, and tuition at a national university rose from 9,000 to 300,000 yen. The postwar generation began to take household comfort for granted; it was education and travel it talked about, but it did not feel *rich*. But while the Japanese consumer made only slow progress, Japanese industry prospered, its natural intense competition channeled by consensus-building techniques.

Japan has a network of networks. There is not only MITI, there is the Industrial Structure Council, the Telecommunications Council, and similar councils, all of which study key industries. The councils have leaders not just from business and government but from consumer groups, labor unions, the press, and universities. They produce a steady stream of white papers, or ''visions,'' and MITI and the other ministries can develop ''elevation'' plans with R&D quotas, production levels for export, and so on. The result is to socialize the risk, to take it from the individual firm and spread it, which makes it easier to have long-term goals. The long-term goal can be to have a dominant position in an industry. One example cited frequently is supercomputers.

The American side of the story is a familiar one, the genius inventor and the better mousetrap. In this case, the genius inventor is Seymour Cray, who left Control Data to start his own firm in the 1970s. No one else could come close to the Cray machines for speed and price, and with no Japanese supercomputers on the market, Cray sold two machines to the Japanese. But in 1981, MITI announced a program to develop a supercomputer. Cray's prospective customers in Japan seemed to disappear instantly, and government research institutes in Japan told Cray not to bother even sending a brochure because the government ministries which controlled their budgets wouldn't let them buy foreign machines. The Japanese government said its research institutes were too small to make use of the Crays. Two years later the Japanese had their supercomputers ready and the research institutes released their orders. A bit later the Japanese makers of supercomputers began an export drive by cutting prices drastically. The Massachusetts Institute of Technology was about to buy a supercomputer from Nippon Electric at a third the normal price, and canceled only when the Commerce Department announced an "antidumping" investigation.

Frictions between Japan and the United States are the subjects of nearly continuous negotiation. We have frictions with the Europeans over agriculture and with the Latins over debt, but supercomputers, semiconductors, and biotechnology will shape the industrial future more than pizzas and chickens. And the United States is not exactly a pitiful helpless giant. The Europeans envy the technological leadership of DARPA, the Defense Advanced Research Projects Agency, a part of the Defense Department, which is able to funnel funds like a mini-MITI. DARPA's money is supposed to produce frontier, leading-edge technology for the military, so commercial applications lag far behind.

DARPA is not to be underestimated as a godfather to innovative research. "DARPA is terrific," said one computer software entrepreneur I know, chairman of a DARPA-godfathered company. "DARPA has people who really know technology, not all of them colonels and generals. DARPA has very deep pockets, and it doesn't have to answer to anybody, as long as you're not talking hundreds of millions. DARPA doesn't make you show a profit next quarter, or even have something that comes out on a bottom line. In a four-hundred-billion-dollar defense budget, you can afford a DARPA. How else would you get Star Wars technology?

"There's a story going around about the Japanese and their fifth-generation computer project, AI—artificial intelligence. This is the project that had everybody scared to death, the computers that think for themselves, and thinking in Japanese, at that. But the Japanese have never been great at software, and let's face it, the name of fifth-generation computers is software.

"The story is that the Japanese had a big drumroll and press conferences to announce the fifth generation, but their real motive was to frighten the Americans. The Americans can't afford to do research that affects the bottom line and doesn't pay off right away, because then Wall Street will raid the companies that don't show profits. But DARPA is immune to all that. The idea was that DARPA would commission some fifth-generation computers, but DARPA only funds advanced *research*. It is not concerned with who applies and makes money from the research, unless it has a direct military bearing.

"So, the story goes, the Japanese idea was that DARPA would fund the research on AI, the American scientists would all publish their papers in the technical journals, those that weren't classified, the papers would be translated into Japanese five minutes later, and the Japanese, with their money and their superior engineering skills, would be the first into AI. Now I'll tell you a secret. I believe it."

DARPA, and the threat of the Japanese were cited in the summer of 1988 by the Office of Technology Assessment, a research arm of Congress, which was looking into superconductors. Superconductors are materials that conduct electricity with no loss of current. The theory of superconductors has been known for a long time, but the technology was impractical because it required very low temperatures to work—several hundred degrees below zero Fahrenheit. Two IBM researchers, working on their own in a Zurich lab and bootlegging their work time, discovered materials that would conduct currents at temperatures much less extreme. Superconductor fans could quickly visualize floating trains, power lines that would carry much more electricity, and superfast computers.

But, said the Office of Technology Assessment, while the Americans had gotten the Nobel Prize, Japanese companies are better positioned to commercialize superconductor technology, because they invest in product research, while the American firms adopted a wait-and-see attitude. Japanese companies, said the agency, already have the lead in superconductor-based trains, and may lead in motors. The Office of Technology Assessment recommended "a civilian DARPA," which could aid high-risk research.

It isn't just that American firms don't want to take chances with next year's profits. Sometimes they have a problem just delivering the product. Here is a table from a Pentagon study with a chilling line in it:

The U.S. vs. Japan: Manufacturing Comparisons

	U.S.	JAPAN
Private investment in plant and equipment as share of GNP	10.2%	17.0%
Average age of industrial base	17 years	10 years
Average annual hours per worker	1,898	2,152
Time between orders and shipments for machine tools	5–6 months	1–2 months
Nonconformance/rework rate in electronics industry	8–10%	0.5–1%

Source: Department of Defense, 1987

It's well known that the Japanese have newer plants, spend more on plant as a percentage of GNP, and have a work force that works more hours per year.

The disturbing line is "Nonconformance/rework rate in electronics industry." This is a *Pentagon* study that says the *defect* rate is 8 to 10 percent, ten times as high as in Japanese industry, which reflects greater attention to detail at every stage, and attention to quality control.

You can see the agitation in the Pentagon now. You want your commanders to press a button and have the gizmo *work*. The American gizmos get sent back, and the mechanic says a new clutch and new O rings and come back a week from Tuesday. If you're ordering up Star Wars—and all the buttons have to work instantly—does that mean you have to subcontract it to the Japanese?

David Kearns is the CEO of Xerox, a company which fostered a new industry, lost a lot of market share to the Japanese, then won it back. Xerox became known as a "samurai company" for having won a battle with the Japanese. I asked Kearns how Xerox had done it.

"The first thing we found is that we had a defect rate as high as twenty-five percent. So we gave ourselves a goal of zero defects. It may cost more in time and resources to do it right the first time, but it's intolerably expensive to do rework."

Kearns said the biggest pressure he felt was in finding an educated work force. American schools—and American parents—simply didn't turn out a labor force with enough skills, so that Xerox was forced into becoming an educator. Kearns coauthored a book, *Winning the Brain Race*, with a program for American schools. Kearns said he wasn't proposing vocational training, just graduates who could read, write, add, subtract—and think.

American firms that take the time and effort to learn how to operate in Japan can eventually do well. American Express has 600,000 Japanese cardholders. Coca-Cola made more money in Japan selling soft drinks than it did in the United States. Lotus produced a version of its 1-2-3 software using kanji characters and graphics adapted to the Japanese eye, and Japan is Lotus's third-best market. Motorola's Japanese division won the Deming Prize for quality. And McDonald's is the biggest restaurant chain in Japan; 12 percent of all the beef and 60 percent of all the potatoes imported into Japan go to McDonald's.

But these don't come near to matching the trade going in the other direction. Most of the American firms selling to the Japanese aren't in manufacturing or in more advanced technologies. Coca-Cola may do well, but the new technologies will be the major businesses in the next decades.

The Sneaker on the Table

Japan's economic performance is the most singular economic phenomenon of the last decades of the twentieth century. In its wake there are the "Little Tigers," Korea, Hong Kong, Taiwan, Singapore. The economists call them NICs—newly industrializing countries. All of them lifted themselves from poverty to comfort in one generation; all of them had populations that worked with the desperation of the Chinese tailors in Hong Kong who deliver your suit overnight. They were lucky in that they had a period of world stability, and a big, relatively open American market to sell into. Korea was a poor, mountainous farming country, devastated by a war, with a per capita income in 1960 of less than $100 a year. A quarter century later that income was close to $3,000, and it was producing computers, automobiles, and panels for the Boeing 747.

I met an American shoe manufacturer in a Seoul hotel.

"I had this idea for a new jogging shoe," he said. "I jog myself. If you have change, it bounces around in your pocket. If you wear shorts without pockets, you have no place to put change for a phone call, or a key. So I had a design drawn up for a shoe with a little pocket, a pouch. That's the kind of simple improvement that, if you market it right, can give you a real edge. So I flew to Seoul and had dinner with my rep and gave him the design. He took the design with him and I thought then we would meet and talk about the costs and so on. When I came down to breakfast the next morning, *the shoe was on the breakfast table by my place.* It was perfect.

"Don't get the idea that the Koreans are just like the Japanese. They are much more volatile. They say they are the Irish of Asia, that they like to knock off work, go to a pub, tell a story, sing a song, get into a fight. I don't speak Korean, so I don't know if that's completely true. And there are a lot of young Koreans who don't remember the war, and take everything for granted. So I don't know if they're the Irish of Asia, except I know you can't take a shoe design to Ireland and find the shoe on your breakfast table the next morning."

Korea's gains came through *chaebol,* huge industrial conglomerates that manufacture everything from spoons to semiconductors. Taiwan, by contrast, is a honeycomb of family companies, literally mom-and-pop.

Like Taiwan, Hong Kong has the energy of Chinese dispossessed from the mainland some generation ago. But in Hong Kong, the frantic activity is played against the ticking of a meter. You could probably get an overnight sneaker in Hong Kong.

*   *   *

We were sitting in a restaurant on the water on the Kowloon side. Across the harbor I could see the peaks of Hong Kong, construction cranes edging up the sides of the mountains like platoons of determined insects. Tugs and freighters and tankers slid by the windows of the restaurant.

"I think you've seen as much as possible in a short time, and you've talked to everybody," said my host. I will call him Ian. "Now, I would like to ask you two questions."

By "everybody" Ian meant the very small establishment of this last outpost of the British Empire. You can meet "everybody" in Hong Kong very quickly because "everybody" is in the chairman's box at the Sha-Tin racecourse on Saturday afternoon. The box is more than well-placed rows of seats over the racecourse; it is also a room that has an elaborate buffet and television sets in case you prefer close-ups and instant replay to the actual running of the races. The chairman is head of the Hong Kong and Shanghai Banking Corporation, which is not only the dominant bank of the colony but one of the twenty largest banks in the world.

The philosophy of the colony has been to have minimal government. So there is nothing in the banking system like a Federal Reserve; the Hong Kong and Shanghai Banking Corporation is the lender of last resort. The colony has a governor, and it has trading companies, or hongs, the oldest and largest of which, Jardine Matheson, is said to be the model for the hong in James Clavell's *Tai-Pan*.

I might have said hello one Saturday afternoon to "everybody," but I was under no illusions. I do not speak Cantonese, and Hong Kong is 99 percent Chinese. I had ridden the beautiful new subway, but I could not talk to the subway riders.

"The first thing I want to ask you," Ian said, "is, how do you feel about the psychological state here?"

Hong Kong has had periodic booms and busts, like a western mining town. I was visiting the Colony in the wake of a panic. From 1975 to 1982 a local stock exchange index, called the Hang Seng Index, fluctuated between 140 and 1820, making the Dow Jones look like a catatonic tortoise. It dropped 40 percent in the fall of 1982. In the Colorado gold towns in the 1880s, people made their fortunes and took them away; Colorado gold towns were not places to stay for a hundred years. Hong Kong is like that. Yet, even the gold towns sometimes would have the illusion of permanence: somebody would throw up an opera house and declare progress and culture. In Hong Kong, however, when people make a lot of money, they put it in a bank account in Switzerland and then they buy condos in Vancouver and San Francisco and New York.

"Everybody is obsessed with the Lease," I said. Again, "everybody" does not include the Cantonese-speaking citizens churning out the watches, the shirts, the radios in the factories of the colony. The Lease—and its expiration—is the ostensible cause of panic, the reason that Hong Kong is not rapidly industrializing like Singapore and South Korea. "Everybody" who is not making a watch or a shirt or a radio talks about the Lease all the time. The Lease expires in 1997, on July 1. On July 2, 1997, Hong Kong will be part of China.

For a long time that date bothered very few. Cheap, hardworking labor came to Hong Kong, and some of the world's swiftest entrepreneurs mobilized it. Before World War II, Hong Kong had been a kind of backwater, in the shadow of Shanghai, where many Western nations had concessions. But after the war, and especially in the 1970s, the capitalist entrepôt found great prosperity. Skyscrapers erupted at the water's edge and worked their way up the hills. Office space in Hong Kong was more expensive than in Manhattan.

Business was still good; in fact, it was so good that it was hard to get Chinese house servants. The Chinese wanted to work in factories, where the pay was better. The Hong Kong bourgeois than began importing Filipinas as maids. You can see the Filipina colony on Sunday morning in the plaza by the ferry station. They gather after mass, showing off clothes more brightly colored than those in the Chinese taste, exchanging gossip, twittering like cheerful birds.

I went to see Sir Lawrence Kadoorie. The Kadoories are a distinguished Jewish family that arrived in China in the nineteenth century and built some of the Shanghai utilities. Sir Lawrence is the chairman of China Light and Power, one of the utilities his family built. He likes to show visitors the silver taels by which payments

were made in prewar China—"that was real money"—and to tell
how his father, Sir Elly, managed to carry such authority in the
Japanese prison camp in which he was interned during World War
II. (The first jacket he grabbed, when arrested, was a morning coat,
and wearing a morning coat in a prison compound carries authority.)
After the war the Kadoories helped to support the Chinese refugees
in Shanghai. Now China Light and Power not only supplies part of
Hong Kong, it sells power over the border into Guangdong Prov-
ince. "To give you an idea of scale," says Sir Lawrence,
"Guangdong Province has the same population as West Germany."
But will China Light be supplying that power in 1998?

"I have seen China through a lot of history," said Sir Lawrence.
He holds his hands together to stabilize a slight tremor; he is in his
late eighties. "Famine and war and revolution. Right now they need
our technology. They have a vast job ahead of them. I hope we can
work things out. I believe that perhaps we can."

"I read recently about Gordon Wu," I said to Ian. Gordon Wu
graduated from Princeton with the class of 1957. Gordon Wu prospered with Hong Kong, in construction and real estate, and he just
gave Princeton $4 million for Wu Hall. I said that $4 million was a
very nice gift to give your old alma mater at your twenty-fifth
reunion.

"Four million dollars is taxi money to Gordon Wu," Ian said.
That made Hong Kong sound like Texas. "Which brings me to my
second question. What would you do if you were me? I've been here
twenty years. I've built up a business. It's been a good place to do
business. It's an interesting place. Winter weekends we go to the
beach in Thailand or Malaysia. Hong Kong has had lots of ups and
downs, and if this is just another down, I'll stay for the next up. But
if Hong Kong really isn't going to make it, then I sure don't want to
be the last one out. If Hong Kong loses its confidence, there will be
a stampede for the exits, and in a year there won't be anyone to sell
to. What would you do?"

My first instinct was to say that Westerners overestimate the
importance of their technologies. When Egypt seized the Suez Canal, it was said there would be no canal pilots to guide ships through.
But in fact there was no break in canal traffic. The citizens of the

Colony tell themselves that the colony earns 40 percent of China's foreign currency and therefore the Chinese will leave Hong Kong's current establishment in place. China is going to be a dynamic part of the world; any gateway will have importance. But the lights go on no matter who flicks the switch.

The People's Republic has had students at the Harvard Business School and associates at New York law firms. In 1997 they may think they can run Hong Kong themselves. Or perhaps exposure to Cambridge and New York will soften the anticapitalist ideology and permit Hong Kong to survive, even if in the twenty-first century it is not the swashbuckling place it has been in this one.

A State Goal in China: *Fa Chai!* Get Rich!

The Chinese invited us to do a television special about the economic changes there. I had last been in China in 1976, and the changes were indeed astonishing. They could mark one of the most important—if not most discussed—developments of this decade.

China's first model after the Communist takeover in 1949 was the Soviet Union. In 1976 that imprint was inescapable. Loudspeakers blared "The East Is Red" every morning; if you were on a train, you might hear "The East Is Red" before each announcement over the PA system. The only newspapers were the *People's Daily* and the Communist papers of Eastern Europe. Radio and television were filled with strident patriotic exhortations. The only foreign movie we saw in three weeks was Albanian, with Chinese subtitles. The hotels were primitive and unheated. I had been warned and arrived in early December with two sets of ski underwear, thermal socks, and a parka, all of which I wore everywhere. If we strayed from our highly organized Friendship Tour, security police suggested we return. Billboards bade the people study the thoughts of Mao Zedong and Karl Marx.

In retrospect it is no wonder that China was in disarray in the mid-1970s, or that the Chinese were cool to foreign guests. The country was just emerging from the Cultural Revolution of 1966–69: Mao's attempt to keep the Communist takeover pure. The Cultural

Revolution had wrecked the economy—which was scarcely robust to begin with—and torn the nation apart. Children were encouraged to denounce their parents for ideological deficiencies. The educated people—teachers, doctors, civil servants—were sent to work on the farms, to teach them humility and the virtues of peasant life. It was as if all Americans with college degrees received government orders to report to a pig farm, or a cotton plantation, and upon reporting were given the most menial jobs possible. Some of the Chinese intelligentsia are still mucking the pigs; recently there was a demonstration by a few who come to Beijing to say it was time they be allowed to come back. The climate would suggest they have a point.

To a recent visitor, the changes are visible and marked. Mao's picture has disappeared from most public places. The billboards extol the virtues of Japanese tape recorders and domestic appliances. The hotels are adequate, and most of all, the heavy feeling of the leaden Soviet style has disappeared from the atmosphere. Not only is the outside world allowed in, you can buy the *Asian Wall Street Journal* and the *International Herald Tribune* in many large Chinese cities.

Wherever we went, people would come up to us and speak to us in English—something no Chinese would have dared to do in Mao's era. In a foreign country one usually tends to shy away from a stranger saying, "Hello, where are you from?" In many places, that would be followed by an offer to change money—or commit some other transaction. But the Chinese merely wanted to practice their English. They listened to the BBC English lessons from Hong Kong. "The Voice of America talks too fast," said one of the Chinese who approached us.

The author of this policy—the opening to the outside—is Deng Xiaoping. During the Cultural Revolution, Deng was denounced as a "capitalist roader," paraded through the streets in a dunce cap, and sent to work as a waiter. A former high official of the party, he began to consolidate power after Mao's death in 1976. By 1978 he was firmly in control, and the *People's Daily* described the Cultural Revolution as a "leftist error." Deng himself said that China needed to bring its economy back up, and that it should reestablish its ties with the outside world.

One of those ties, it turned out, was the invitation from CCTV, China Central Television, to come and look at the Chinese economic reforms. Deng Xiaoping's reforms have been simply to let market forces work. Deng is from Sichuan, a rich agricultural province; Zhao Ziyang, the premier of China, was first secretary there. Mao had always preached that the strength of the country was in the peasants, and Deng allowed the peasant farmers to pick the crops they would grow and to keep the profits, once they had contributed to a quota or tax. The government still owns all the land in China, but Soviet-style collectivization is fading.

With the reforms, farm productivity doubled, and the Chinese—who once starved periodically—exported corn as far as the West Coast of the United States and are expected to produce the largest wheat crop in the world this year. The rich village farmer became a model—the "ten-thousand-yuan farmer." So did the entrepreneur, even in a society still officially Marxist. With the aid of our hosts at CCTV, we heard many stories of vigorous entrepreneurs.

In Beijing we visited a privately owned restaurant that was prospering. In the United States we take for granted the right to open a new business, a new restaurant, even a McDonald's, but everything in China was owned by the state until recently. It wasn't hard to find the restaurant. CCTV had already featured it. We got there in time to shoot the patrons watching a dubbed version of *Calamity Jane*. We visited a shirt factory. Some of the shirts were for Arrow, and already had the labels in them. The factory workers got 29 cents an hour, and the factory manager wanted to increase productivity by a bonus system.

In Shanghai we spoke to Wang Dao-han, the mayor. Wang was very proud that McDonnell Douglas was going to come to Shanghai to build its MD-80, a version of the DC-9. He had also helped to sponsor a new airline, Shanghai Airways, which was to compete with the state airline. There was even some talk that the old prewar Shanghai Stock Exchange might reopen. Even so, we were told that Wang Dao-han was on his way out—because he "didn't move fast enough."

In Chongqing we had a banquet with the people from the Television Authority there. The managing director was a middle-aged woman who wanted to know how they could make better television commercials. Only recently had they begun to produce commercials, and some of them were charming. A local doctor marched up, faced the camera, and said he was a good doctor; then he gave his address and invited you to consult him if you were sick. Chongqing is in the mountainous province of Sichuan, and is not up to Beijing's sophisticated standards. The local commercial the Chongqing people liked best was an animated cartoon for Sichuan Cola. Asking people from American public television about commercials is probably not the most direct route to snazzy commercials, and to tell the truth, I like the Chinese commercials just the way they are.

One of the mottoes you hear in China could be coming from many recent American college graduates. The characters are *fa chai*— "get rich." It is now an encouraged state goal. Bo Chin, vice-minister, has said that with a hundred million rich people, China could catch up with Japan. To get rich through labor is glorious, says another slogan in China.

It is a bewildering turnabout. Only fifteen years ago, even the slightest twitch toward profit was criminal. It was against the public good, it corrupted the purity of Marxism, it could get you the label of "capitalist roader," and that label got some people shot. Today you have to remind yourself that we sent troops to Vietnam not only to help the South Vietnamese fight off the Communist North Vietnamese, but to teach the Chinese that the dominoes in Southeast Asia were not to be pushed over. And here are the Chinese with a banner that could be flown from the Reagan White House.

I mentioned this irony to Ying Ro Cheng, who played Willy Loman in the Beijing production of *Death of a Salesman*. Arthur Miller had been critical of a business society; yet here was China speeding headlong toward the very same business society.

"At first, early in the play, the audience was confused," Ying said. "They would say, 'What's the problem with this guy? He's got a refrigerator. He's got a car. He's got a house!' But by the end, they were all moved. Children would send their parents to see the play. So the message does get across. With the new reforms, people in China want to be getting rich. We had two people in this theater company who started a fast-food business. Now they help support the theater. But we are aware—as in Arthur Miller—that getting rich is not the whole answer. Here, you are the experts—in getting rich. Maybe we will have to learn from you.''

These economic reforms—a small class of entrepreneurs, a few more freedoms—do not mean that China has ''gone capitalist.'' It is still a Marxist country. Recently there has been some pulling back from the ''open door.'' The people who backed Mao so fervently are still around, except for the most ardent of his cohorts, and China has a history of political volatility. But Deng's successor, Zhao Ziyang, is in place, along with whole tiers of ''pragmatists.'' If they carry out the reforms with a good sense of the reactions in the countryside—retreating when necessary—the reforms will last.

And that has significance because of the sheer size of China. One out of every five people on this planet are Chinese. Lifting a billion people to even modest prosperity creates a huge force—and a huge market. And the Japanese are already present, as the premier trading partner. Japan has technology, China has a powerful labor force.

The Rim of Asia turned up as a military problem for previous generations of Americans who saw war in Japan, Korea, and Vietnam. This generation is watching the discipline of the Asians as the Rim is forged into economic power.

China Central Television dubbed our hour-long special into Mandarin and broadcast it at nine o'clock on a Wednesday night. A correspondent wrote us that there wasn't much on the other channel, and there are only two channels. The audience was 350 million. For one night, we had seven times the audience of ''The Cosby Show,'' but Madison Avenue did not break down the door. We got a cassette of the show as broadcast, and in New York I sat with a Chinese translator to see what the Chinese had changed. We had said, after all, that no one knew if the reforms would last, and that the Mao hard-liners were still around. Would they leave it in? The Chinese broadcast it as it was. They had deleted only a single sentence, out of the entire hour. It was the one that said that in the Cultural Revolution, when Mao wanted to humiliate Deng, he called him a ''capitalist roader'' and sent him to work as a waiter.

Lee Kuan Yew: Surviving on the Rim

Singapore! My problem with Singapore is literary images. I think of Somerset Maugham. Singapore should be a planter from upcountry, waiting under the lazily circling ceiling fans in the long bar of the Raffles Hotel. The planter is dressed in white linen and he is in love with the wife of another planter, and the Chinese barman is going to be witness to the scene. On the waterfront there is the honk of tramp steamers and the smell of cloves and cinnamon and pepper.

But I cannot smell the spices, because this taxi is air-conditioned, which also cuts down on the honks from the tramp steamers in the harbor. The airport is spanking new and glistening, but chimes announce the flights and the destinations still sound romantic: Kuala Lumpur and Penang and Bali and Kota Kinabalu. The airport is called Changi, the same name as the Japanese prison camp in which George Segal was King Rat.

And when did Singapore get freeways and soaring bank buildings and begin to look like Dallas? The Raffles Hotel is still here with its louvered doors and long bar, but it is eclipsed by the Hyatt and the Shangri-La and the Holiday Inn and the Mandarin. The Mandarin has squash courts and a gym on the fifth floor, and a revolving rooftop bar on the fortieth from which you can see three countries. In the lobby, the display of daily events announces meetings of Digital Equipment and IBM. The Westin has a bar on the seventy-third floor. On a clear day you can see halfway to Penang. If Switzerland had palm trees, it might look like this.

Singapore is a republic, largely Chinese, independent since 1965. It is one of what are called NICs—newly industrializing countries, the southern anchor on the Rim of Asia. The Rim is the most rapidly growing part of the world in terms of economic development. The economies in the Rim are growing twice as fast as the rest of the world's; when steel mills shut down in Pennsylvania and the Ruhr and the British Midlands, the steelmaking moves to Korea and Japan. The shoemaking moves from Massachusetts to Tennessee and then on to Korea and Taiwan. You can buy a computer in Malaysia that looks suspiciously like an Apple, only it is called a

Pineapple and pays no royalties to Cupertino, California. In Taiwan there is a $500 computer called an Orange, 256K and all that. The logo has very familiar, cheerful colors.

I began to feel the reality of the Rim when watching the weather lady on Singapore television. Morning television news programs in the United States, like *Today* and *Good Morning America,* show you a national weather map, largely horizontal: it is 58 degrees and raining in San Francisco, it is 30 degrees and clear in Chicago, it is 41 degrees and brisk in New York. That way you know whether to take your lined raincoat when you travel. The weather map in Singapore is largely vertical, because the Rim is a vertical crescent.

"It is thirty-two degrees and clear in Seoul," says the weather lady, "forty-five degrees and raining in Tokyo. A period of intense thunderstorm activity is moving across eastern China and will reach Guandong and Hong Kong this afternoon. Bangkok is seventy-four degrees and cloudy, and in Singapore it is eighty-two degrees." (The weather lady speaks in Celsius. I have translated into Fahrenheit.)

I was in Singapore to speak at a conference; its sponsors called it the Adam Smith Conference, and the theme was disinflation—who benefits and who is penalized when inflation abates. The other speakers and the panelists were bankers, academics, and government officials from around Southeast Asia, and the audience was a mixture of high-level government and business people. I had my keynote speech well prepared, with slides and graphs. But I was wondering how sophisticated to make my dinner speech: how much about the American economy would I have to explain?

Then I heard the morning news broadcast in my hotel room. "In the United States, the Federal Reserve has lowered the discount rate half a point, and the overnight Fed funds rate was nine," said the announcer. "President Reagan's budget is in trouble with certain congressional leaders. The President returns tonight from California." I bought a newspaper. The *Straits Times* carried not only the New York Stock Exchange but also "Peanuts" and "Beetle Bailey."

The "shuttle" to me is a disagreeable but convenient service between New York and Washington and New York and Boston. There is another, more agreeable shuttle, between Singapore and Kuala Lumpur, the capital of Malaysia. Flight time: forty-five minutes. In the airport I had run into a classmate, an architect commuting from Texas to Malaysia. "I'm just about to hop on the shuttle," he said. "Come to K.L. for the weekend."

I did. Unlike the New York–Washington shuttle, the Singapore–K.L. shuttle has stewardesses in cheongsams, saronglike dresses, serving drinks. In K.L.—which has gotten to look more like southern California—the talk was of whether Texas Instruments would build a new plant, and how K.L. was spreading up the Kelang Valley.

Images recede grudgingly. The Kwai River is in Thailand, but my image of the River Kwai comes from the great movie with Alec Guinness and William Holden and Sessue Hayakawa, when Hayakawa was the Japanese officer who said, as I recall: "English prisoners! Be happy in your work!" *The Bridge on the River Kwai* was actually filmed in Sri Lanka. But tourist buses bring the tourists to Kanchanaburi, where there is indeed a bridge on the River Kwai. During "River Kwai Festival Week," the drama is a light-and-sound spectacular. The tourists see fires on the riverbank, recalling the burning of cholera victims during the epidemic among the English prisoners. "Allied bombers" dive for the bridge. Mock rails collapse into the river below. I do not particularly want to see that bridge on the River Kwai. The Thais I met were all talking about their big offshore gas field and what kind of industry to build when they get the gas piped ashore.

In Singapore the manager of the Hyatt has pictures of other Asian Hyatts on the walls. Here is one on the beach at Kuantan, on the east coast of Malaysia. Did not the poor women prisoners of *A Town Like Alice* have to walk to Kuanton? And here is a Hyatt on the water at Kota Kinabalu.

Where, I ask, is Kota Kinabalu?

"Sabah," says the Hyatt manager. Seeing me still look tentative, he says, "Eastern Malaysia. On the north coast of Borneo. Very modern city, Kota Kinabalu. It could grow like Singapore."

The manager's wrist shoots out, and looks at his watch. He throws some papers in his briefcase. Apologetically, he says, "I have to catch the three-ten to Taipei."

There are some aspects in which Singapore does not resemble Dallas. It has wonderful Chinese cuisine. It also has acres of public housing, uniform high-rise apartments, some owned by their occupants, some rented from the public housing authority. Lines of washing are strung from point to point. With all this prosperity, can Singapore not afford dryers?

"We don't make them here," says my local colleague in the taxi, "and our people still think sunlight is good for the clothes."

One thing is remarkable and every visitor comments on it: Singapore is so clean. "Well," says the local colleague, "we have a five-hundred-dollar antilittering law, and it is strictly enforced. When they passed it, the word went out, uh-oh, they mean it." One squints, looking for a beer can or a candy wrapper or a cigarette butt.

The American ambassador is Harry Thayer, a tanned, bearded career foreign service officer, a specialist in China who speaks Mandarin. "Lee wanted to make it into a Switzerland," he says of Singapore's prime minister, Lee Kuan Yew. "Banking and insurance and clean. The penalty for littering is five hundred dollars, and the penalty for dealing in heroin is death. You can walk anywhere in this city safely."

I asked if the American ambassador ever had to cope with wandering American kids dealing dope. He sighed.

"There are always some," he said. "Somehow there are kids who don't read and don't get the word. Not too many, thank God."

I asked what he did when he did get one. He looked glum.

"I hand them a list of competent local lawyers and tell them the penalties are severe, and I do what I can."

"It sure is a clean city," I said.

"Oh, it's clean," said the ambassador. "Very clean. And you can drink the water."

The architect of independent Singapore and its thrust to be a Southeast Asian Switzerland is its trim, almost-crew-cut prime minister, Lee Kuan Yew. At Cambridge he was called Harry Lee. We are talking on the grounds of the Istana, the government residence. The name above mine in the guest book is Valéry Giscard d'Estaing. The British high commissioner used to receive people here.

Lee Kuan Yew has been in power since 1959, when he was thirty-six. He has been reelected six times. His longevity in office makes him a statesman.

"We had a new country, a small island," he says. "We made a list of our resources, and it was quite short. We have a harbor, and an entrepôt, and people who are willing to work hard." The prime minister discusses productivity almost continuously, and exhorts his people in frequent speeches: "Productivity is the only way we can survive."

One of his New Year's messages was entitled "The Future Is Grim." "It is traditional to wish you a happy New Year, although I know the future is grim," said the prime minister. Grim because it is hard to survive as a city-state, without resources. Singapore must be restructured into high technology, to get out of the trap of competing against countries with lower wages that are working on lower-technology machines, producing textiles and simple electronics. The answer? Productivity. "More and better machines per worker, more highly skilled, better-educated workers, positive attitudes. From the British we inherited a tradition of labor antagonism; we have to imitate the cooperation of the Japanese. We will make technicians, engineers, and managers out of each Singaporean who has the inborn attributes to make the grade." Computer camp for twelve-year-olds costs $1 per two-day session.

The prime minister's other theme is security. Every Singaporean does national service of two years. "Beirut was a banking center, a prosperous oasis in the Middle East," says the prime minister. "Look at it. Cambodia was an oasis in Indochina. Now a third of the Cambodians are dead and its cities are in ruins. After thirty years of war, the Vietnamese are still suffering, risking their lives in small boats to get out. So we are resolved we will not be boat people. We will have the best air force, the most advanced equipment in the area."

What worried the prime minister most? He seems to have built an island republic with high growth, low inflation, low crime, and nary a cigarette butt on the street.

"It's the next generation," he said. "We were not safe, and we had to work so hard. But the young people—they are growing up taking for granted safety and prosperity. How will they learn to run lean?"

Confucian Capitalism

The Istana is a majestic white building amid palm trees and rolling green lawns that look as though they should be graced by peacocks, an oasis in the middle of busy Singapore. It is the prime minister's residence, about the only image left of the days of Somerset Maugham, except perhaps the Raffles Hotel. There are now few people in Singapore who can remember when Lee Kuan Yew did not live at the Istana, since he is the only prime minister Singapore has ever had. Lee has said he will step down sometime soon, and there is speculation that his son, Lee Hsien Long—called B. G. Lee, after his rank as brigadier general—may succeed him someday. B. G. got high honors at both Cambridge and Harvard, and is certainly involved in the government of Singapore, but has taken himself out of the succession talk, so, say the Singaporeans, the next prime minister will probably be Goh Chok Tong, the current first deputy prime minister and minister for defense. Thus the future is "Father, son, and holy Goh," they say, but not necessarily in that order.

Lee—Prime Minister Lee—still speaks in clipped Cambridge tones, and is still lean and crew-cut. I had a second visit with him, doing a survey of the Rim of Asia. I asked Lee what the biggest failure of his tenure was.

"I underestimated the Chinese mother," he said.

Lee was talking about his social engineering, and he was not totally serious, but the social engineering has been a failure in one respect. When Lee became prime minister back in 1959, he wanted Singaporeans to have fewer children, lest a population explosion overwhelm the island. But by 1985 he found educated Singaporeans were not reproducing themselves, and now the government wants to encourage *that*.

"We have had equal education for men and women here," Lee explained. "And that produced a problem I did not foresee. The Chinese mother is a great force for education. She will make sure each child has a desk. She will nag about homework and keep the television off. But the Chinese mother also tells her *son* that he must be the master in his own house. Then he grows up and doesn't want a wife who has a master's or a Ph.D. because he might not be the ruler of his own house. So now I have a generation of spinsters with master's and Ph.D's. I underestimated the Chinese mother."

Lee's point has to be seen in a larger context. His country had to survive the turbulence of the Vietnam War, left-wing riots in the streets, and the departure of the British fleet. Nonetheless, the government is now running parties at which bachelors and spinsters can meet, and sponsors a "love boat" cruise of the harbor for singles. All you need to get on board is a college degree.

Lee created a prosperous city-state, neater than the Switzerland after which it was modeled. It is efficient, practically corruption-free, and tidy beyond belief. It now has so many sleek glass towers that there is talk of preserving a few blocks of the old Chinese district— maybe putting a dome over it—like the western frontier street in Disneyland.

Lee has tried to apply the same kind of tidiness to politics as well. When the *Asian Wall Street Journal* and the *Far Eastern Economic Review* wouldn't print the letters of government ministers, or when they reported on opposition to Lee's People's Action Party, Lee restricted their circulation. His technique of dealing with the annoying foreign press has not been not to ban it but to hold the distribution to five hundred copies. You can get a numbered copy of the *Asian Wall Street Journal* at your hotel, if you call at the newsstand early enough, and the libraries have it, so this is hardly a Soviet-style repression. It is more in the nature of take-that.

"This isn't America," Lee told one journalist. "Put two and a half million Americans here, and the place wouldn't last six months."

I asked Lee about the opposition. There seemed to be so little opposition, and Singapore is so prosperous, and the people are scarcely in political turmoil. They are all talking about their boats and their bank accounts.

"That is what it appears," Lee said, "but I never forget where we have come from. We are a small state, and we have a racial mix that is three-quarters Chinese, 15 percent Malay, and the rest Indian and other Asians. We all get along, and we have a meritocracy. We have all races in the government. We have religious tolerance and no state religion.

"On one side, just three miles away, is Indonesia, a large Muslim country, one hundred and eighty million people, I think the fifth most populated in the world. It has had a series of military governments. Across the causeway is Malaysia, which has had a lot of racial tensions—another Muslim state. We have a lot of young people who don't remember the riots here, but I remember, and I remember that Cambodia was once so prosperous that a third of all the days were holidays," said the prime minister, repeating a theme he'd used before, "and Beirut was once a banking center in Singapore. So I take nothing for granted." Singaporeans, said the prime minister, must work harder, must get to be better educated. Lee has a long worry list. Malaysian politics, Indonesian generals, and those spinsters with Ph.D.'s who put off potential husbands.

The largest multinational firm in Singapore is Seagate Technology, a maker of computer disk drives based in California. Seagate followed the pattern of many American high-technology firms: design the product in Silicon Valley, take it "offshore" to manufacture. "Offshore" almost always means the Rim of Asia. As Seagate went to Singapore, RCA went to Taiwan.

"We went to Taiwan the same way a lot of American manufacturers have gone to Asia," Thornton Bradshaw, the former chairman of RCA, told me some time ago. "We went because we could make TV sets cheaper in Taiwan than in the United States, and we expected that. Then we found that this was a well-educated work force. Engineers were coming out of the local universities who could produce and design as well as some RCA engineers in the States, but their salaries were much less. So we came for the cheap labor and stayed for the engineering, some of which is quite innovative."

*   *   *

If you are tempted to ask why all this attention to the Rim of Asia, remember that we are now the world's largest debtor, and many of the creditors are in Asia, and all of this has happened in just half a generation. The jobs do not migrate from Michigan and Illinois to Peru, Morocco, or even France. They move to East Asia. When you're a major creditor, you can call in the assets behind your chits from time to time. So the Rim of Asia is in our future.

Why did the Asians succeed? It isn't cheap labor. Mexico is cheap—cheaper than the Rim of Asia—Peru is cheap, Bolivia is cheap, Bangladesh is cheap, Malawi and Ethiopia are right off the scale. The East Asian countries are in better shape than Argentina, a country self-sufficient in oil and food and considered, at the turn of the century, the equal of the United States. But Argentina's economy is in deep trouble. Mexico and Brazil have had rapid growth, and have vast resources, but even with great resources they have severe problems.

There is a theory that the cultures of the East Asian countries are the engines of their success. All of them share Confucian values that spread out from China 2,500 years ago. These values encourage diligence and harmony in the workplace, strong family ties, and a passion for education. The diligence in the workplace is described as "a hungry spirit." We have seen it in the United States in Silicon Valley, famous for its ninety-hour weeks, but in few other American workplaces. When was the last time you ran into a plumber or an electrician who would work late or call the next day to make sure everything was working all right?

David Halberstam, in his book *The Reckoning,* describes a scene in which an American manufacturer visits a Japanese auto plant.

"Where are your inspectors?" he asks.

"The workers are the inspectors" is the guide's reply.

The biggest success in dollar terms for the Asians has of course been in the production of Japanese automobiles that the world will buy. In retrospect, it was easy. In the period following World War II, Japanese cars were considered junk, but within a generation they were operating in a world where British workers had developed an "I'm all right, Jack" attitude, and Americans began telling one another never to buy a Detroit car built on a Monday or a Friday. Eventually it became apparent that the Japanese cars simply required less service and did not break down so quickly. The rest, as they say, is history.

Confucius valued the educated man, the self-advancing man: so do Asian families. Two blocks from my hotel in Taipei I found a little street the locals call "cram-school alley." It houses the schools that will tutor you for the GREs and GMATs and the other tests necessary to get into American graduate schools. More than half the doctoral candidates in science and engineering in our graduate schools are now foreigners, most of them Asians. They are getting advanced degrees in a second language—English. New Yorkers have noted in the last decade the proliferation of Korean grocery stores that stay open virtually all night. Mom and Pop who run the stores may not speak English, but the children by golly are going to Caltech and MIT. What percentage, would you guess, of first-year graduate students in physics at U.S. universities are foreigners? Try 42 percent.

In looking around for the villains that cause our trade deficits, senators and congressmen often say these are caused by the NICs and Japan keeping out our goods. "We need a level playing field" is the phrase often used. It is true that custom and bureaucracy— what are called "nontariff barriers"—have helped keep American goods out of Japan. Hong Kong and Singapore have always been more open to U.S. products.

But what can we say when the Asians start to give us trouble because of their engineering—because of the superior levels of skill in their work force? Korea was desperately poor thirty years ago, torn apart by the Korean War; today it too is producing automobiles and computers. Korea has taken the steel and shipbuilding business away from the Japanese and has begun to lose the low-tech items such as shoes and clothing to still cheaper places—Sri Lanka, Bangladesh, and China. The Japanese are moving up to supercomputers and artificial intelligence. Moving up the ladder of industrial sophistication requires an educated work force. When the Japanese move up to supercomputers, jet aircraft, and artificial intelligence, what's left for us?

It is also said: What's wrong with our schools? But Laurence Steinberg, a professor of child and family studies at the University of Wisconsin, points out that the problem isn't just in the schools. American mothers, he says, don't push their children like Japanese mothers—especially when the mothers are working. American students also don't get praised often by their peers for academic achievements—in fact, if you study hard you are a nerd, or worse. When you finally get down to it, the Asians simply do more homework. For example, when it comes to homework on Saturdays, American fifth-graders spend seven minutes on homework, the Japanese thirty-seven minutes, and the Chinese eighty-three minutes.

What does this mean for *our* future? Well, we might hope that talented Asians will settle and work here; the recent breakthroughs in superconductors, for example, were made largely by people of Chinese origin. And we might hope that affluence in the next generation will slow down the Asians on the Rim. But finally, we must realize that in the knowledge-intensive late twentieth century, Confucian—and Calvinist—characteristics pay off. We knew them once; we may have to learn them all over again.

That means we have to pay attention to hard study and hard work. American industry is already beginning to learn these lessons. But American industry is receiving recruits who cannot always read and write with skill. The answer is not merely government policy—though government can help with consciousness-raising. School policy is determined on the state and local level, by voters—and parents. And too many American parents have, naturally, the same goals of athletic prominence and social success that their children do. We do not need to go to the extent the Asians have in their disciplined work and study, but we have to move in that direction. We have to have some "Japanese Jewish mothers" or some "Chinese mothers" who make sure each child has a desk and that the TV is turned off. It may be curious to think that the industrial future of our country depends on such things, but this is how we got to preeminence in the first place.

4 WHAT REALLY GOVERNS?

This Idea Is Going to Come Back
Under Another Name

The countries of the Pacific Rim that challenged the United States had no great natural resources, but they mobilized themselves with a kind of Confucian capitalism. The response has ranged from Bash Them to We Need a Plan. As soon as you have a national plan, you have something that suggests—especially to those that fear it—an Industrial Policy.

"Industrial policy" is not a phrase that naturally brings a song to the heart. I thought for a while that if the Democrats could give it an *image*, they could make it their riposte to the "supply side" of the Republicans. A while back, the neoliberal Democrats bounced the term around, hoping it would pick up a clean, high-techy look, like the landscaped single-story glass buildings of Silicon Valley. The neoliberals were using the phrase to show that the Democrats were not simply the same old 1930s New Deal crowd, labor and minorities and so on, but the new yuppie crowd, zooming down the road to a future with fifth-generation computers and biotechnology, and at the same time having the heart and compassion for poor folks that the Democrats have always prided themselves on. "Industrial policy," though, never meant any one thing: its beauty was that it meant many things to many people, and as you might expect, that turned out to be its fault, too, because people don't get enthusiastic about something vague when it sounds as boring as "industrial policy." And now the phrase "industrial policy" seems out of date, failed, but the *idea* is still in currency.

The thesis of the supply-siders was fairly simple—you got the government out of the way, and the magic of the marketplace produced wealth. The natural tendency of the marketplace was to mobilize goods and services and people efficiently. Robert Reich, the diminutive Harvard professor who wrote the industrial-policy thesis in *The Next American Frontier,* said supply-siders were just "ideological neurotics." Neurotics can't see the world as it is, and "no matter how much you explain and reveal that there was *never* a free market in this country, these people won't believe it. Government intervention sets the boundaries, decides what's going to be marketed, sets the rules of the game through procurement policies, tax credits, depreciation allowances, loans, loan guarantees, and a thousand different schemes." The choice, as he put it, is not between the free market and planning, "the choice is between preservation and adjustment."

The IP crowd says that not only does the government intervene, it frequently contradicts itself. We accept, for example, that the government subsidizes tobacco farmers and also subsidizes cancer research. Given the political facts of life, maybe we have to accept that, but there are many areas where the government is contradicting itself and, naturally, producing confused results. So if the government does intervene—and even supply-siders say it is not going to get much smaller on the national scene—then let it intervene *coherently*. In order to have it behave coherently, some sort of national board is necessary that combines business, labor, and government and establishes goals and priorities, along with ways of moving toward both. What puts some people off about industrial policy is that it provides an opportunity for traditional liberal Democrats to distance themselves from the pressures of the unions. And once the national board decides on a proper course, it can use compulsion in what may amount to painful choices.

The IP crowd seems to me frequently to have the Japanese in mind. The Japanese project the image of coherent policy, even if there are internal squabbles we don't know about. The Japanese Ministry of International Trade and Industry, MITI, is well known around the world for its ability first to set national targets and then, through the carrot-and-stick inducements of loan guarantees, subsidies, and export quotas, to nudge Japanese industry along the path marked by the consensus of elite government technocrats and the representatives of various groups. The critics of this idea say that Japan runs by consensus, and we run by butting heads and competing with one another, and that each culture has to run its own way.

Not long ago I met with Ira Magaziner, who places himself at about the midpoint of the IP crowd. Magaziner is a lean, angular fellow with tousled hair who runs a consulting firm specializing in business strategies. The firm has offices in Paris and Melbourne, but its headquarters are in Rhode Island, a state Magaziner has energetically adopted as his own. A '60s activist, a Rhodes Scholar, and later a trustee of Brown University, he helped create Brown's popular curriculum. Magaziner coauthored a book with Reich, *Minding America's Business*, that helped put him into the dialogue.

"We see industrial policy as pragmatic, not ideological," he said. "The mission is to keep the United States a strong international trading nation. We can, more or less, handle business cycles. What we haven't handled so far is long-term development. Whoever is President next will face a huge trade deficit as well as a huge budget deficit. Seventy percent of our national output is subject to international competition. We hear a lot about how we're becoming a service economy, but it was our manufacturing and trading base which allowed us to add the service jobs. We hear a lot about high tech being the wave of the future. Take robotics. Look where robots are used—autos and steel and machine tools, and if you don't have those industries, you're not going to have robotics. In the 1960s and 1970s we pioneered the high-growth industries—robots, computers, CAD [computer-aided design], specialty chemicals. But we've almost lost our technological edge. Our patent position is declining, and in many of our technical schools fifty percent of the students are foreign.

"What's wrong is actually in the culture of business. The stock market is dominated by institutions who want instant results. They want earnings to grow every quarter—not in five years. They want a high return on investment. A company can get a high return on investment by increasing its income, or by lowering investment. If you lower the investment, you look better at the moment and that pleases everyone in our instant-gratification society, but then you're not a competitor in the long run.''

But, I suggested, did we not have a probusiness administration that passed a tax bill several years ago precisely to encourage business investment through tax credits and advantageous depreciation schedules?

''Business managers are much better off—I'm better off, anybody who makes money is—but the Reagan tax policy was too blunt an instrument. For example, computer keyboards and tools and auto parts can all be made abroad—General Motors can move a plant to Japan, bring the goods here, and use the tax benefits to build the warehouses that house the imports.''

Could a bunch of technocrats in Washington make better decisions than the marketplace?

''The marketplace works, but only in a very lumpy way. For example, we have protected industries in this country—cars, textiles, steel—but the quotas or tariffs are all decided in an ad hoc way, without a clear rationale. We pretend we exist in a world of free trade, but having advised American companies trying to sell in Japan, I can assure you the playing field isn't level and both teams don't play by the same rules. So we need a clear policy in that area. Government in the nineteenth century provided the infrastructure here—roads, railroads, the Morrill Act that created our land-grant universities. It has to do the same in the twentieth, only now the infrastructure is in research and education.''

Like some other proponents of an industrial policy, Magaziner believes we need a federal agency that looks to the future—encouraging the ''sunrise'' industries in high technology and genetic engineering. ''We would have loan guarantees and loan banks, just as we have in the housing market, and tax incentives where we need them, just as we had for the oil industry. But we can't just say goodbye to all of our older industries—they make up half of the economy, and they are going to be around for a while.''

If all of this is so logical, why is industrial policy not greeted with open arms?

"We have a strong populist streak in this country, and if you say, 'Big business and big labor and big government, sit down,' a lot of people feel threatened."

The defense industry, I pointed out, has some clear priorities, and "military-industrial complex" certainly means a consensus between government and industry. But in defense, most of the dollars—and the loan guarantees, and so on—go to the established giants, not to small or even growing enterprises.

Magaziner had an unusual experience for a theoretician—he got to test a program at the polls. He put in a lot of time and energy, *pro bono*, on a program that would help arrest the decline of Rhode Island's economy, a matter about which he is understandably concerned. Rhode Island's textile industry has long departed, and unlike Massachusetts and Connecticut, it has few white-collar and sunrise industries. The Murray Commission, as the program was called, emphasized a climate for research and new industry. The state would set up four "greenhouse" areas with tax incentives for new industries that brought in revenues from outside Rhode Island. One interesting inducement was that an entrepreneur who created a payroll would have his personal state income tax forgiven—and so would any partners, in the start-up stage.

The "Greenhouse Compact" won unusual breadth of support. In a state marked by stormy labor relations, bank presidents and labor leaders marched side by side through the streets of Providence in a demonstration. The Chamber of Commerce, the executive board of the AFL-CIO, the Rhode Island Baptist Ministers' Alliance were all on one side, and only some recalcitrant Brown economics professors and conservative businessmen were on the other. The reaction of the voters was to turn the Greenhouse Compact down solidly.

"Our timing was bad," says Magaziner. "Buddy Cianci [the former mayor of Providence] and Buckles Melise [former deputy of public works] were indicted in the same week, and the people said anything government gets is going to stick to the fingers of these guys. The people were just against anything the government was involved in." They seemed to have the attitude of the supply-siders:

give the officials more money, and some of it will stick to their fingers, so don't give it to them.

Admittedly, Magaziner and the Greenhouse people had some particular problems in Rhode Island. Vince "Buddy" Cianci received a suspended sentence for having beaten a man said to be having an affair with Cianci's wife, and the police were diving into the rivers and bays looking for missing city trucks and backhoes that were in the domain of Edward "Buckles" Melise. Perhaps the citizens of Rhode Island could be forgiven an aversion to any plan, no matter how ingenious, that allowed the officials of Providence anywhere near it.

But still—the people of Rhode Island turned down a plan that had the support of the whole Rhode Island establishment. Didn't that have some echoes or implications for the national scene?

"I guess it does. We couldn't explain industrial policy very clearly. It's a complex idea. Many good ideas are. The opponents had a bumper sticker that said, 'Greenhouses are for flowers, not taxes.' I guess a lot of people just saw it as more taxes and more government, even though I know the benefits would have paid off for Rhode Island."

Industrial policy, on the national level, is always being worked at, ad hoc, by pressure and bargaining and the stress of events. It is not even a new idea. Someday it will come back again under a different name. I do concede that it would be neater if there were a neat agenda, but the national mood is not for it. We are going to need some ordered priorities, whether or not we need another federal agency. But if even the tip of the idea is to get across, the proponents will have to be able to communicate it better—maybe even come up with some good bumper stickers.

Million-Dollar Wands

"Industrial policy" brings visions of bureaucrats sitting around a table in Washington, deciding things for us arbitrarily. We prefer life at the village level. The Federal Government can equate to mail (late), the IRS (inhuman, computer errors, impossible to talk to), and regulations eight feet high. Why do we let Federal Government keep growing? I suspect we invite it to, when other institutions fail.

Let's consider wands, million-dollar wands. A corporation waves a wand over a lucky, well-placed citizen, and a million dollars appears in his or her pockets! Magic! What are the implications of such magic?

Consider what happened in the city of Omaha when various bidders for the local cable-television franchise arrived in force. The Omaha city council looked them over and awarded the franchise to a subsidiary of Cox Broadcasting. Cox is a gigantic Atlanta-based movie-production-and-television chain with considerable experience in cable. It was estimated that $36,879,000 would be needed to build the system; of this sum, Cox would supply $36,878,800. Eight Omaha investors would fill the $200 gap. In other words, the eight locals would put up $25 each.

What would the eight local investors get for their $200 investment? Twenty percent of the profits. And, after five years, the locals could, by contract, force Cox to purchase their interest at a "pro-rata share of total value." Cox's calculations were that a 20 percent interest in the system would be worth $12 million after ten years. Just in case it wasn't, the locals were protected by another clause specifying a floor price of $1 million in five years, regardless of results.

What inspired Cox to give the eight locals such a handsome deal? Were these people technological geniuses, contributing to the wiring and connections? Or programming talents who could generate what the people of Omaha wanted to see? No, the eight locals were simply those citizens of Omaha who Cox thought would help its bid for the franchise as substantial local partners.

This story comes from Warren Buffett, a sixth-generation citizen of Omaha whose father was the local congressman. As an investment manager and a newspaper publisher, he is one of the outstanding successes of the last twenty-five years, well known for his plainspoken approach. Though his net worth has climbed into nine figures, he still lives in the modest house he bought twenty-two years ago in midtown Omaha. His investment philosophy has been based on value, not on market timing or on projections of the economy;

and the Omaha cable-television situation plainly rankled him. One reason was that another cable-television bidder, a national cable operator, had invited Buffett into a partnership. Buffett's cash contribution, he recalls, "would have required us to forgo a night at McDonald's." The letter that offered him this participation, he said, "wasn't a letter you would have enjoyed reading to a civics class." That's a way of saying the nineteenth-century railroad robber barons have found a new incarnation; the battle between public interest and private gain is again joined.

After the national cable company spelled out that it would supply all the money for constructing the system and that the locals could come in for 20 percent of the action for the cash equivalent of a bunch of Big Macs, it suggested what it would like from the locals: "We view the local investors as full partners, particularly with regard to developing the strategy to obtain the favorable vote of the city for the award of the franchise. . . . The winning of a cable franchise is essentially a political campaign. . . . The ability of local investors to take the political temperature, make introductions and appointments on a timely basis, and to lend their personal credibility to our formal business proposal is vitally important to the success of our proposal."

The Omaha case is not at all unusual. Perhaps the only noteworthy event in the application procedure was that one of the influential local citizens did not take the royalties he had been offered; he spoke up instead. Nothing illegal went on. In Houston, on the other hand, a federal grand jury is investigating the procedure by which that city granted its cable licenses. The grand jury is seeking to determine whether the cable applicants had met and agreed to cut up the market beforehand, thus violating antitrust regulations. With almost no public debate, the Houston city council handed out contracts to five local firms, two of which quickly sold out to national conglomerates in multimillion-dollar deals. In cable deals, the money always seems to be there; in San Antonio, when the city council was running short of funds for street and sewer repair, it asked UA-Columbia, a cable operator, to advance $1 million against future franchise fees. UA-Columbia agreed with dispatch and got the franchise.

How is it that the cable companies have a magic wand to create instant wealth? Obviously, it isn't their own money that they give away; the money comes from the *future* users of the service. Once the subscriber is hooked up, nothing governs additional charges; the franchise agreements usually cover only the basic cable rate. "Imagine the fun the telephone company could have," says Warren Buffett, "if only local charges—the 'basic service'—were subject to regulation, and they were free to establish whatever prices they wished for such 'extras' as phone directories and long-distance service."

Cable television began simply as a mechanical device to bring reception to those small communities that had no TV stations and that were beyond the range of good reception. The monthly cable charges were small, the regulation was fragmented, and nobody much worried about it. But now cable is becoming large and urban, and the monthly charges are no longer $7. The cable operators are hardly local entrepreneurs merely boosting a signal from the nearest big city: Westinghouse paid $646 million for Teleprompter, a cable operator; and Time, Inc., American Express, and General Electric are among the suitors of major metropolises. The cable operators naturally exert their best efforts to keep regulation at a level that was suitable when cable was a village operation, and they are more than willing to wave those million-dollar wands for the local citizens who are able to open the gates. "If the rate of return is effectively regulated," says Buffett, "there is no windfall to be distributed."

Ideally, the local officials who vote on license applications could demand all sorts of benefits for their communities: local programming, public service, open access. But many of them don't even know what questions to ask, and the consultants who are sometimes hired to evaluate franchise proposals frequently hold stakes in the cable companies. Cable, says *Newsweek*, frequently produces inflated rates, shoddy maintenance, and a dearth of quality programs.

Conservative, successful businessman Buffett wants clean, proper rate regulation; *Newsweek* wants the federal government to have "national franchising standards." Local government has been too weak, the industry is not likely to regulate itself, and the consumer is getting ripped off. Aha! Note that "federal" and "national" mean "strong" and "incorruptible," much the way they did in the 1930s, when the government began to grow in size. Under the New Deal, federal agencies could do what locals could not; federal law enforcement made the FBI a glamour agency.

I bring up these cable stories not because I am particularly agitated about the cable consumer, or because I think "federal" means "noble." I want to point out how we call on the federal government when business and local government do not do the job themselves. Last year, the National Cable Television Association negotiated with the National League of Cities over a code of good franchising practices, but the cities withdrew when the cable people came out for a bill that would limit local control. Congress is in a mood of deregulation, but I am sure that the Federal Communications Commission would be glad to hold hearings, run surveys, hire more bureaucrats, and start policing cable with national standards.

We are told that the federal government is a monster on our backs, an engine of inflation, a blanket on productivity; that agencies divide and grow like the brooms of the sorcerer's apprentice; that federal jobs multiply like cancer cells. Milton Friedman would have private post offices and let parents bid for the schools they want. In any election, the post office and Amtrak are sure to come in for calumny. Yet the dairy farmers want their milk supports, congressmen campaign boasting of how they have produced federal dollars for their districts, and the *Federal Register* grows in size.

Cable television is a local affair. Cable television takes up little space in the *Federal Register*. But if your cable company crosses you, you can scarcely call a competitor. You could call your local government—but are you sure its members aren't $25 partners of the cable company? Then where do you turn?

If cable takes it place in the *Federal Register,* who ends up paying for the regulation that curbs the million-dollar wands?

5 SLICKEMS

Slickems

Back to getting and spending, in a moment. For perspective, we have to recognize context, the context in which we live, even if we don't think about it much.

Consider: overhead, at all times, flying continuously, like the *Flying Dutchman*, is an armed SAC plane (not always the same plane, I grant). In the plane is a SAC general, because for this particular plane and its particular mission, the thumb on the button has to belong to an officer of flag rank.

Our citizens work at different metiers. There are weavers and spinners and CADCAM engineers, and the people who arbitrage between them. I have a friend, a political scientist, whose trade, he says, is "death and destruction." He is a specialist in arms control and arms parity, in megadeath and rocket delivery, and he is a highly paid consultant in think tanks and in our defense establishment. "Death and destruction" occurs as lightly in his papers as "assets and liabilities" or "price earnings ratio" in more familiar surroundings. A sample sentence from a recent "death and destruction paper" reads:

> The major military effect of the Soviet buildup to date has been to increase the amount greatly of death and destruction the Soviet Union could produce in the United States, by either a first or

second strike, without significantly affecting the amount of death and destruction the United States could produce in the Soviet Union.

It was the casual use of "death and destruction" that impressed me, but if you're used to it it's no worse than blood to a surgeon.

Happy New Year

On my friend's desk was a kind of slide-rule calculator. It came from TRW, a leading defense contractor, and it was called The ICBM System Effectiveness and Survivability Slide Rule. "Multiple Aim Point Basing Promotes Stability," it says. If you're in the death-and-destruction trade, TRW sends you one of these just like your insurance man sends you a calendar. Not just TRW, either. Other major defense contractors send you their desk aids, just so you don't forget them. Boeing will send you the Vulnerability Assessment Calculator. RAND will send you the Bomb Damage Effect Computer and the Damage Probability Computer for Point Targets with P and Q Vulnerability Numbers.

My friend liked best the Missile Effectiveness and CEP Calculator, made by the Electronic Systems Division of General Electric. CEP is Circular Error Probable, a number corresponding to the radius of the circle within which your missile has a fifty-fifty chance of falling. Enthusiasts of the cruise missile, for example, believe it has a ninety-foot CEP, which is uncannily accurate.

What these calculators produce are equations and numbers. Some of the numbers are quite large and not easily translatable into flesh, bone, and blood. My friend's thesis that the United States has retained its second-strike capability translates this way: originally, back in 1964, the Soviets could have inflicted about 30 million deaths on us in an all-out nuclear war, and now they have increased that capability to 100 million to 120 million, whereas our second-strike death-and-destruction capability has remained at 100 million to 120 million—that is, 120 million dead.

One difficulty for the casual visitor to this world is that the acronyms are pronounced before the visitor is quite sure what they mean. There was, for example, much enthusiasm for what sounded like "Slickems" and "Alchems." "Slickem" suggests a rubber raincoat, and "Alchem," the ancient process of turning lead into gold. Actually, "Slickem" and "Alchem" are the same cruise missile, but the SLCM (Sea-Launched Cruise Missile) would ride on a submarine or a surface ship and the ALCM (Air-Launched Cruise Missile) would be slung under a B-52. Both Slickem and Alchem have TERCOM (Terrain Contour Mapping): to find its way, the missile scans the surface as it tools along, recognizes the terrain, and matches it against the pictures in its computer. And the missile has that wonderful ninety-foot Circular Error Probable. Those in favor of the cruise missile also point to its relatively low cost and to its "high survivability." Because the cruise missile flies at extremely low altitudes, its proponents claim that it cannot easily be detected by enemy radar; and because it is so small, it is supposed to be difficult to shoot down. Opponents, on the other hand, say that the deployment of the cruise missile will make the monitoring of arms-control agreements more difficult, since cruise missiles can be outfitted with either conventional or nuclear warheads. Neither the United States nor the Soviet Union would then be able to verify which kind of warhead was loaded into the other's cruise missile.

Proponents point out that cruise missiles will add warheads to inventory, which is good, except that you can't just match numbers against numbers. "The strategic debate," warned political scientist Warner Schilling, "has focused on numbers of missiles and warheads as if they were living creatures whose survival was of value in their own right . . . [instead of] potential differences in the war outcomes among which statesmen might actually be able to discriminate in terms of values about which they do care."

So the Russians have caught up with us in sheer numbers. Was there anything we could have done about that? Well, if we had pushed for the building of even more warheads and more missiles and if our 1964 ratio had been maintained, we would now have 12,000 "delivery vehicles" and 50,400 warheads, instead of 2,058 vehicles and 9,200 warheads. What we have now are options flexible enough to take out 100 million to 120 million people—death and destruction—on a second strike, so the extra 41,200 warheads might have been a bit redundant. And then we negotiated the Strategic Arms Limitation Talks. I wanted to know how we would know whether the Russians were cheating. I remember when the spy-satellite photography got so good it was said to bring pictures home of the olive in Khrushchev's martini. Now it's even better.

MIRVing

What else could we have done? We had two other choices as the Russians built up. Should we have MIRVed our missiles? MIRVing makes them multiple independently targetable reentry vehicles and gives you many warheads where before there was one. We MIRVed the ICBMs in 1970 and the SLBMs (Submarine-Launched Ballistic Missiles) in 1971. The Russians MIRVed their ICBMs in 1975 and their SLBMs in 1978. Neither side has tried to ban or limit the MIRVs.

The other choice we had was to increase our defense: Make the Russians use more missiles to knock us out. We decided against that for several reasons. First, it could only lead to an arms race without any positive military gain. Second, the technology of the ABM (Anti-Ballistic Missile) seemed a bit shaky. And third, as for civil defense, fallout shelters, and all that, the public wasn't having it. The public doesn't like to be reminded of death. The first ten years of the Soviet buildup coincided with the Vietnam War, and the public didn't like Vietnam. Vietnam was inflation and disruption enough, without the addition of ABM.

What disturbs American policymakers is not necessarily that the Northern Hemisphere would get charred in a missile exchange. Not much you can do about that. What disturbs them is the vision of the Soviets counting up warheads and getting bold. We have substituted nuclear strength for conventional arms vis-à-vis the Soviets, and now the Soviets are at parity. Maybe the Soviets would blackmail our allies, if not us, and, what's more, the allies might just cave in, so the Soviets would win without even fighting a nuclear war.

When the policymakers looked at Europe through the '80s, that continent looked as if it had just arrived in the late '60s. The longhairs were now marching in France and Belgium and Germany and Britain, chanting "Nukes out." Somehow the Americans have been made the bad guys, wanting to fight to the last European, whereas the original point of having Americans there was to ensure that we were in it with the Europeans if they were attacked.

If the tone of this essay seems light for so heavy a matter, that is deliberate, if defensive. To a drop-in civilian, the whole business is appalling. I know perfectly well the Russians are up to mischief in many corners of the globe. But the equations—from those desk aids that tell you how many megadeaths with what variables—deal only in cold numbers, not in real lives, real people with noses and ears and cavities in their teeth. Even Russians get cavities. I think it is with some other kind of *perception* that the breakthrough must come, not merely the piling up of more warheads and more sophisticated systems. An alarming article in the *Journal of Conflict Resolution,* one of the political-science journals tracking this field, asked: Do arms races escalate to all-out war? The statistics show they do. "The findings support with hard evidence the intuitive fears of those who argue that an intensification of the superpower arms competition could lead to . . . a major confrontation . . . likely to result in . . . all-out war."

Study the Taboos?

Kenneth Boulding, the distinguished economist, wrote that in the Great Depression, economists wrote about unemployment as if it were a bad hailstorm; then the Keynesian revolution gave some hope that nations could do something about the "economic blizzards" that had previously been considered as random as the weather. Right now we consider peace and war like the weather, something to be fatalistically endured. What, Boulding asked, could the elements of peace be? Should we study the taboos that inhibit primitive tribes? Or what? We study so much war, but "no government at the moment has anything remotely resembling a policy for peace. All of them have a policy of defense, but that is something quite different. If the peace research community [could inquire] as to what a policy for peace would look like, even on the part of a single government, we might be able to lift ourselves out of this slough of sterility and impotence into which we seem to have fallen."

Since these lines were first published, General Secretary Gorbachev has created something of a different atmosphere with *glasnost* and *perestroika*. Gorbachev sent the chairman of his Joint Chiefs, Marshal Sergei Akhromeyev, to the United States. Akhromeyev spent a week in the summer of 1988 with Admiral William Crowe, the chairman of the U.S. Joint Chiefs, touring military bases—an astounding event, the first such in forty-five years. Crowe introduced Akhromeyev at a foreign policy meeting I attended. Akhromeyev, who is also first deputy minister of the Soviet Union, is a slim, balding man in his sixties, not the beefy Soviet general of political cartoonists.

"I told Admiral Crowe," said Akhromeyev, "that we were scared of the Slickems."

We had earphones that permitted simultaneous translation. Marshal Akhromeyev actually said "Slickems" in his Russian sentence. The translator did not translate "Slickems." The acronym for "sea-launched cruise missile" is apparently colloquial in both languages, in the death-and-destruction crowd. Nobody blinked.

"But he said he was scared of the SS-18s," said Akhromeyev.

Marshal Akhromeyev was asked whether he thought the fail-safe procedures at the U.S. bases he had visited were better than those in the Soviet Union.

"I think they're about the same," he said.

Akhromeyev said the Soviet Union's posture was being shaped so that it was totally defensive, and he said he would like advance notice of major NATO exercises, just to avoid accidents. Some of our Soviet experts, after Akhromeyev left, said that the indications were the Soviet Union was leaning to a defensive strategy, maybe for budgetary considerations.

"We had a good week," said Admiral Crowe.

*   *   *

It will take more than a good week, considering the momentum in the Pentagon and at Langley and their Soviet counterparts. But perhaps the perceptions are beginning to change. I am happy to have Frank Carlucci, Secretary of Defense, riding in a Soviet Blackjack bomber and touring the Soviet bases, and glad to have Marshal Akhromeyev touring here. Secretary Carlucci said he didn't believe the Russians were switching to defense. We have spent a trillion dollars on defense in recent years. The CEP is probably down to thirty feet, and the next set of desk aids sent out by TRW and General Electric and Boeing and RAND will no doubt have the computing power of the first Cray. I bet the death-and-destruction crowd has computations that blot four hundred million people, with a very small deviation, in a second. It's so easy to think in units of a hundred million people when you have a handy desktop calculator with the missile exchanges already keyed in. There are no monopolies in this business, so you have to assume that the Soviet defense contractors are sending the Soviet planners their happy-new-year desk aids that start with how you take out a hundred and fifty million Americans. The rockets that rise in Central Asia can target an area not much bigger than the room you are sitting in. I wish the desk aids on both sides came with pictures of children. The Soviet and American economies could both use a breather from arms; there are other uses for the money. *The Journal of Conflict Resolution* is still doing its algebra. I am not so sure Kenneth Boulding is wrong when he says we spend so much energy studying war, what would a policy of peace look like?

And if that phrase, a policy of peace, sounds hopelessly naive, what does that say about our conditioning and the context from which we operate?

Is the Game Still *Kto Kogo*?

That *Flying Dutchman* overhead is not there because of the Italians or the Brazilians. We are in a relationship called *kto kogo*, according to the Sovietologists I have been visiting. We were talking about

Central America, and I suggested Bhutan as a good yardstick for thinking about Nicaragua. Our concern about Nicaragua could be kept in perspective by this phrase: There is no crisis in Bhutan. Let me explain. Bhutan is a small kingdom in the Himalayas, once a protectorate of India. The State Department may have a subexpert on the Asian desk evaluating Bhutan, but even the editor of the newspaper you read does not know whether Bhutan is a monarchy, a dictatorship, a people's republic, or has merged with Brigadoon and will not be back. There are no TV correspondents, no U.S. forces, no Soviet forces, and, while there may be students in the streets, there is no crisis as we think of crisis.

What has this to do with Nicaragua? Nicaragua was run and virtually owned by one family, the Somozas, the country having been occupied by American troops. El Salvador is still owned by a handful of families. It is getting rather late in the twentieth century for that kind of operation. Change does not have to be disagreeable to us; there is no crisis in Bhutan. Why the crisis in Central America? Perhaps the questions we should ask are about the Russians: How does Central America fit into their strategy? Are the Soviets competing with us for influence there? Are they prepared to risk deterioration in Soviet-American relations to accomplish this? How much of what is currently happening in Central America is signaling between the superpowers, like the drumming of competitive grouse?

I spoke to the Soviet experts in Washington at the Wilson Center of the Smithsonian Institution, a fellowship program that does advanced research in international politics and the humanities, to those from the Kennan Institute for Advanced Russian Studies, and to those from the International Security Studies Program.

Like so many of our Soviet experts, Jiri Valenta was born not in the Soviet Union but on its periphery; a native of Czechoslovakia, he studied nuclear technology there before emigrating to the West, and his permanent job is at the Naval Postgraduate School at Monterey. Valenta has written about the signaling and maneuvering that go on between the United States and the Soviet Union. For example, in 1956 the Soviets invaded Hungary because reform-minded Hungarian leaders were replacing conservative Communists. The month before the invasion, John Foster Dulles, elsewhere a master of brinkmanship, indicated there would be no U.S. intervention. "Does anyone in his senses," he said, "want to start a nuclear war over Hungary?" When the Soviet tanks rumbled into Prague in 1968, the Johnson administration, preoccupied with Vietnam and domestic racial tensions, sent no signals at all, and thus lost an opportunity, though it could not have prevented the invasion. Valenta says the Carter administration knew of Soviet mobilization in 1979, before the tanks rolled into Afghanistan, but the Carter administration sent no clear signals. Only after the Soviet invasion did it establish a grain embargo and cancel American participation in the Olympics. On the other hand, President Carter sent Brezhnev a firm note when Soviet forces mobilized on the Polish border in 1980, and then mounted a worldwide campaign focusing attention on the Soviet buildup. The American action helped check the Soviet momentum, and Poland is a major problem for the Soviets.

What is happening now?

"Americans sometimes think of foreign affairs as a separate category," said Valenta. "The Soviet view is based on *borba*, struggle, a part of the culture. Lenin's famous phrase is *'Kto kogo?'*—'Who can get whom?' So that game is very basic. The policy is to support Leninist regimes. What is a Leninist regime? It has one party, a disciplined party, the dictatorship of the proletariat, and it supports other Leninist regimes, the proletarian international. The Soviets see our military posturing in Central America the way they see themselves in Eastern Europe, where they move the tanks along the borders to express displeasure with political events. In fact, their press says of Central America that now we have learned from them."

"Then this kind of posturing serves a purpose?"

"It is better than not reacting, but what we are doing in Honduras is extravagant and silly. The administration has a frantic reaction, which does send one kind of a signal. But it doesn't put the situation in context, it doesn't look at the situation that *produced* the revolution. We always should have two topics of examination: First, what created the regime? And second, what is its attachment to the Soviet Union?

"The Soviets have moved fairly tentatively in the Caribbean, but

I think in Nicaragua the moderates have steadily been silenced. Our trouble is that we have only one rather gross response, a massive force. We are dealing ad hoc, and only in military terms. We need a political and social response as well.''

"I see the Russian view this way," said another Sovietologist. "The Soviets see themselves as the historic leaders of a historic process, rather like spiritual leadership. The historic process is the arrival of socialism. I believe they see their camp getting stronger. In two decades they have built their armed forces up to a point where they can project power all over the world. They have a Marxist regime on the Arabian peninsula, South Yemen. The Cubans have been the foot soldiers and the East Germans have been the brains of some of the movements far from Russia. The East Germans show that the Afrika Korps is alive and well, and the Germans are very good at setting up police forces—and secret-police forces—and concentration camps. We think the Russians are weaker because their economy does not work well. But that is secondary to them. You don't have much consumer agitation in the Soviet Union, especially because things are better than they used to be. It is true that the military had sort of a blank check for a decade, and now there is competition for those investment rubles, both to develop energy and to supply consumers.

"I think what worries the Russians is the Reagan military budget; they thought it would fade and it hasn't. So they are worried about their own political perceptions. Japan is becoming a worry, because it might rearm and be more independent of the U.S. and it has the second-largest economy.

"So I don't think of the Russians as pushing over dominoes in the Caribbean. But they will train people and supply people and hope for enough discomfort that we get pinned down, and that puts a strain on NATO and the relationship with Japan. You have to keep perspective in mind, and perspective is Western Europe and Japan.''

Like many of our defense intellectuals, I have used the image of a world chessboard. But that analogy is false. The two superpowers influence but do not control the board, and the various knights and bishops, while they may have various shades of identifying color, are frequently independent and sometimes change sides. What disturbs us about Central America? Why do we worry about Nicaragua? Is it the vulnerability of our neighbor Mexico?

Of course, we worry about Mexico. Mexicans can walk into the United States along an undefended two-thousand-mile border. Hispanics are the most rapidly growing part of our population. The Mexicans owe most of that hundred-billion-dollar debt to American banks, and the big lenders at Manny Hanny certainly know the flight schedules to Mexico City. Universities that want to have a seminar about Mexico, and draw a crowd, title it, Mexico: Another Iran?

But Mexico's fate is not determined by what goes on in Nicaragua, or in Washington, or in Moscow. They may all have an influence, but for influence I would rather bet on the birthrate in Mexico, the price of oil, the world price of money, the future of the PRI party, and I would listen to the experts in Latin America and Central America as well as the Sovietologists. The Soviet economists I meet say the new policy is to pull back from *kto kogo* because, pragmatically, it didn't work so well. But the Sovietologists are skeptical.

The problems that cause change in Latin America are not going to go away, nor are the clients of the other superpower. Lenin's game, *kto kogo,* may last a hundred years, but it won't be decided just by muscle.

That doesn't mean I want the *Flying Dutchman* to come down.

6 FORTUNES

T. Boone: Sail Ho!

Some time ago I was riding across the country with T. Boone Pickens in his Falcon 50. T. Boone has a tight schedule, but he courts the press, so riding around in his jet as he made his calls seemed like a good way to catch up with him. T. Boone was in a good mood at that point. Out in Bartlesville, Oklahoma, the citizens were having prayer meetings in their churches. They did not exactly pray to God to deliver them from Pickens, the way the coastal villagers of medieval England rushed to their stone churches on sight of a Viking sail—"O God, deliver us from the wrath of the Norsemen." But the Bartlesville citizens prayed that the board of directors of Phillips Petroleum be granted the wisdom to know what to do about Pickens, since Pickens was threatening to take over Bartlesville's largest employer. I asked Pickens how it felt to have the aid of God sought against you.

"I was hurt," he said, pouting slightly, barely able to contain a grin. "After all, I'm a native Oklahoman, born and bred, went to college in Oklahoma, my wife's from Oklahoma, did they think I would shut down the whole town? Those people had things on backwards. They thought the *town* owned the *company*. The town didn't own the company, the *shareholders* owned the company, and the shareholder is the forgotten man. That Phillips management didn't even own one tenth of one percent of their own company."

With or without the aid of God, the board of Phillips Petroleum decided to "restructure" the company. It issued more debt, offered some of its assets for sale, bought back the block of stock Pickens had acquired, and, in effect, paid him $89 million to go away.

Pickens scooped up his chips and tried the next company. Unocal, the Union Oil Company of California. Since 1982, Pickens's own company, Mesa, has made investments in—and attempted takeovers of—a number of oil companies far larger than Mesa, with results gratifying to Pickens. On its stock in Cities Service, Mesa made $31.5 million; on General American Oil, $43.6 million; and on Gulf Oil, $404 million. The grateful Mesa directors, all picked by Pickens, voted their chief more than $24.1 million in deferred bonuses one year. That is a respectable figure even in the state of Texas, where they talk in terms of "units," a unit being $100 million. It was said around the oil patch that Pickens had found more oil in other people's balance sheets than the great wildcatters had found in the ground.

T. Boone is, of course, not the only takeover artist in town, but he is the most visible. He is fun to be around, if you are not his target. He knows exactly how to play the Texas Robin Hood. President Reagan joked about him in a press conference; cartoonists have found him a great subject. All this is just fine with T. Boone; his sense of theater is acute. He could, after all, have remained Thomas B. Pickens, Jr., just as the playwright Tom Williams could have retained that name instead of rechristening himself Tennessee. But the name fits the persona; Pickens wanted to suggest the brave, lonely frontiersman, who he says is a distant ancestor.

This is not mere vanity, though Pickens likes to talk about Barbara and Phyllis and Bryant and the other talk-show hosts. Visibility is credibility. When Pickens started Mesa, it was a tiny one-horse oil company scratching for funds. Now bankers fall all over themselves to lend to it so it can do its "paper drilling."

Boone likes to build the image of himself as the man with a rifle, looking for a target. He likes the sensibility of the predator.

"I was at a meeting of institutional investors in New York," he said, "and there are all these big-time money managers, and what they want to hear is some *hint* of what we're looking at. So I said, well, I think I can *trust* everybody in this meeting, so if you will all lean *forward*, I will *whisper* the name of the next *targit*. One young lady down at the end of the table said, 'Is he kidding?' ''

Boone paused, relishing the moment. "But they all leaned forward!''

Boone laughed. He loves the image of the money managers straining for a tip. It is all told in a pleasant good-ole-boy Oklahoma drawl.

The Falcon lands at the airport at Boone's hometown, Amarillo, Texas. The wind is whistling and roaring off the flat, treeless plain. Boone shows us around Mesa's headquarters. He is very proud of the gym, and the racquetball courts. Boone loves to play racquetball with his staff.

"We have to be *fit*," Boone says, " 'cause when we go after a *targit* we might have to stay up all night.''

There is a statue of Boone in the Mesa headquarters. Boone the statue is tense, knees bent, racquetball racquet in hand.

"The employees put that statue up,'' Boone says. "I sort of objected, but they wanted to.'' Boone later shows us around his house. He has built an indoor tennis court. He has collected Texas art, realistic scenes of oil towns and bird dogs. Boone loves a good bird dog. "That dog won't hunt'' is one of his favorite expressions.

Boone tells us how he started as a young geologist, working out of his car. He tells us about meeting the woman who was to become his wife. He took her hunting on his Oklahoma ranch, and she became a bit breathless. She also lit a cigarette.

"When she saw it might get serious, she got fit and gave up smoking,'' Boone said.

Pickens and other similarly styled investors have had a profound influence on the American business scene in the 1980s. Corporate board members now meet to consider "shark repellents,'' which make it more difficult for a raider to accomplish his job legally, and "poison pills,'' which make the firm less attractive if a raid has already begun. Five-hundred-dollar-an-hour lawyers work late into the night, devising legal minefields and booby traps. Investment bankers, scenting the fat fees that come with mergers and acquisitions, prowl the corporate corridors, lining up possible "white knights" that can save a target from a presumed black knight. The investment bankers and lawyers are mercenaries, ready to take either side, and while they may battle each other one week, they may be allies for another client the next.

"All the companies that we invested in have things in common," said Pickens. "One, the market price of the stock wasn't where it should have been. It was selling at too big a discount in relation to the assets of the company. You need to go through the assets, the reserves in the ground, the refineries, whatever, and determine the value. We believe the stock price ought to sell, per share, close to that. But their stock didn't. Why? The management just didn't care about the shareholder. They cared about their hunting trips in Spain and Norway, that's what they cared about, and if you ask about the stockholder, they say, 'Well, we pay him a dividend, don't we?' "

Actually, it is not unusual for asset-rich companies to sell stock in the marketplace that is worth less than their assets. They tend to sell on the basis of the current earnings, or their current cash flow. To liquidate or sell a company's assets—the only way to realize the full value—takes time, and once it's done, of course, there *is* no more company. That is exactly what the raiders threaten: to sell off all the assets, and thus realize the present worth of the company. Managements oppose this not only because their jobs are at stake but because they are thinking—eptly or ineptly, as the case may be—about the future of the company.

"The second characteristic," said T. Boone, "is that the managements of these companies were arrogant and cold and aloof and out of touch with the people. That's the image of the oil industry, and it comes from the big oil companies."

Few would dispute T. Boone on that score. If you went through the roster of American corporations—and various polling firms have—the most unloved are large oil companies. Like major chemical companies—also unloved—they have very few people for each dollar of assets; that is, there are assets—sometimes in remote, difficult-to-reach places—and engineers who deal with the assets, but the smooth, everyday stroking of people is not part of the culture of the company. Major oil companies have usually been run by engineers or geologists, remarkable for their toughness, their tenacity, their willingness to gamble, rather than any ability to be sensitive to people.

For many years, Texaco had a reputation—in the financial community and elsewhere—for being very difficult to deal with, and there were those who said this helped grease the slide to bankruptcy after the Pennzoil case.

Fred Hartley, the former president of Unocal, Pickens's 1985 target, is generally thought to have done a creditable job building Union Oil. Yet Hartley will always be remembered for one of the great ungracious remarks in American business history. A Union Oil well blew in the Santa Barbara channel some years ago, sending thick black oil through the water and destroying marine life. The people of Santa Barbara rushed to the beaches and began trying to sponge the oil off the feathers of the gasping and dying seabirds. The Santa Barbara channel has become a symbol for ecologists all over the world, from the Great Barrier Reef in Australia to the oyster beds of Normandy. "I am amazed at the publicity for the loss of a few birds," Hartley is reported to have said. "What's a few oily birds?"

"And finally," T. Boone said, "management owned [hardly] any stock—just like in the Phillips case."

This is certainly true—the managements of major oil companies own little stock. They are salaried executives, not founders or entrepreneurs, and the market worth of their companies is far greater than their admittedly handsome salaries. And just as they are frequently not sensitive to people in the public-relations sense, they have, just as frequently, been indifferent to the nurturing of the shareholder community.

But Unocal proved a bridge too far for Pickens. In a somewhat surprising judgment, the Delaware Supreme Court backed Fred Hartley and Unocal, successfully warding off Pickens's bid for the huge oil company.

But Pickens had left his mark. Unocal took on so much debt in repelling the boarders that it listed in the water, and is still spoken of as a takeover target. So Boone was not popular around the headquarters of the major oil companies, nor in Pittsburgh, which had been the headquarters of Gulf Oil. Gulf, as its defense, chose to be carried off by a white knight, Chevron, and later Chevron closed down Gulf's Pittsburgh headquarters.

But Boone is certainly popular in Wall Street. Takeovers generate wonderful arbitrage opportunities and fat commissions, and even retail brokers can sometimes do a turn by squinting at the horizon and shouting "Sail ho!" even if a Jolly Roger is not being run up the mast. Investment bankers have certainly been known to drive the fat merchantmen into the lanes of the pirate brigs. Boone was even honored at a dinner in New York, in which Mayor Ed Koch gave him a crystal "Big Apple."

Boone did make corporate managements more aware of their shareholders. But there is something that bothers me in this mania of raiding and restructuring. The whole focus is on the *present* price of company stock—even at the cost of the *future* price of the stock, should the company continue to exist. For example, one recent defense against takeovers is for the target company to take on more debt; it buys in some of its own stock, or pays out a higher dividend, or buys another company. Interest on all that new debt has to be paid. If it buys in its own stock, the return on equity may well go up. For a mature company, with no growth prospects but adequate cash flow, that may be an option. The money that goes into paying interest and amortization can't go into the growth of the company. It's true that debt used to be considered a good thing to have in periods of high inflation—you could pay back with cheaper dollars— but now the lenders are wise and the interest goes up faster than inflation. Going into debt as a kicker to the stock price, rather than as a source for future earnings, is ultimately a crippling defense.

Let me grant that "ultimately" may not be tomorrow. Boone and I had an exchange of correspondence: *he* did not load up companies with debt, he said, *he* did not strip assets. I must be thinking of some other guys. Boone was right; he didn't borrow and didn't strip because in the last few years, he hasn't taken anything over. Sometimes just running the old Jolly Roger up the mast does the job; the stock goes up at the sight of it.

Eventually some of the bank loans and the "junk bonds" that financed the takeover mania will turn sour, and the takeover phase will be over, just as previous fads have died away. But at present the concern with the fast buck—the next quarter, rather than the next ten years—is paramount. The demand is for instant gratification on a macroeconomic scale. It reflects a shortsighted attitude that is not new in America, that extends even wider than T. Boone and his friends, and that leaves a bill to be paid in the future.

How to Do an LBO

Boone became a media hero. He was popular because he managed to bill himself as the hero of Joe Six Pack, the small shareholder. "I am out there working for Joe Six Pack, and I get letters from him all the time," he would say. "I got a letter just yesterday from a Joe Six Pack in Louisville, said, 'Dear Mr. Pickens, I own stock in this company that hasn't done a damn thing and I wish you would take it over.'" The interviewers also liked the way Boone said, "That dog won't hunt." In truth, it was the arbitrageurs and the managers of billion-dollar funds who were Boone's allies. Carl Icahn and Asher Edelman did not say, "That dog won't hunt," but they learned quickly to use the press to speak of fat-cat managements, the necessity to get "lean and mean" and maximize shareholder profits.

The latest wrinkle—but probably not the last—in this ongoing game is the *leveraged buyout*, accomplished frequently by insiders. "Leverage" simply means the use of debt. Back in more serene times, a high level of debt was not considered a good thing because you had to pay the interest and amortization, and that had to be paid before research and bonuses and other goodies. Entrepreneurs built up their companies, paid down the debts, and would achieve the milestone of their careers when they sold stock to the public. Frequently they would enshrine the newspaper announcement of the public sale of stock in plastic and hang it on the wall.

But in the upside-down world of the Roaring '80s, debt has suddenly become a good thing, and the favorite game is not just to take private companies public, but to take public companies private.

Levi Strauss, the jeans maker, Mary Kay Cosmetics, and R. H. Macy have all gone private. The biggest leveraged buyout we've heard of so far was $6 billion, to "privatize" Beatrice, the conglomerate that owns everything from Tropicana orange juice to Samsonite luggage. The key instrument in many of these buyouts is the junk bond. Today's junk bonds are simply bonds piled on behind all the other company bonds, so that they have the first exposure to real risk. In a recession, if the company's earnings falter, the junk bonds would not be secured by assets and would not pay the interest due. A junk bond is not necessarily new—when Chrysler approached bankruptcy, for example, investors sold the bonds because they feared they would not be paid off. Chrysler's bonds evolved into junk, but subsequently improved. Junk bonds produce higher yields—interest coupons—than well-rated bonds; they have to, in order to entice investors. And there seem to be plenty of buyers, in spite of the risks.

Let's say you and I are the president and vice-president of Slice 'n' Dice Cutlery, whose stock is selling at $10 a share. We own only 1 percent of the stock, but we're on the board and the other directors are friends. Looking ahead, we see many years of increasing prosperity. We go to a firm that does leveraged buyouts, and together we offer the shareholders $15 a share. Our leveraged buyout firm has in the meantime gone to some banks who will lend us the money in return for some fat fees and high interest rates, and a piece of ownership in the company. Our going-private firm also owns a kind of shell company—not much in it—but it issues some junk bonds secured by the firm to help buy back all that $15 stock from public hands. Our going-private firm gets 40 percent of the ownership after the deal. The bank gets 30 percent. You and I and the senior officers and directors get 30 percent, even though we haven't put up more than $1.50 of our own money.

Why will our shareholders give us all their stock for $15 a share? Because it's a very fast 50 percent profit on each dollar. Because, if they are investing institutions, like pension funds or mutual funds, they must show results quarter by quarter, and this gives them a quick pop. They don't care if Slice 'n' Dice Cutlery might be worth $25 in two years—they operate by the old Casey

Stengel philosophy: win today; tomorrow it may rain. Our go-ing-private takeover will also be aided by arbitrageurs, who will lope in for a quick turnover, buying stock on the rumor of our deal and, they hope, selling it a few days later at a higher price. (The arbitrageur can buy the stock in the market at, say, $14 and sell it to us at $15, because the stock price doesn't go up to $15 all at once.)

Ben Stein, a Los Angeles columnist, is critical of managements doing leveraged buyouts. "Officers and directors are fiduciaries," he said. "They must be trustees for the shareholders. If they pay the shareholders x and can restructure the company to make it worth two x, they are required to do that for the shareholders, not themselves. They are like the trustees for an orphan who inherits a lot for which his grandfather paid five hundred dollars. The trustees offer the orphan six hundred dollars, a profit on the books. Of course, the lot is worth one million, but the orphan doesn't know it."

The defenders of the leveraged buyouts say that the stockholders get an immediate and handsome profit—and that the new company assumes far more risk carrying all that debt, and the new sharehold-ers are taking the risks.

But if you and I (and the bank and our buyout firm) can hang on, the company will pay down the debt out of its own revenues, our 30 percent will be worth millions, and maybe we can sell the company back to the public, making millions more, and then we can start the whole game over. Of course, we will have to fire some people and sell off some assets to get "lean and mean." But you and I will be richer.

"It is a situation like the 1920s," says Stein, "in which powerful figures in the financial community lend themselves to the process of looting shareholders, compounded by the looting of the American taxpayer."

But it is all legal. What is going on, all through the American financial scene, is the substitution of debt for equity. Corporate debt now exceeds the net worth of all our corporations. Our tax laws encourage this. Interest is deductible—so Slice 'n' Dice Cutlery, which now pays taxes, will not pay taxes after the new deal is completed because its debt will be so much higher that the interest on it will eat up all the profits.

We can pull this off because there is no difference between a shareholder who owns the stock for five minutes and someone who has owned it for twenty years. Many of the shareholders of Slice 'n' Dice Cutlery were the tax-exempt pension-fund managers pressed by clients to judge people on ninety-day results, encouraging a short-term point of view.

I anticipate criticism from the buyout crowd, and I know that there are good managements and bad managements, good buyout deals and bad buyout deals. I talked to the chief honchos of Drexel Burnham Lambert, the main purveyors of junk bonds. They said the next recession will wipe out a lot of junk bonds, but not *our* junk bonds. The leveraged buyout firms say, sure, the next recession is going to wipe out a lot of *companies* with all this new debt, but not *our* company. Someone else's.

Meanwhile, the fees in these activities are the highest since the Berlin banker Bleichröder got a percentage of the French reparations in the Franco-Prussian War of 1870–1871. The fees from Pantry Pride–Revlon exceeded $100 million, for work done within the space of a few weeks.

With rewards like these, it is no surprise that brainpower and talent are flocking to the manipulation of pieces of paper, and not to the hard work of manufacturing products that can compete on the world market. As a nation, we are getting very good at piling up debt, both public and private. The best business minds of the country are preoccupied with paper tactics—offensive or defensive or both. The Japanese must be giggling at their good fortune. They have very few lawyers; they just *make* the cars, the television sets, and soon, jet airplanes.

Why is this happening now? It stems from the current climate of deregulation, from the attitude in Washington that government does best when it does least. Of course, even though this is the attitude, the government itself has grown, but the watchdogs of government—the Justice Department, the SEC, and so on—have a more relaxed attitude toward the financial world. Some lawyers have suggested—quietly, lest the fees go away—that a junk bond is not really a bond when there are so many layers of debt, but rather a more junior security, a common stock. If it *were* considered a stock, then its payments would be dividends, not interest, and they would not be deductible. Even just a nuance in the law would make a difference. If the payments were not deductible, you and I would not be subsidizing this activity, for we pay in taxes what the junk-bond issuers do not. But the Washington watchdogs have not pressed this issue.

Of course, not all leveraged buyouts are done by management. I've been a director myself of a company that began life as an LBO. A major oil service company wanted to streamline, and it sold its chemical division. It was sold not to another company, but to two executives with decades of experience in the chemical business; they had already run a major chemical firm. They bought the division, using a debt package put together by a group of venture capital firms. Gradually they bought other small firms, or divisions of larger ones, that fit, and built a solid proprietary chemical concern. The debt wasn't onerous, and the assets didn't have to be sold to meet it. The acquisitions were all friendly, there was no major "lean and mean" publicity, and the operation was successful, even if nobody got terribly rich.

But in the case of management buyouts, I wonder. I know a man who bought the company of which he was president. He is, to my limited observation, a good, competent, aggressive executive, and he had worked for his company for many years. If the LBO fad had not come along, he would have worked for his salary, his bonus, his options, his stock appreciation rights, his perks, and in the end he would have turned the company over to his successor and retired on a handsome pension. But the LBOs did come along, and he got some friends and directors and a package of debt and bought the company. They took it private, they owned it all. The next year, they sold a good hunk of it back to the public. It was the same company in stage one, stage two, and stage three, public, private, public, except that when it got back to the public the second time it had a lot more debt. My acquaintance made a handsome salary as CEO, but in the public-private-public exercise he made more than $300 million. But can every CEO do this? What about the *next* CEO? Can he do it too?

Henry Kravis Would Make $400 Million! Without Lifting Anything Heavy!

It took serious sums to raise eyebrows in the bloated '80s on Wall Street, but one Monday morning, my phone began to ring and kept ringing—

"Did you see the numbers on the Beatrice deal?"

The phones actually started ringing on Sunday morning, because the Sunday *New York Times* had carried a feature that spelled out the fees and profits on Beatrice. The numbers weren't secret, but here they were, all lined up in rows on a neat chart.

Beatrice began life many years ago as a Nebraska dairy-products company. In recent years it had become a conglomerate; it owned Tropicana, the juice maker, Samsonite, the luggage company, Avis car rentals, Playtex, and a host of other companies. The company hit a turbulent period, and the board bounced out Beatrice's president, Donald Kelly. But Kelly came back, and with heavy backing—investors led by the firm of Kohlberg Kravis & Roberts, which specializes in lining up debt and taking over companies. The buying group was able to borrow $4 billion. It offered enough to the shareholders— public shareholders owning the company—to take it over, and the group then began to sell off the various companies within Beatrice.

Here are some of the numbers that caused so much talk:

For its skills in arranging the buyout, the firm of Kohlberg Kravis & Roberts took a fee of $45 million and stood to make $2.4 *billion* when the deals were finally complete.

For lining up the package of debt, Drexel Burnham Lambert took $86 million and stood to make $810 million.

Donald Kelly, the former president of Beatrice, would get fees of more than $20 million and might make as much as $277 million.

And in their wake were the firms of Kidder, Peabody, and Lazard Frères, which would make $15 million and $8 million, mere taxi fare by comparison.

What pulsed through the phone lines that Sunday and Monday were some emotions familiar enough in the world of high-velocity money: envy, greed, and rage. KKR was going to make $2.5 *billion* dollars, and it had only eighty-five people! It had only twenty partners! Henry Kravis would make something like *$400 million* in sixteen months! And he hadn't even lifted anything heavy! He hadn't struck oil, or invented the Polaroid camera, or spent twenty years building a business; he was just skilled at buying, selling, and packaging. He got some investors, bought a company—a big company—and sold off the pieces. Forget Dan Rather and his lousy $2 million a year! Forget Michael Jackson and Eddie Murphy and James Michener and Bill Cosby and Lawrence Taylor and Larry Bird! Hackers all, when it came to money! Henry Kravis ran rings around them—and that was just one deal! And, of course, money chases money; KKR has now raised $6 *billion* from investors to do *more* deals. They get 1.5 percent off the top for office expenses—that comes to $75 million a year for phones and stationery—plus a piece of the action! Out in Middle America, John and Jane Jones are waiting to see their boss to discuss what a good job they've done—to get a $5,000 raise. They're not even on the same planet!

"It's lucky I love my work," I said to a friend, "because otherwise I would think I was in the wrong business."

"This morning, everybody in America thinks he is in the wrong business," said my friend, "and maybe that's what's wrong with America."

Why is something like the Beatrice payoff so big? Ben Stein, the Los Angeles syndicated columnist, explains it this way: "Management knows the assets of the company. So although they borrow millions—in some cases even billions—to buy the company, they know the assets are worth even more. They don't do the deal if they don't see a profit. That's why the people doing these leveraged buyouts get so fabulously rich. You have a company owned by thousands of people—but it's undervalued. You bid their stock away at a slight premium, but you know the company, so you know it's worth much more. You know you can get hundreds of millions more if you dress it up and turn it around and sell it. But now that value isn't spread over thousands of people—*it's spread over three or four or ten*. Those few people are simply appropriating the value that should belong to all of the shareholders.

"We have a basic myth in this country that the market is constantly analyzing the prices of stocks, and that the prices are close to their actual value. But the fact is that many companies are priced inefficiently. Managements know their own businesses, and they have investment bankers coming by who tell them what they really can sell for. So management has inside information that the stockholders don't have. I think management buyouts should be illegal, and if there is an outside buyout, the stockholders should get the benefits of the liquidation.

"This is all happening now because of the atmosphere in which we operate. Investment bankers certify the deals because they get fat fees. The issues are too complicated for 99 percent of federal judges to understand. Someday there will be a judiciary that will enforce the laws. But meanwhile this is becoming a two-tier society—the Wall Street movers and shakers, and the rest of us. Wall Street and the leveraged buyout phenomenon are turning American industry into a vast junkyard of corporate spare parts, and this is hardly what we need to compete in the world market."

Businesses have always been bought and sold, and the use of debt has long been standard practice. What is unusual now is the *size* of the company that can be taken over. Ten years ago, no group of individuals could have borrowed $6 billion to buy a company they didn't own. Then Mike Milken and Drexel Burnham popularized the "junk bond." Ten years ago, institutions might have been afraid to buy junk bonds lest they default, but we have had a recent period of prosperity and rising bond prices, and the early junk bonds survived well. Junk bonds pay more interest than high-rated bonds, but if you're going to buy Beatrice and sell off the pieces, these few extra percentage points don't matter. Banks and insurance companies have come to like these loans as well, because they get more interest. The loan officer can book a high fee, and if in a few years the loan goes bad—well, that loan officer could be at another bank by then. Win today, tomorrow it may rain.

With so much money whirling at such high speed, such critics as Ben Stein have seemed like lonely Isaiahs, shouting into a high wind. The official word—that is, the common consensus in the business community—has been that leveraged buyouts help the country, because they "add wealth"—the company is now more properly valued—and the managements are better motivated. And when managements are better motivated, they pay more attention to the details of the business, they work on Saturdays, they think of better ways to compete, they work as hard as, well, the Japanese. One might well ask—I have—if managements get high salaries and stock options and stock appreciation rights and corporate perks, why isn't that enough? But the question itself is naive. It might be enough if there were no other option. But since there *is* another option—the leveraged buyout—why not go after it yourself instead of leaving it to those faceless stockholders?

Of course, companies bought with a lot of debt have to have a flow of cash high enough to pay the interest on that debt. Hence a company newly bought in one of these transactions isn't always the nicest to work for if you're lower down on the ladder. It will be looking for ways to cut corners, to fire people, to trim research— anything that will get the costs down so that the debt can be paid. One might argue—people do—that in the long run it makes the company a survivor, that if the company was originally just a division of a big company, it had "layers of fat" lost to the corporate bureaucracy, and so on. But others conclude that a small, swift group of that very corporate bureaucracy has, in these cases, made off with the "fat" without earning it.

William Simon was formerly secretary of the Treasury, and he has since made a fortune in the hundreds of millions of dollars through leveraged buyouts. In a way, he helped popularize the phenomenon, because of the publicity that greeted one of his early coups: Gibson Greeting Cards. Simon and his partner put up less than $1 million in 1984, borrowed $79 million more, and paid RCA $80 million for the company, which was then one of its divisions. Within a year and a half, they were able to sell the company back to the public at a value of $290 million. Simon went on to do a number of other deals, also at great profit. Now he says this success involved a certain amount of timing and luck.

"When I started," he says, "you could find a lot of bargains selling at seventy percent of book value, of what they were worth.

Inflation was in double digits, the stock market was in the ash can, interest rates were up to twenty percent. Then inflation came down, interest rates came down, the stock market went up, and we were able to take advantage of the market. So we did well, and we were lucky. Now there is a lot more money out there chasing many fewer deals, and I would say the bloom is off the rose. In fact, if inflation heats up, or if we have a recession, a lot of companies will be in real trouble because they won't be able to pay the interest on their debt. Meanwhile, we have all the familiar problems compounding—the balance of payments deficit, the budget deficit, the declining dollar. We're going to have a correction sometime that won't be pleasant. So I'm retreating at the moment, and when times get tough, I intend to be there to pick up some pieces of deals now being put together that will someday blow apart.''

Simon's view is that there is a natural cycle that cures the excesses.

Richard Cunniff and William Ruane, who have run the successful Sequoia Fund for decades, also see a cycle. They wrote in a 1988 quarterly report: ''The Greater Fool Theory has historically played a role in almost every financial excess, each time appearing in a new guise.'' In the 1970s, it was ''one decision'' stocks, companies so powerful you could pay fifty times earnings for them. But the prices of those stocks collapsed in the 1973–74 recession. ''We believe this insidious theory is with us today,'' wrote the Sequoia managers, ''in the form of ridiculous prices being paid for *entire companies.* . . . It has clearly paid handsomely to date. . . . But near the end of this chain-letter process, the average buyer will be making an unsound investment.''

The LBO packagers had a fortunate wind through half of the '80s: they had declining interest rates. They could refinance the debt, and major fortunes were quickly created. The LBO packagers could buy a company, get their pictures in *New York Magazine,* sell off divisions to the next tier of buyers, who would in turn releverage the companies, show off their art collections, work on getting onto the boards of the Museum of Modern Art and the Metropolitan Museum, and repackage the business for sale to the next tier of buyers. . . .

Cycles: "Greed Is Healthy"

The LBOs were all legal, a phenomenon of the time. They opened wonderful opportunities for arbitrage, and the arbitrageurs made money. One of the most prosperous arbitrageurs was Ivan Boesky. Boesky was doing well, but apparently not grandly enough, when he began to seek and use inside information. Before he went to jail, he decided to cooperate with the authorities and walked around with a microphone under his Hermès tie.

Boesky had not yet been branded on the covers of national magazines when he gave the commencement address at the University of California School of Business Administration in 1985. In the tradition of graduation speakers, Boesky had some words of advice for the new graduates. "Greed is all right," he said. "Greed is healthy. You can be greedy and still feel good about yourself." These remarks were received, it was reported, with laughter and applause. Both the speech and the reaction seemed normal for the Roaring '80s.

At the time, Boesky was considered a brilliant arbitrageur: the SEC had not yet penalized him $100 million and he had not gone to do time at Lompoc. No one has paid that kind of ransom since horse-borne, sword-carrying kings were captured in battle. Boesky may actually have been good at his craft, but his quest for megamillions—not just millions—led him to pay for inside information. No one could possibly *spend* the kind of money Boesky amassed; what he hungered for, it seemed, was a kind of Establishment respectability.

Boesky wrote a book about arbitrage, published in 1985, and I did a television interview with him in his office. Television monitors enabled him to keep an eye on key employees, and he liked to talk on two phones at once. He wore a very well-cut, traditional three-piece suit, and his speech was soft, almost apologetic, as if he were burdened by a great-grandfather who was a Vanderbilt or a Rockefeller, not a delicatessen entrepreneur. He liked to talk about his charities—the money he had given to Harvard, the money he was going to give to Princeton, where his son is a student. He was very proud of his Princeton son. Later, we went off to play squash. (There, I can report, Boesky was dogged and competitive, but a latecomer to smooth squash strokes.) I doubt that Boesky has read *The Great Gatsby*, but he seemed to me much like that flawed Fitzgerald character. Gatsby was a kind of symbol for the Roaring '20s; history may make Boesky a symbol for these times.

Some Wall Street glamour figures of the 1920s also ran afoul of the law. The president of the New York Stock Exchange in the late 1920s was the handsome, gregarious, sports-loving Richard Whitney. In 1937, Whitney went to Sing Sing prison for his financial machinations. It is said that at Sing Sing he was the only prisoner ever to be called Mister by wardens and prisoners alike. A fine athlete as well as a popular fellow, he was elected captain of the baseball team. Whitney wasn't the only titan to raise eyebrows. Albert Wiggin, president of the Chase National Bank in 1929, sold *short* the stock of his own bank using the bank's credit, so that as the stock collapsed in the crash he made a very tidy fortune.

There were small-time offenses, too, relatively speaking. In 1929 the author of "The Trader" column in the *New York Daily News* planted tips in his columns; more recently, the hapless *Wall Street Journal* reporter R. Foster Winans divulged the contents of his "Heard on the Street" column for a return of mere thousands.

In every major rising market, plutography abounds and the practitioners of adept speculation are given the kind of reverence that goes to scientists, generals, and charismatic politicians at other times. In 1929 John J. Raskob, a director of General Motors, wrote in *The Ladies Home Journal*, "Everybody Ought to Be Rich." These days, the *Forbes* 400 Richest Americans is a favorite front-page story. It doesn't matter whether they invented something, traded real estate, syndicated old television shows, or moved pieces of paper on Wall Street—the reverence is bestowed.

So American economic history has a kind of ebb and flow. There are periods when riches, the gathering of riches, the spending and display of riches, are the dominant theme. Then success leads to excess, excess leads to reform, and the climate changes. The Vassar girls of the 1930s did not want to admit that their fathers were bankers;

better, they fantasized, to be supported by some honest workingman. The college students of the late 1960s took for granted the prosperity of their parents and adopted egalitarian jeans as a costume.

I don't mean to suggest that all of Wall Street—or all of America—is caught up in a shark frenzy of greed, nor that historical cycles are the only force in play here. We have witnessed an explosion of money and credit. Nearly all the government banks in the world are so fearful of recession that they turn on the money taps with each economic slowdown, and the sheer volume of money loosed upon the world is harder and harder to control.

Wall Street is the place where major fortunes have most recently—and visibly—been created. When inflation was rampant in the 1970s, the securities business suffered, but oil and real estate, the more traditional inflation hedges, prospered, and the real estate entrepreneurs began to make the Forbes 400.

One reason that certain segments of Wall Street are so well rewarded is the rise of the institutional investor and a certain style of investing. Institutional investors—primarily pension funds—control $1.5 trillion. It will soon be $2 trillion. They own a third of the equity of all the publicly traded companies in the United States and maybe *half* the equity of some of our major companies. Of the thousands of corporate pension funds, a few very big ones have the others playing follow-the-leader.

If a company's pension fund performs badly in the stock and bond markets, the company must contribute to that fund out of its earnings, and its reported earnings go down. If the pension fund does well, it meets the actuarial schedules on its own, and the company can report higher profits to its shareholders, to Wall Street, and to the world. So companies naturally put terrific pressure on their pension fund managers to perform well and to perform well *now*. Many companies give their pension funds to several managers, say, five. At least once a year—usually more often—the audit committee and the chief financial officer of a corporation sit down and look at the computer sheet that lists the performance of the pension fund. All the managers are rated—and it's a common practice to lop off the worst-performing manager and entertain solicitations for a new one. Forget the long term, it's this quarter that counts.

Now, let's say Alden Grenville, of Jones, Smith & Grenville, has a number of pension funds under management contract. He can't just buy great old American companies; he has to stay ahead of the other four managers who have divided up the XYZ pension fund. Grenville deals with a number of brokers; the brokers have armies of analysts. Research reports flow out, and computer screens flicker their numbers. But something has to give Grenville the edge, other than sheer investment genius, of course (which would be difficult to practice under this kind of pressure).

You can see why the Grenvilles of the world have their telescopes to their eyes, scanning the horizon for the skull and crossbones of raiders like T. Boone Pickens and Carl Icahn. If T. Boone is after the company, the stock will pop. When the company itself spots T. Boone or whomever, it will twist and turn and start up its defense tactics. It may take money out of its treasury and buy in some of its own stock or sell some bonds to buy in its own stock. It may sell off some assets and use the money to buy off the raider, or reshape the company in such a way that the stock moves.

Of course, if the company borrows to buy in its stock, it can't use that money for bricks, mortar, research, engineering, drilling, training, or what-have-you. If it sells off a division, it can't turn that division into a big money earner. But never mind. The *appearance* of the old skull and crossbones flapping in the wind sends the blood coursing and the stock rising higher. Let tomorrow worry about itself.

It doesn't have to be an unfriendly raid, of course. Raiders capture the imagination, but there are more friendly takeovers and mergers than unfriendly ones. In each case, the shareholder of the company being taken over must be offered a premium to induce him to sell. If Acme Widget is selling at 10, Universal Widget must offer 15 to make sure it gets all the stock—and indeed to make sure that no one else comes along with an even higher bid. Usually, on the announcement of the proposed merger, Acme Widget will move to only 14 or so—it isn't worth 15 until the actual moment it is tendered, and something may go wrong, the deal may fall through, in which case Acme may fall back to 10. So arbitrageurs like Ivan Boesky step in, buy the stock at 14, take the risk that the deal will go through, and tender it at 15.

Finally, Grenville is happy. The mere *presence* of swift-moving brigantines has made Acme Widget more eager to sell, even if no one has fired a shot across its bow. Grenville sells his Acme to an arb, and he is all right for another quarter. As his share of the fees, Grenville will take home a million or two for managing money, which pays for the Tagamet and leaves a lot left over. The arbitrageur earns his money by taking the risk. Ivan Boesky apparently tried to cut the risks by paying for the information.

Two trillion dollars is more than the total market value of any stock market in the world except those of the United States and Japan. With so much at stake, it is no wonder that Wall Street number-crunchers fresh from business school can get $100,000. The highest skill in the land, as measured by society at this moment, is keeping Grenville happy. Those who create the financial instruments, sell the bonds, line up the bank credits, and get the securities to the market can make many times what any CEO does, to say nothing of a poet or a police chief.

But this will change. Congress is already asking what the current takeover climate has done to American competitiveness in the world. It isn't clear that takeovers are necessarily harmful, and T. Boone Pickens is still something of a folk hero. But the discrepancy between the rewards for financial skills and other skills will narrow.

An executive from northern New Jersey contacted me recently. He lives, he wrote, in an area where commuting investment bankers abound. At a party, "one guest told how a commodity trader's subordinate appeared in his office in a rage. The man threw his bonus check on the floor, actually spat on it, and cried to heaven at the injustice of its paucity. The check was for $2.1 million.

"All of this folderol contrasted dramatically with a recent experience in my own company [at] one of its plants in New Jersey. We advertised to fill the vacant position of production manager. A tough, demanding, twelve-hour day; hands on; pressure; for a modest salary of $32,500. A single ad in the Sunday *Star Ledger* drew 175 applicants, many with graduate engineering degrees. We ended up with a short list of ten finalists, all of whom would have done the job."

Later I called my correspondent. He was still astounded at the gap between working America and paper America. When I asked him about all the job applicants, he repeated how qualified they were. "I'm talking about engineers with science degrees from Princeton, M.B.A.s from Wharton, and twenty years of experience. We would tell them they were overqualified, and they'd say, 'Please interview me anyway.' When we checked with their old employers, the employer would say: 'This guy is terrific, first class, but these are lean times and we had to downsize.' "

As my correspondent so aptly pointed out, the glamour is now in trading, not making. This is not a stable situation in an economic superpower, and sooner or later Newton's second law comes back from lunch.

When Franklin D. Roosevelt delivered his inaugural address on March 4, 1933, he promised to drive the money changers from the temple. There followed a wave of congressional hearings and reform. I don't expect anything so dramatic—for one thing, we haven't lost a third of our banks recently. But the climate will change. And it may turn out that Ivan Boesky's commencement address will have been the high-water mark of another era when self-interest was king.

Why Did Ilan Do It
If He Never Took the Money?

Ilan Reich was standing before Judge Robert Sweet in a Manhattan courtroom. Sweet happens to be a friend of mine. Reich was, even at the young age of thirty-two, a superstar lawyer. He was paid $500,000 a year by Wachtell, Lipton, Rosen & Katz, one of the major New York firms involved in mergers and takeovers. Martin Lipton, one of the senior partners of the law firm, the inventor of the "poison pill," one of Wall Street's most famous anti-takeover devices, had said that Reich was so smart and so creative that he, Lipton, sometimes couldn't follow him and would ask Reich to write out or diagram his ideas. Reich was not in the courtroom as a lawyer, however. He was there, this January day, to be sentenced. His career was about to come to an end.

Robert Morvillo, Reich's lawyer, said that his client had already suffered enough. He had lost his job. He had lost all of his assets—in a fine imposed by the SEC. "We don't treat people who commit treason, people who violate narcotics laws, as harshly as the SEC on the civil side is now doing to the people who engage in the practice of insider trading," Morvillo argued.

Morvillo said that unlike some of the more notorious people in the insider-trading schemes, Reich came away without a penny in his pocket. Further, he had withdrawn voluntarily from an insider-trading scheme—without being forced, without law enforcement breathing down his neck. He had done that because he believed what he had been doing was wrong. Some credit should be given to Reich for that. He himself began the process of his own rehabilitation long before law enforcement had caught on to the scheme.

Judge Sweet asked Reich if he wanted to say anything. Reich said he was saddened for the pain he had caused his family and friends; he was ashamed for having betrayed the trust his clients and partners had placed in him. He said he would never again do anything wrong, and he begged for leniency in his sentence.

Judge Sweet said that all of the letters he had received since proceedings had begun supported what Morvillo said. Reich had indeed not profited a penny; he had indeed walked away.

"Why do we find ourselves here on this sad and tragic moment?" said the judge. "If this sentence involved just you and your family, the outcome would be that you have suffered quite enough . . . but unfortunately the sentence involves all of us, and the strength of the laws of our society. . . . You will never, I am absolutely confident, betray your country's trust or the laws again. . . .

"I impose a sentence of one year and a day."

Reich's pregnant wife wept quietly. Robert Morvillo asked if Reich could defer reporting to begin his sentence for sixty days, so that he could be with his wife when she had the baby. She and Ilan already had a two-year-old and a four-year-old at home. Judge Sweet said that he could.

Out of all the insider-trading cases, this one seemed peculiarly haunting. Reich never took the money. He had withdrawn voluntarily. When I saw that Robert Sweet was the judge on the case, I began to follow it, and I have already acknowledged my relationship with him. His secretary sent me, at my request, all the public records, and a complete transcript. *The American Lawyer*, a trade publication, said Sweet was a fair-minded jurist, neither soft nor draconian. But—a year in jail?

Ilan Reich is not one of the major players in the insider-trading schemes that have come to light. He is Rosencrantz or Guildenstern rather than the Prince of Denmark. But some aspects of his case interested me. Why would a fast-rising young lawyer risk his career for no profit? This was not a credit-card theft, where the thief suddenly lived on champagne and caviar or bought a Ferrari. *Reich never took the money.*

The question *why* is pervasive throughout the insider-trading cases. In many of them, the insiders were doing well before anything happened—they had to be, to have access to the information. They were rising investment bankers and lawyers, doing brilliantly by any standards. Soon after and not because of his illegal actions, Reich was making half a million dollars a year, with many years ahead of him as a noted lawyer. Dennis Levine himself was making a couple million a year as an investment banker. Martin Siegel, handsome, well-liked, smart, was making a reported $2 million a year at Kidder, Peabody.

In Reich's case, he was seduced by Dennis Levine, whose arrest in May 1986 began the year's avalanche of insider-trading scandals. The underlying concupiscence was money, not sex, but otherwise the scenario was a seduction.

Steve Brill of *The American Lawyer* reported this scene after talking to Reich:

Reich meets Levine in a conference room during the negotiations for a friendly merger of two cement companies. Reich at this time— 1980—is less than a year out of law school, a junior associate. Levine is richly dressed, a pinstriped banker from Smith Barney. He proposes lunch. They lunch. At the fourth lunch, Levine proposes something new. What he proposes is that Reich tell him what impending mergers are being worked on at Wachtell, Lipton.

Reich says no, it's illegal, it leaves a paper trail, you'll get caught. Levine says everybody does it, that the key to not getting caught is to get the information well ahead of time, so that it doesn't flag the SEC, and that the proceeds of the gains will be put into a network of foreign bank accounts. Reich is worried enough that he won't even hear this at lunch—he hears it during a walk in Central Park. And that sets the pattern.

Levine sets up an "account" for Reich, with a share of the "profits," and periodically Reich and Levine lunch. But the lunches are only shoptalk, the market, their families. Not until they go on their walk does Reich tell what information he has. Each time, Reich told Brill, "I felt sick about myself." After giving Levine information on eight deals, he withdrew.

The miscalculation made by the inside traders was made because they were not mafiosi. The Mafia—at least we read this in novels— imposes an oath of silence, the *omertà*, which carries the most horrible penalties for violation. But there were no oaths in the insider-trading scandals. There was simply temptation by the enormous amount of money sloshing back and forth through the system. Hundreds of millions of dollars were being made by people who did not hold a patent, or put a brick upon a brick, but performed some marketplace activity like arbitrage. Whom would it hurt, to get a bit of information ahead of time? But the insiders were not bound to each other, and the SEC had to nab only one, because "everybody does it." The songs to the D.A. intermeshed with other songs, the voices that turned up on the hidden cassettes of the informers were the same voices on still other cassettes. Hermès ties hid tiny microphones, and the whole opera played out.

I went to lunch with Judge Sweet. Sweet has tried other of the insider cases and has been a federal judge for eight years. A Yale law graduate, he was formerly an assistant U.S. attorney, deputy mayor of New York, and a partner in a major law firm. He has four children and four grandchildren.

Judge Sweet had said he hoped that when Reich had served his term, Sweet's remarks might help get Reich reinstated to the bar.

"If that's in order, I wouldn't have any hesitation," he said. "This fellow is a good lawyer—even a brilliant lawyer. Someday, somebody will hire him."

But why jail? I asked. There were muggers and burglars and drug dealers out there getting off by plea bargaining, and no one seemed to think Ilan Reich was a threat to society.

"You have to set up a deterrent. Forty weekends of community service? That's not enough of a deterrent. If you're going to have laws on the books, then you have to have them obeyed. This fellow had been privileged by society, he went to Columbia Law School, he should have known better—he *did* know better, that's why he felt guilty enough not to take the money. He was a skilled lawyer, an interpreter of the laws."

"Are you holding lawyers to a higher standard than other people?" I asked.

"Maybe I am. Insider trading doesn't seem as bad to some people as burglary, because it doesn't involve a physical threat. And some economists, I know, say the whole notion is fallacious—that we should have *no* rules on insider trading. But we the judiciary don't make the laws, the legislature makes them. Once they're on the books, though, we have to enforce them or the system comes apart.

"Right now the laws on the books say that the public has to believe that markets are fair, and in order to sustain that faith, there has to be no information passed on what is not yet public information."

I asked Judge Sweet how he had decided the sentence.

"Every judge gets a report from a probation officer who investigates the accused," he said. "The probation officer investigated, and he said, 'This guy works—he works all the time—and that's all he does. He's a workaholic. I'm convinced he'll never do anything wrong again.' There are rough guidelines, and if he serves his time well, which I'm sure he will, he will be out in less than a year. But nonetheless, a jail, any jail, is a traumatic experience for an educated, upper-middle-class person."

Judge Sweet, in the courtroom, made these remarks: "Here is the crux of the problem: that element in our world which has abandoned all that we used to cherish—integrity and honesty—an element that ignores reality and the law of the land, an element which exalts form and discards substance, which is only for the appearance, and the appearance is success.''

In most cases, Wall Streeters involved in insider trading learned to take on the appearance of material success. Ivan Boesky lived like a grand duke, with a magnificent estate in Westchester and a handsome apartment. He was in the process of endowing prestigious institutions when the whistle was blown. Martin Siegel built himself a $3.5 million house on the water in Connecticut.

And yet these insiders pursued money not only for what it could buy—but for the money itself. Like children overdosing on candy, they could not keep their fingers from getting sticky. How else to explain Martin Siegel, already making a fortune annually, taking a grand total of $700,000 in cash—in a suitcase—like some furtive drug runner? The elements of pathology rise to govern the scene. And for some future playwright, the minor character Ilan Reich becomes interesting; his tortured conscience will not let him touch the money.

Lord Keynes, an astute observer of both men and money, wrote, ''The love of money as a possession—as distinguished from love of money as a means to the enjoyments and realities of life—will be recognized for what it is, a somewhat disgusting morbidity, one of those semicriminal, semipathological propensities which one hands over to the specialists in mental disease.''

Judge Sweet had said in the courtroom, ''. . . an element that ignores reality.''

I asked him what he meant.

''Ilan Reich confused illusion and reality,'' he said. ''He was seduced. He had an emotional need—he wanted to be part of the world he thought Dennis Levine represented, and he thought Levine really cared about him. But all Levine wanted was money.''

Illusion and reality—an interesting phrase for a judge. I thought of all the situations in which many of us blur illusion and reality— the love affairs that end badly, the jobs, or the relationships within the jobs, that are not what they seem. A universal problem—but we do not go to jail for our mistakes.

''No, we don't,'' said Judge Sweet, ''because somewhere there is a line we do not step over.''

*   *   *

The rationale for sending Ilan Reich to jail was that he had violated the law of the land, a comparatively recent body of law. Those laws are there, as Judge Sweet said, to sustain the faith of the public that markets are fair.

Yet there were phenomena in progress that would jolt the faith of the public more than the handful of inside traders who got so much publicity.

Crash!

In every generation, there are certain landmark days during which time seems to slow down and the details are etched very slowly and clearly. Everyone of a certain age can remember where they were and what they were doing when they heard John F. Kennedy was shot on November 22, 1963. For another segment of our society, the same is true of October 19, 1987, the Crash of 1987.

On October 19, 1987, the stock market collapsed 508 points in a single day, a drop of 24.77 percent. The Brady Commission reported that the decline had been accelerated by institutionalized trading by computers and by sales of derivative instruments, such as futures and options. Markets, of course, fluctuate. For two generations, the Crash of 1929 had endured as the great mythic catastrophe; this was a greater drop. Recently I talked to a number of prominent people in the financial community. Each can remember exactly where he or she was, and to a person, there was a new fear in them that came from having looked into a void.

John Phelan has been the chairman of the New York Stock Exchange since 1984. Before he held that job, he was a specialist on the floor of the Exchange, a member of the firm his father founded. He was named president of the Exchange in 1980. I asked him what he was thinking about on Monday morning, October 19.

"By eleven o'clock," he said, "we knew we were going to have a new volume record. There were orders from all over the country, and they were predominantly sell orders. We called the SEC in Washington. We wanted them to know what stresses we were feeling, and we wanted them to touch other people, talk to other exchanges, talk to member firms so that we could get a feeling of what was happening.

"We were looking for leaks, a seam bursting somewhere."

"What kind of a seam?" I asked.

"Well, first," Phelan said, "the system itself. A computer failure. Then I called the Federal Reserve and said we should keep an open line because this was going to be an unusual day. Then Howard Baker called me from the White House and asked how things were going. Jim Baker of Treasury was in Germany, but I talked to George Gould, and Alan Greenspan was on his way to Texas but I talked to Corrigan in New York. I tried to set up a control center so I could see what was going on—like monitoring a patient, taking his pulse, seeing how his heart is doing, how his blood pressure is doing, and so on."

"About one o'clock there was a rumor that David Ruder of the SEC was going to ask the Exchange to close. Had you been talking to him?"

"Yes. He went out to give a speech and I think that remark was taken out of context. When I talked to him earlier, he said he had no intention of asking the Exchange to close. He agreed it should stay open."

"Then the market kept falling. What were you thinking?"

"We thought our capacity was about four hundred and fifty million shares, and by two in the afternoon, we were running at a clip that was one hundred and sixty million shares over capacity, so we were in a free-fall as far as volume was concerned. We had system delays bringing orders into the Exchange, and delays in reports going out as well. But we didn't have to shut down [stop trading in] very many stocks.

"After the market closed on Monday, I sat there and looked at the screen—six hundred million shares, 508 points, and I couldn't believe it. It's easier to imagine the six hundred million shares than the five hundred and eight points in one day. I thought, 'How did we do six hundred million shares without a meltdown?' A *trillion dollars* was gone from equity values.

"That night I had trouble sleeping, and I got up and looked out my apartment window at two in the morning, at people walking in the street, and the cars on the street. I thought, 'What does this mean for each of these people, what kind of effect will it have on the institutions and on the economy itself?'

"At six-thirty A.M. I was in the elevator and a fellow said he heard the Exchange might close. He'd said to himself, 'My God, it can't be that bad, can it?'

"That renewed my desire to keep the Exchange open. If one individual thought that, what would the rest of the world think? When I talked to the government people and the White House, I think we had all agreed it was important for the worldwide perception of this country that the markets continue to function even though we had a crisis. So on Tuesday that became the focus. If we had had another day like Monday, we weren't sure what would happen."

"People say that Tuesday morning was the real crisis," I suggested.

"Well, Tuesday, the Federal Reserve told the banks to go ahead and lend money, they would push the money out to any borrower who needed it. The banks opened their windows and said they'd worry later about getting paid back. But no one thought we could sustain another day like Monday. Tuesday started with a rally of about two hundred points, but by noon the rally had rolled over and there were sellers again. The imbalance in orders was too great in a lot of stocks; at one point we had one hundred and sixty or seventy stocks shut down. Of course, fourteen hundred and fifty were still open, but when you can't trade in one hundred and seventy stocks it's serious. There was great concern that another avalanche was yet to come—maybe another five hundred points."

"What would have happened if you had had another avalanche?" I asked.

"We would have had an interesting time," Phelan said, "and interesting problems, but I'm glad we didn't have to try."

"What were you thinking as the stocks shut down, one by one?"

"That this place cannot close. I went down on the floor and talked to the floor directors and said, 'We have to get these stocks open.' "

"How do you get stocks open when the trading has been shut down?"

"Well, you indicate them. If the last sale is at thirty-five, and you had to shut it down, maybe you say the market is twenty-five to thirty, bid twenty-five, ask thirty, and assume somebody is watching and at some point a value investor will come in again. That's what you're really looking for. So we put up these indications, and you could almost feel the market crawling along, trying to feel its way along the bottom. By twelve-fifteen or so it began to move up, imperceptibly at first, but at least it wasn't going down. It began to get a little strength, and so it wasn't off a hundred, it was off seventy, sixty, fifty, forty—you could feel it beginning to gain strength, as if the wind had been knocked out of it and suddenly it could breathe again."

"Did you go on the floor at that time?"

"Yes, several times. There was great concern. Sometimes in your life you see real fear in people's faces. But I also saw resolve that we had to keep this thing going. I had [a floor member] call me and say, 'Listen, we're taking in five times the volume we had, we don't know what we're doing, we have to shut down.' I said, 'Listen, we gotta keep this open for God and country.' He said, 'Okay, I just thought I'd make the pitch.' He went back and kept his post open."

"You sound like a football coach at halftime."

"That's part of leadership when you get into a crisis. If the head guy doesn't think you're going to make it, you're not going to make it. Out on the floor stocks were down, but the volume was drying up. It was like the eye of a hurricane. When I came back up and looked at the computer there wasn't the same pressure and [the market] was beginning to turn around."

"So you were back from the brink," I said.

"On Tuesday morning firms looked at the margin requirements of their customers and at their own capital and said, my goodness, if we sell all this out, what will happen? A lot of people faced the terror in their own way and came through it, and the reason the system came through is that a lot of people and a lot of firms put a lot on the line in courage and guts."

"If it hadn't turned around Tuesday—"

"I don't know. Major firms could have failed. Banks that loaned to the major firms could have been in trouble. You never know where the dominoes stop. But they stopped."

"Could it happen again?"

"Sure. You'll always have declines in the market, and every once in a while, you'll have a crisis. Each time is a bit different, but there are similarities. People try hedges that are supposed to work and don't work. There's a lot of leverage, debt in the system that people don't anticipate and don't know is there. And there was an enormous amount of money moved by a small number of big institutions."

"You're talking about Fidelity, and the General Motors pension fund, and so on."

"I'm not naming names. But if you look at the volatility we've had, the ups and downs, it really began to increase in 1985, an it's not just program trading and portfolio insurance. It's an attitude among institutions that each has to have the greatest possible return in the shortest period of time. The big institutions can't hit the exit at the very same instant, much less two hundred institutions. The irony is that most of this money comes from pension funds whose stocks are listed on the exchanges. In trying to get a better return by quick buck investing, they created instability for their own shareholders."

"So what is a small investor supposed to think?" I asked.

"Small investors are worried, and we're concerned about them," Phelan said. "There are forty-seven million share owners. But institutions, too, are becoming concerned. We don't want these people to leave the market. So we've got to go back to basic questions. What's the real purpose of the market? Is it fulfilling its function? If not, how do we correct it? If you don't want to correct it, what are the consequences? The consequences affect every American because the development of both new companies and existing companies affects every American. If we're going to change the system radically, we'd better pause every once in a while and ask, 'Where are we going?' "

Who were the buyers on October 20? In many cases, they were the companies listed on the New York Stock Exchange, the very companies whose stocks had been shut down by an imbalance of sell orders. Their managements knew the perils of falling stock prices; raiders lurked to take advantage. Many of them had already authorized stock buy-back programs. Their investment bankers urged them to buy in their own stocks. Telephone board meetings were called, and the orders went out—when they could get through the jammed telephone lines. The "value buyers" were the companies themselves. But if the market had fallen another 500 points, would they have continued buying? Many had already exhausted their war chests.

Alan Greenspan, the chairman of the Federal Reserve, and the Federal Reserve Board got high marks for their handling of the crash. I went to have lunch with Greenspan at the Federal Reserve. You would not call the cuisine world-class. In fact, it was the same menu Volcker had had, a bit heavy on the fried chicken with gravy and biscuits. "Paul is such a Puritan," Greenspan said, "and he really doesn't notice what he eats. I'll do something about it later.

"When I got this appointment," he continued, "I did some reading. I had a couple of weeks, and while I had to wind down my own office, this was one topic I boned up on. I went through all the previous crashes in American history. One thing was common to all of them—liquidity vanished. The money the brokers borrow—the call money—would suddenly spike up to forty, fifty, sixty percent. It's a natural tendency—the lender who loans to a broker is nervous in a crisis, and he wants his loan covered, and if the ratios start to come apart, he wants his money back, and that accelerates the downward spiral. If the brokers fail, so could some of the lenders. So I determined, after this reading, that the system would be prepared—should something happen, it would be there. Monday night, some of the banks were ready to pull back. We told them if they kept the money out there, we would keep the window open."

Keeping the window open at the Fed is like leaving the porch light on and a key under the flowerpot.

"Could it happen again?" I asked.

"You tell me," Greenspan said. He put his fork down, smiled, and took on his official tone. "We believe that the actions of the Federal Reserve System were appropriate, and that they helped to maintain the stability of the banking system, and of the financial community."

*   *   *

Is this it? The American financial community—even the world financial community—had had, deep in its collective unconscious, the fear that things *could* collapse, even though 1929 was a fading memory. The elders who had lived through it had retired. 1929 was not simply an event on Wall Street in New York, though at first it seemed to be. The market rallied through the spring of 1930, and recovered half its loss. Then it ebbed away, month by month, until, in June 1932, it was down 90 percent from its peak, and one out of every four Americans was unemployed. There were many parallels between the 1920s and the 1980s: the compounding of debt, farm failures, trouble in the banking system, giddy times on Wall Street. But farms were a much smaller part of the economy of the 1980s. And the Federal Reserve in the early 1930s *contracted* the money supply, and thousands of banks failed. Some of the literature of the time speaks of "a healthy purge of excesses." The Federal Reserve of the 1980s had read its own history.

To much of America, the October Crash was like hearing of a nuclear meltdown in a faraway utility, like Chernobyl, or that SAC went on an alert, and the bombers were in the air, but it turned out to be a computer glitch. Industrial production did not fall, as it had in 1930.

Authorities debated the role of the computer-driven trading and the synthetic instruments. The volume of trading in futures and indexes had grown to where it was larger on some days than the "real" stocks underneath.

The twenty-three leading stock exchanges of the world all went down in October 1987. Some had related trading in futures and index options; some did not. They all went down. The partisans of computer programs said that some of the exchanges with computer-driven trading went down even more than New York, but then the markets in Milan and Wellington were thinner. The opponents of computer programs said the "Chicago crowd" which made the market in futures and options had so much political clout that it was able to turn the New York Stock Exchange into a big commodity pit, that the shares of American industry were now traded with the fervor and volatility of pork bellies.

Computer programs were one issue. The behavior of the stock

exchange specialists was another. The New York Stock Exchange operates on a monopoly system. It grants a post to one firm to make a market in a particular stock, to buy when there are no other buyers. It was these specialists that John Phelan had rallied. During the Crash, some of the specialists stood at their posts, trying to make some order of the markets. Others, when frantic sellers descended upon them, disappeared to the men's room. A couple of the specialist firms did not survive. When the statistics were toted up, the specialists had had a scare, but as a group they had all made money! Even with the October crash, 1987 had been a good year.

Federal agencies squabbled for jurisdiction. One thing was certain: the swiftness of the crash, and the publicity given to institutions and their computer-driven programs, sent many small investors—and many institutions as well—to the sidelines.

The New York Stock Exchange once had an institutional advertising campaign that proclaimed, "Own a share of America." Somehow, in the 1980s, that notion began to seem old and quaint. Computer jockeys, academics who could run equations at Berkeley and MIT, had become fashionable on Wall Street as "quants." The quants sold services that enabled even giant institutions to hedge their portfolios with futures, flip them, spin them—all to get the last percentage point of return. But in the process, the whole institution of the marketplace began to lose some of the faith of the parishioners, the faith that the market would always be there, there would always be a buyer. The parishioners became agnostics, rather than atheists; they did not deny, but they hoped. No one wanted to live through another crash. But no one would say we have seen the last one.

Warren Buffett: Two Billion Dollars, and He Still Makes It Look So Easy

Q. Could we have another crash?
A. Anything can happen. That needn't concern the investor. To the extent that silly instruments cause silly prices, he can take advantage of them.

The pilgrims have flown into Canterbury, only Canterbury is Omaha, Nebraska. They are the shareholders, five hundred or so of them, of Berkshire Hathaway, the holding company run by Warren Buffett. They could have dropped their proxies in a wastebasket, like the shareholders of most companies, especially since Buffett and his wife own 42 percent of the stock. But the shareholders have come for a tribal experience. They have read the annual report, which is picked up from London to Sydney—no pictures, good numbers, Buffett's annual essay. They mill around on the steps of the Joslyn Art Museum, asking each other where they are from and how long they have held the stock. Then they file into the auditorium. They are all happy.

The meeting itself takes seven minutes. Directors are nominated, rules are followed, and the minutes are approved. Then the shareholders take to the microphones. Some ask detailed questions about Berkshire's investments. Berkshire has put $700 million into Salomon Brothers, the investment banking house. But isn't Wall Street risky and isn't Salomon having a particularly turbulent time? Buffett says that he thinks Salomon will do all right. Berkshire's investment is hedged because it's a convertible preferred. Some ask about the outlook for inflation, deflation, a stock market with computerized trading. Buffett says he's not smart enough to know *where* the yen and the deutschmark and interest rates are going, but inflation is a bet on the fallibility of men and governments.

This is the annual audience with the chairman, and Buffett handles the questions with easy humor. Then the shareholders board a bus to visit the Nebraska Furniture Mart, which Berkshire bought in 1983. Buffett knew the sales per square foot back in the early 1970s. (There is an account in *Supermoney*.) Mrs. Rose Blumkin started the store fifty years ago with $500. Today it is the biggest of its kind. Now ninety-four years old, Mrs. Blumkin works seven days a week, patrols the store in an electric golf cart, and says she is having a ball. It is the kind of investment Buffett likes.

As shareholders say goodbye to each other in the lobby of the Red Lion Hotel, there is an implicit question: Can he still do it? Can he do it again? Can he do it from *here?* But the answer almost doesn't matter. None of them would sell a share. To own a share of Berkshire shows you are a member of a select and knowing group.

In 1965, one share of Berkshire stock was worth $12. Today it is worth $3,900. Since 1974, when the stock was under $50, it has risen in value almost a hundred times. Those who had invested $10,000 in Buffett's original partnership in 1956—and only a few citizens of Omaha did—now own stock worth something like $15 million dollars.

When I first met Warren Buffett two decades ago, he was not famous in the business world, and I had no idea he ever would be. He was known to a limited circle as a good "value" investor who had a small investment company. He had infectious good humor, an extremely sharp intelligence, and a gift for metaphor—J.P. Morgan, dressed as Will Rogers. And of course, I was struck that while eager Wall Street players nervously traded both securities and stories by the minute, Buffett did everything from Omaha, without a Quotron, a ticker tape, or a computer. His research was painstaking and dogged. After the salad-oil scandal at American Express in the '60s, he sat behind the cashier at Ross's Steak House, counting American Express card receipts to see if American Express was affected. (It wasn't, and the stock soared.) From time to time, like a good instructor, he would send me a packet of information to see if I could find the right nugget. Why should the bonds of the Indiana Turnpike sell for less than those of the Illinois Turnpike? (The Indiana Turnpike had more money than it appeared—road maintenance was overreserved—and the bonds moved up.)

Today Buffett still lives in Omaha in the same house he bought years ago for $32,000. He is the best-known investor of a generation, worth almost $2 billion, all earned through slow and quiet stock market investing. But the companies Buffett invests in are no longer New England textile mills like Berkshire Hathaway. (The original mill was sold in 1985 but the company retained the name.) His investment in Salomon Brothers helped that leading investment house stave off a hostile takeover. His investment in Capital Cities Broadcasting enabled it to buy the ABC TV network. He has spent years on the board of the Washington Post Company, and his face has turned up on the cover of a business magazine.

But it is no accident that Buffett stays in Omaha, or that he never talks to analysts, or that he has never split the stock of Berkshire to make it easier to buy. To him, the shareholders are important. They are rational, patient shareholders. Some years ago, he used one of his metaphors to describe the importance of working at your own cadence.

"In the securities business," he said to me, "you're a batter in a game in which there are no called strikes. They can throw you General Motors at forty and you don't have to swing. They can throw you IBM at one twenty and you don't have to swing. They have to keep pitching but you don't have to swing. So if you're patient, the odds are with you. You can wait until you get one right where you want it."

"You might not swing for six months," I said.

He said, "You might not swing for two years. If you have impatient shareholders, they start hollering, 'Swing, you bum.' "

"Most institutional shareholders are not so patient. So you've always worked for yourself. Isn't it boring, standing with a bat on your shoulder for two years?"

"It can be, and boredom limits the capabilities of many money managers."

Buffett says he has always followed the principles of Ben Graham, the author of the classic textbook *Security Analysis*. In fact, it was Ben who actually introduced me to Warren. Graham's textbook first came out in 1934. He had already retired by the time I met him and he was translating Greek and Latin classics. *Medius tutissimus ibis*, he said, when I asked his counsel. You go safest in the middle course, Phoebus Apollo's instructions to Phaeton. Graham preached that the first rule of investing was not to lose. Simple enough. You invested only when you found an investment that was selling for less than a rational buyer would pay, by a wide margin of safety. According to Graham, following the market is like having a manic-depressive partner. Sometimes Mr. Market becomes so giddy he will ignore all reality and offer you outrageous sums of money for your part of the business. When Mr. Market is manic, you should sell him your part. Sometimes Mr. Market falls into despair, seeing no end of problems, and he will offer you his share of the business at a discount that would be silly. So you buy it. In between, you keep your bat on your shoulder. It seems too simple to be true.

"Well, it seems too simple that if you eat less and eat the right kinds of foods you lose weight," Buffett said, "but there are new diet books sold every year."

Buffett was rejected by the Harvard Business School. He studied with Graham at Columbia University Business School, after graduating from the University of Nebraska. He sought out Graham, he says, because reading him was like an epiphany.

Academic economists have written that no one can beat the market consistently, because the market is "efficient"; all the information is already in the prices. But Buffett's performance confounds that theory.

"Not just my performance," he says. "Everyone I know personally who stuck with Graham's principles has done better than the market."

But Buffett has added his own interpretation to Ben Graham. Graham had a statistician's view; he looked at numbers, he liked to buy assets at less than their value and trust the market to someday recognize their value. The assets might be bricks and mortar, or machinery. But Buffett likes the power of a franchise, something more intangible.

"Valuing a business is part art and part science," he says. "Logically a business is worth the present value, however much cash it is going to distribute between now and Judgment Day. If you own a water company, you might be able to figure the earnings fairly closely. If you own a shipbuilding company, it might be difficult. I don't understand the shipbuilding companies but I do understand the water companies, and they're hardly ever attractive. Somewhere in between I find something.

"I look for a business where I think I know what in a general way is going to happen. If you buy a U.S. government bond, if it says the coupon is nine percent, you know what the income will be for thirty years. Now when you buy a business, you're buying something with coupons on it too. The only problem is that they don't print in the amount. It's my job to print in the amount on the coupon."

"So what does that lead you to?" I asked.

"Businesses whose products I understand. I mean, I understand what a Hershey bar is and I've got a pretty good idea where Coke or

Pepsi will be in five years, but I have no idea where any high-tech company will be in five years."

I'd been through the Berkshire report, and there was nary a share of Coke, Pepsi, or Hershey.

"So you'd never own IBM," I said. "But you don't own Hershey, Coke, and Pepsi, either."

"No," Buffett said, "but I look at them. Under certain circumstances I might own them. If I go into a store for a chocolate bar, and it's fifty cents and it's a Hershey bar, I'm not going to go across the street to find one for forty-five cents . . . I don't shop for a chocolate bar. That's a franchise. The limiting factor is me. If I were smart enough, I could evaluate every company on the Big Board, and I hope I could evaluate just ten percent of them. You don't need very many good ideas. If I can get one good idea a year, I'll be batting better than I have recently."

"Did you have a good idea last year?"

"No. It's been a while since I've had a good idea. I know a number of good businesses, I just don't know good businesses at good prices. You have to wait until both are present."

"Do you ever get a big hit buying ordinary businesses?" I asked.

"Yes," Buffett said, "but not very often. Occasionally, sensational businesses are given away, and more often unsensational companies sell at prices that should be reserved for sensational ones."

"Can you think of an example?"

"Sure. In the mid-'70s, the Washington Post Company's stock sold at a market price of eighty million. But the properties—*Newsweek,* TV stations, the newspapers—were worth four hundred million. No one would have argued about the value of the properties, but people were focusing on whether the market was going up or down, and whether the stock was going up or down, instead of where the *business* would be in five years."

"You've been talking this way for years. Why doesn't everybody do it?"

"It takes patience. People would rather be promised a lottery ticket next week than get rich slowly. If we're right about the business, the stocks will take care of themselves. The stock market is closed on Saturday and Sunday but the businesses go right on. If we're in the right businesses, they could close the stock exchange for two years."

Buffett's annual report has its usual aphorisms.

"In your annual report," I said, "you say that if you're in a poker game and in the first half hour you don't know who the patsy is, *you're the patsy*. How does that apply to investing?"

"If the market goes down ten percent and that upsets you, that means you think the market knows more about your business than you do. In that case, you're the patsy. If it goes down ten percent and you want to buy more, because the business is worth just as much, *they're* the patsy."

Buffett's rhythms—and rationale—are very different from the blinking-light computer-terminal world of contemporary Wall Street, and much quieter than the trading pits of the Chicago exchanges where bids are shouted out for futures and index options— the new "synthetic" instruments. Several years ago, Buffett published a letter addressed to Congressman John Dingell, chairman of the Energy and Commerce Committee, warning that index futures would be detrimental to the securities markets and to the public.

"Our capital markets function quite well," Buffett said. "They have enough liquidity. If you and I and ten other people were stranded on a desert island, we'd probably have a couple [of people] work on clothing and shelter, and a couple would work gathering food, and maybe one would be a doctor. I don't think I'd take the three smartest and have them over there on the beach trading index futures on the output of the rest of us. Not if we ever expected to get off the island."

Is Buffett, then, against the whole development of computerized synthetic instruments?

"I'm not a big believer in synthetic instruments. If people decide they should own General Motors for the next five years, they can either buy it or sell it. The more instruments are designed, the smarter the players have to be. If you build a big casino and it has all the glamour of low margins and fast action and has the stamp of government approval, that will be telling the American public this is not a bad place to be."

Was the Crash of 1987 an aberration, or could it happen again? "Anything can happen in stock markets. That doesn't have to concern the investor. To the extent that silly instruments cause silly prices, he can take advantage of them. The rest of the time, he can ignore them. If I'm a farmer in Washington County, and the farm next door is selling at a silly price, I don't say, that's a terrible event. If I have the money, I buy it; if I don't, I watch somebody else buy it. I don't go out and buy six newsletters to find out what's going to happen to my farm."

Two years ago, Buffett caused something of a stir when he revealed that though he loved his three children dearly, he wasn't going to leave them any money when he died. It wasn't fair to them, he said, and it wasn't fair to society.

Buffett chuckled. "I hear children of the rich or the rich themselves talk about the debilitating effect of food stamps on welfare mothers and they say it's terrible," he said. "You hand them all these food stamps and then they don't bestir themselves and it causes the cycle to repeat itself. But of course, when a very rich child is born, when they leave the womb they're handed this lifetime supply of food stamps. And they have a welfare officer, only he's called a trust department officer and the food stamps are little stocks and bonds. And no one seems to notice the debilitating effects of that particular form of lifetime supply of food stamps. I think, by and large, if I'm going to be a sprinter I will be a better sprinter in life if I sprint against everyone else leaving the starting blocks at the same time than if I say I'm Jesse Owens's child and I get to start at the fifty-yard line."

I asked Buffett how his children felt about this.

"I think they feel pretty good," he said. "I'm not as draconian as I sound. Close to it, but not quite. I think kids should have enough money to be able to do what they want to do, to learn what they want to do, but not enough money to do nothing."

Buffett's daughter Susan was at the Berkshire meeting, with his newest grandchild, Michael, two months old. I asked her what it was like growing up with Warren.

"Well, he's a great guy," she said, "and we grew up completely normal. We didn't even get cars at sixteen, or anything like that. For years I didn't even know what he did. They asked me at school what he did, and I said he was a security analyst, and they thought he checked alarm systems. He's indifferent to clothes and he still lives in the same house and he just reads all the time.''

"He compares money left to kids to welfare checks," I said.

"I know," Susan said. "It can have a debilitating effect and that happens to a lot of people, especially too much money at a young age." Susan thought wistfully for a few seconds. "I kind of think I'm old enough now not to be debilitated," she said.

"Your parents have over a billion dollars, and you don't have any of it. Wouldn't some of it help in fixing the kitchen?" I asked. She laughed.

"Sometimes, I have to tell you the truth, it would be nice. But I understand him and what he says and it does make sense."

Though Susan was totally charming, I didn't get the feeling she was totally convinced. Still, I think the kitchen might get fixed. I had asked Warren what he would do with the money.

"Eventually ninety-nine-plus percent is going back to society, through a foundation. I'll try to find the best people in the world to manage the foundation and then let them try to do very bright things with it. Basically I have a bunch of claim checks on society and those claim checks can go back to society."

I asked Buffett whether he worried about the trade deficits and budget deficits and all the other problems that upset the financial community.

"We would certainly be happier and our growth rate would be higher if we could close the deficits," he said, "We've traded consumption—those cars and VCRs—to the foreigners and they have claim checks on us and they can cash those claim checks. So every few weeks the Japanese buy another office building. When they bought the ABC building in New York, that one hundred and seventy-five million dollars was one day's trade deficit. So we're trading real estate for trinkets like VCRs, but there's a certain amount of justice in that because Peter Minuit originally got Manhattan by trading trinkets for it. It took just three hundred years to complete the circle."

So how will we come out, then?

"Either we will make the IOUs the foreigners hold considerably less valuable by having a lot of inflation, or eventually we will produce more than we consume.

"I like the gas tax because oil is a resource we're running out of. We keep sucking it out of the ground like a giant soda we've stuck straws into. If we don't close these gaps, there's real intergenerational unfairness. We consume more than we produce, the foreigners have the claim checks, and they can present them to the next generation."

So for the moment you're not pessimistic?

"It's an enormously rich country, and we can continue trading it away for a very long time. It's a powerful machine, and it can take a lot of abuse."

There has been so much freneticism in the Roaring '80s, so much money churned up in trading, so much champagne and hangover, so much concern about getting and spending that it is a relief to be with an ebullient citizen like Warren Buffett who does not display his wealth, a citizen who has been well rewarded for doing what he likes best.

"Money is a by-product of doing something I like to do very much," Buffett says. "If Ted Williams was getting the highest salary in baseball and hitting two-twenty, he'd be unhappy, and if he was getting the lowest salary and hitting four hundred, he'd be very happy. That's the way I feel about this job.

"I pick managers in my businesses who love what they do and who aren't trying to build a résumé or even make money for themselves, they're wedded to what they do and they keep doing it even after they have a lot of money. I'd like to be like Mrs. Blumkin is in her store. Every day, when I get to the office, so to speak, I do a little tap dance."

7 THE ROARING '80s

So much money sloshing around in the system has an impact on the mores of the time. "God gave me my money," said John D. Rockefeller, and he believed it. The investment bankers believed they were worth a million dollars a year, and the security analysts believed they were worth half a million. Plutographic magazines recorded the getting and spending and rarely questioned the sources of the means.

The Popular Culture Association, academicians who scrutinize cultural trends, reported a blurring between fame and notoriety. "Never before," said Professor Ray Browne, of Bowling Green State, "have Americans been so desirous of brushing up against the notorious and the wealthy. We're mad to be in the same room with them, to let a little of the danger they engaged in rub off on us. If they're well born like von Bülow or the Mayflower Madam, well, that makes it even more wonderful because we're trading up." Count Claus von Bülow was accused—and acquitted—of the attempted murder of his heiress wife, Sunny, who remains in a coma. Sydney Biddle Barrows, the Mayflower Madam, was a former debutante who remained in the Social Register even while she ran a string of call girls. Count von Bülow did not retire his dinner jacket during his troubles, nor did Ivan Boesky. "All my good friends," said Cindy Adams, a *New York Post* society columnist, "are indictees and worse." But then, that was reported in the *Times*.

Why Is One Master's Degree Worth So Much More Than All the Others?

Lois is in her mid-twenties, and she works in New York in that nexus that composes the world of words: publishing, magazines, advertising, public relations. She shared a house at the beach last summer with a large group of single men and women. Most of them were M.B.A.s, she said, and she had some trouble getting along with them because of their "M.B.A. mentality."

I asked her what an M.B.A. mentality was. After all, an M.B.A. is just a master's degree in business administration. We do not think of masters in English or architecture as particularly having a caste mentality. Lois herself has a master's from Stanford, so she was just as highly educated as her housemates. But her degree is in English, and the M.B.A.s considered themselves superior. Why?

"Because they make more money," Lois said. "Sometimes I think we're living in a two-tier society. There are M.B.A.s, and there is everybody else. The M.B.A.s think of everyone in terms of money. They rank everyone they meet by salary. They look up to those who make more money and down on those who make less. If you've been to a famous business school like Harvard or Stanford, you outrank people from the other business schools—until the people from the other schools start to make a lot more money or get a more prestigious job. To an M.B.A., it's important to have the right kind of car, to live in the right kind of neighborhood, to wear the right kind of clothes. M.B.A.s have no time for artists—unless the artist is very famous. They would never date a musician or a teacher or a research scientist—unless the research scientist was about to invent a product that could make a lot of money.

"M.B.A.s have a condescending attitude toward people with inherited money, though they enjoy associating with them. M.B.A.s want money because it buys power, prestige, and the right possessions. Money is the measure of their success, but it is not the only measure; it's the *victories* in business that count. If you ask M.B.A.s why they want these things, they don't even understand the question.

"So what got to me was feeling I was at the wrong end of the telescope. Somebody would say, 'This is Lois,' and the M.B.A.s would say, 'Hi.' Then one sentence about the weather or the beach, and then: 'Where do you work?' I would tell them I worked for a publisher. They would way *'Oh,'* even though publishing is an interesting business—in fact, it's so interesting that the salaries are low because of high competition for the jobs. They would say *'Oh,'* and then they'd want to go meet somebody else. I guess you could get their interest if you said, 'I'm James Michener's editor, and he just promised two million to Swarthmore,' but it would be the two million they'd be interested in. Needless to say, I'm not James Michener's editor, and my writers are not in a position to give anything to anybody—they have a hard enough time with the rent.''

Lois lit a cigarette. She has stopped smoking several times, but apparently she found the recall of summer scenes stressful enough to reach into her purse.

"Now, these are fast-track M.B.A.s, I admit,'' she said. ''Maybe there are others who aren't quite like this. The fast-track M.B.A.s are the ones who got the invitations their second year at business school. Companies woo these students at recruiting time—and students come back and compare notes. Shrimp or salmon at your dinner? Chocolates or liqueurs after dinner? What kind of car did they give you? What hotel did they put you up in? If these students have any kind of grades—or outside business experience—they think of themselves very, very highly, and they want the best. There is apparently so much demand that new M.B.A.s can make two or three times what non-M.B.A.s make. They can start right out of business school at fifty thousand a year if they had some experience in business before school. I know one who got eighty-five thousand a year.''

Lois was oppressed by the intensity of the M.B.A.s in her house and relieved to be away from them.

"I know they work hard,'' she said. *"Too* hard. Sometimes they didn't get the whole weekend off, even in summer. In a lot of Wall Street firms they have to get there earlier than the partner they work for and have the papers read and the work prepared, and some of those partners get there at six-thirty or seven in the morning. It's not at all unusual to work until eleven at night. Naturally, your social life develops in the firm or company—who else do you meet? I know a woman who had a honeymoon one and a half days long—then she had to fly to Cleveland to close a deal. The work itself becomes a drug, and then they don't know how to do or talk about anything else. You should have seen them—on Sunday night people have been to the beach, somebody wants us to listen to a new tape he bought, somebody else has seen a great movie, and the M.B.A.s are in the kitchen talking deals and percentages and clients. So what I want to know is this—just what the hell is it they *do* that is worth so much money?''

What is it they do that is worth so much money? I have told Lois's lament at some length because she asked a profound question, and the answer says something about the kind of society we live in. It is the social order—the tax laws, the customs, even the attitudes of the times—that produce these money discrepancies. We take for granted now, for example, that doctors make a lot of money. It has not always been this way; Lewis Thomas writes that when he graduated from Harvard Medical School in 1937, the advice from older physicians that appeared in a reunion yearbook was that young doctors should have rich wives, because while medicine was a noble calling, one could scarcely make a living from it. Doctors are much richer now, but not because their education lasts so long or because illness, life, and death have become more important. Doctors are richer because of what is called "third-party insurance." Society decided that medical care was a *right*. It did not decide this overnight; some of the contracts won from corporations were subjects of fierce negotiation by unions. The federal government has offered Medicare and Medicaid only since 1965. Fifty years ago, if you got sick, you got sick at your own expense, and poor sick people did not make for high—or promptly paid—medical bills. But doctors can now collect from Travelers or Prudential or the federal government, and health care accounts for 10 percent of the GNP—that's $37 billion a year. It's a lot easier to be a rich doctor than it used to be.

We used to think airline pilots made in excess of $100,000 a year because they were responsible for our lives when we flew with them. The image grew up of the silver-haired, responsible, competent father figure, with the Chuck Yeager tones on the intercom—"This is your captain speaking." Then People Express come along and proved it could pay pilots $36,000 a year to fly a 727 jet 1,500 miles and the pilot could say "This is your captain speaking" just like the $100,000 pilot. (People Express has been absorbed by Texas Air, but many of the pilots are still there.) Much of the flying public seems more influenced by low fares than the experience or salary of the pilot. We still respect pilots, just as we respect doctors—we still have our lives at stake in each case. Airline deregulation permitted the entry of lowfare carriers that needed low costs. Society wanted deregulation, and a skilled profession is affected, just as third-party insurance made for rich doctors.

Lois's fast-track M.B.A.s were either in consulting with one of the major firms or on Wall Street. Consulting has traditionally paid high fees to recent business school graduates. The Wall Street M.B.A.s from Lois's summer house were—judging from the hours they kept and the money they made—in investment banking and underwriting. An underwriter sells issues of stocks or bonds. The skill involved is that of sizing up the opportunity in the marketplace, mobilizing the client to take action, and marketing the security. Underwriters' fees are large not because the hours are long or life itself is at stake, but because their fees are a percentage of the dollars at stake in the deal. If you bring me your company, which is making $2 million a year in profits, and I bring off a deal that gives a market value of $60 million to your company, you're not going to quibble when I send you a bill for $1 million, and I may be able to do all the work in a *week*.

One activity of investment bankers is to buy and sell companies or divisions of companies. This is slightly more complex than buying or selling a house, but it doesn't necessarily take more time. I have a friend who is an investment banker who used to buy companies for ITT when that giant bought all sorts of enterprises. ITT bought Avis Rent a Car and Wonder Bread, among others; I can't remember now which deals my friend worked on, but he got quite rich. Now ITT's stock is down, and there are rumors that another management may take it over and sell off all the companies—or at least some of them—that were acquired! ITT goes up and ITT goes down, but the investment bankers make money in both directions. And the fees?

Well, when Texaco bid for Getty, the investment bankers were estimated to have made $45 million, because the value of Getty was $10 billion. Plenty of cash there to pay hardworking young M.B.A.s.

Will it always be thus?

Investment bankers will always prosper more than poets and archaeologists, and the bankers who help the world to function will always be rewarded. There will be worldwide investment banking firms, just as there are worldwide ad agencies. No one wants to deny real talent its due, whether Larry Bird or Leonard Bernstein or Dr. Edwin Land. Presumably skilled and talented investment bankers belong in that group. But it is certainly no secret that many run-of-the mill investment bankers have made millions of dollars a year. If our system works, profits like that will invite competition, and competition will reduce profits. One day some corporation may simply pay its bankers $600 an hour, like its lawyers, instead of a percentage of the assets moved. Or the climate will change; a different tone in Washington, in the Justice Department, in the tax courts, and the merger business may not be such a bonanza.

Finally, the attitudes of the "summer shares" may change. Lois will be at another stage of her life by then, but other groups of young men and women will be in those same beach houses, and the conversations may be different. The M.B.A.s may not be so fashionable. There are times when getting and spending are very important, and times when public purpose surpasses private interest as the accepted goal. The Reagan years will be remembered as money-value years.

But What Do Investment Bankers *Do*?

My lunch guest was, I would say, about forty. He had sent me an article he wrote five years ago, so I asked him to lunch and asked what business he was in. He said he had been to business school in the early '70s, had been given a small stake by an uncle to buy into a company, and now had a collection of companies in a variety of mundane businesses. And he wanted me to know how well he had done.

"Now my net worth is in the middle eight figures," he said.
It took me a minute to figure out.
"You mean fifty million," I said.
"Give or take," he said.
"You have done handsomely," I said.
"I have," he said. "But you know, you look around, and all of a sudden there are a lot of guys with fifty million."
Were there really? Did it bother him?

"Well, we've always been used to the idea that people who start successful enterprises get rewarded—Edwin Land invents the Polaroid camera, Steve Jobs starts Apple in a garage. And I'm not saying I invented anything, but we've been up and down with these companies, and it's taken a long time. But when I look around, I see a lot of people with a lot of money who have just moved paper around."

The Roaring '80s have been characterized, like the '20s, by an amiable hands-off attitude in Washington, and by rising financial markets. It is not only okay to be rich; it is okay to flaunt it, to be photographed in sleek magazines with the new furnishings in your $5 million apartment. It is also an age of plutography—writing about and recording the wealth—and shortly after my lunch date, I came across an article in a financial magazine that supported the thesis of my guest.

This article tried to estimate the income of various Wall Streeters. There was Mike Milken of Drexel Burnham Lambert's Beverly Hills office. Mike makes somewhere between $50 million and $100 million *a year*. Call it $6 million a *month*. He popularized the "junk bond"—that is, he helped to sell institutions the idea that low-rated debt was safe. If $50 million a year seems hefty, it is a small proportion of Drexel's $75 billion bond business. Then there are Messrs. Kohlberg, Kravis, and Roberts, of New York and San Francisco. They are the specialists in leveraged buyouts; that is, they put together a package of debt and with the debt they buy entire companies from their public shareholders, after which they sometimes sell them again. They are not newcomers to this business. With this technique, KKR bought Storer Communications and Union Texas Petroleum, each for *$2 billion*, and then their landmark buyout, Beatrice Foods, for $6.2 billion. The companies go right along producing after KKR buys them; the only difference is that they owe more money. Last year, KKR divvied up something like $190 million.

Then there are the traditional investment-banking firms, like Morgan Stanley, Merrill Lynch, Salomon Brothers. At Goldman, Sachs, a 1 percent partner is said to be able to pull in close to $5 million a year.

The most profitable part of investment banking has been M&A— mergers and acquisitions. Companies, in the course of business, want to sell divisions; other companies may want to buy them, and the investment bankers are in the middle, like real estate agents selling a house. The deals, of course, are more complex than selling a house—the securities have to be worked out and tailored—but then the fees are handsomer because, like those of the real estate agent, they are based on a percentage of the deal. When General Electric took over RCA—itself a huge company—the deal was valued at $6.4 billion, and one of the two investment banks involved took home fees of $9 million. If investment bankers were paid like lawyers, on a per-hour basis, they would still be very well paid, but they would get nothing like the millions they now receive. The corporate chieftains who pay these fees do not change the custom of paying a percentage of the deal because (a) it isn't their money, it's the company's, (b) their outside directors need the imprimatur of a major investment-banking house for protection against suits in any deal, and (c) even an improvement of a small fraction—fifty cents a share in a deal, let's say—can pay for the fee of the investment banker. And if an investment banker is skilled enough to earn the company that extra fifty cents a share, then everyone wants that top investment banker—people do not shop around for the cheapest fees.

But notice, nothing in particular is getting *built*. Real estate agents are crucial to maintaining a good market in the buying and selling of houses, but they do not put a hammer to a nail. Dr. Edwin Land created a fortune with Polaroid, but first he had to create instant photography. Then he had to build a factory, hire the engineers to staff it, arrange to get the cartons in which the cameras could be shipped, sign deals with distributors, sign contracts with retailers, devise a whole marketing and advertising program, establish health and pension plans for his employees—in short, all the grind and details of building a *business*. Along the way, he had to solve all the problems—the rollers in the cameras sticking, patent infringements, key employees leaving—that were also part of the daily grind of a business. Creating a fortune took years.

In contrast, the paper fortunes of the '80s seem to take neither time nor huge amounts of capital. It takes capital to have an office, but that is nothing like the capital needed to build a factory. The skills rewarded are uniquely those of the marketplace—the ability to read the market well, to have access to financing. In fact, the profits of the financial fortune hunters are possible partly *because* there is so little capital involved. KKR, with its skill at lining up billions, employs few people, yet it reportedly made a profit of $190 million; it would have taken a standard industrial company sales of at least a billion to achieve the same result. Of course, a big investment-banking firm does invest a lot in people; Drexel Burnham now employs close to nine thousand. And it is the fat profits of the investment bankers that make possible the salaries of $100,000 for M.B.A.s barely two years out of school.

With numbers like that floating around, it is no wonder that 400 of the 1,250 graduates-to-be of Yale applied to a single firm—First Boston—for jobs in investment banking. It set some senior money managers to thinking that maybe what was going on was the re-arranging of deck chairs on the good ship United States, a point which has also occurred to Robert Reich, the Harvard political scientist.

"Takeovers, mergers, and other forms of asset-rearranging are important up to a point," he says. "Assets have to be redeployed to their highest and best use, and every economy needs a certain number of people to oil the wheels of commerce. The problem is, we've gone way overboard. The best, brightest, most talented individuals in our society are attracted to the paper professions. All this asset-rearranging will not enhance global competitiveness; it's going to do quite the opposite."

I asked Fred Joseph, CEO of Drexel Burnham, whether investment banking was bleeding off the best talent. He said, "Only one half of one percent of the seventy thousand graduating M.B.A.s last year went into investment banking. Investment bankers have been pivotal in the past six months in raising about two hundred and eighty billion on an annualized basis for corporate America. That's not deck-chair rearranging. This is a cyclical business. As the markets move up and down, our business is going to move up and down. There is a good chance that it's peaked.''

I suspect Joseph is right about the cycles. Business-school graduates flock to where the money is, where the higher starting salaries are that year; they seldom have the perspective to figure out that if four hundred of their classmates are applying to the same firm and even a few of them are hired, it's going to be very competitive, even for those who survive the high degree of stress and the ninety-hour weeks. I filled in as a substitute instructor one year at the Harvard Business School when the stock market was boiling; most of the class that year wanted to go to Wall Street. Five years later the market had collapsed and no one was interested in Wall Street, so ironically, that was the time to go there, if you could get a job at all.

It's nice to think you can go to Wall Street and make $25 million a year, but this is a time when the real incomes of many have gone down. Perhaps more of the $25-million-a-year people will adopt entire classes from Harlem schools and send them to college, as the industrialist Gene Lang did, but I haven't seen any sign of it. The $25-million-a-year people walk through streets policed by people who make $25,000 a year, if that: if they get sick they are nursed by people who make $25,000 a year, and they send their children to schools where the teachers—even at elite schools—get $25,000 a year. Something is missing. That gap will never close completely, but it is uncomfortably wide—and getting wider—all the time.

"You *Ought* to Get Rich"

Albert Hirschman, a distinguished economic historian at the Institute for Advanced Study in Princeton, argues that since the Industrial Revolution, Western societies have alternated between public interest and private action. The public interest is that of the citizen in his community; private action means the individual working for his own gain—that is, for money. "The world I am trying to understand in this essay," Hirschman writes, "is one in which men think they

want one thing and then upon getting it, find out to their dismay that
they don't want it nearly as much as they thought . . . and that
something else, of which they were hardly aware, is what they really
want." Hirschman's essay is called *Shifting Involvements*. The first
things people want are necessities: food, clothing, shelter, mobility.
Then they want excitement and luxury. "[A] recent advertisement
for a BMW," Hirschman writes, "blurts it out: MEETING THE DEMANDS
OF SOCIETY [read: safety and pollution devices, fuel economy] IS NO
EXCUSE FOR BUILDING A BORING CAR." The more basic the needs that are
met, the less one is satisfied. In other words, when everybody has a
BMW, everybody has transportation but BMWs become boring.

According to this view of history, in the acquisitive, money-ori-
ented part of the cycle, individuals say, "Me, me, I want more." In
the booming 1880s robber barons were told by their ministers that
their wealth was the will of God. Russell Conwell, a nineteenth-century preacher and educator, delivered an enormously popular speech
on the Chautauqua circuit called "Acres of Diamonds," which did
not merely exhort self-help, but indicated a *duty* to get rich. "Opportunity lurks in everyone's backyard," said Conwell. "Everyone
can and should get rich." Conwell delivered "Acres of Diamonds"
more than six thousand times to admiring audiences, and earned
from it $8 million, in an age when a beer and a sandwich cost five
cents. One was to get rich not merely to be rich, but to help others;
Conwell himself founded Temple University. Affluence, though,
breeds restlessness in the children of affluence. Think back to the
movie *The Graduate*. Benjamin's graduation party features all his
presents, his parents' swimming pool (in which he later tries out his
scuba gear), and a family friend saying, "I'm only going to say one
thing to you, Ben . . . plastics." The tone of the movie in that
respect is satirical.

Now think back to the ads for the Peace Corps. Pictures of strong,
kindly young Americans in the African bush, the South American
tropics. They were digging latrines, building schools, planting rice.
What did the Peace Corps promise those who signed up? "The
Toughest Job You'll Ever Love." Hard work, long hours, low
pay—and satisfaction. The Peace Corps volunteers were motivated
by public concern, not private gain. The Peace Corps, even though

it is still with us, was very much a '60s phenomenon, as was the concern about the environment and pollution. In the '60s, fashionable dress for younger people was the cheapest and most utilitarian available: jeans, boots, Army fatigues. Two governors of California symbolized the contrasts: Jerry Brown slept on a mattress on the floor, drove a plebeian blue Plymouth, and went off to a Zen center in Marin County for contemplation. Ronald Reagan's advisers were the rich businessmen of Los Angeles, and he took some of them to Washington, where they restored the white tie and tails as a mark of the presidency. In the election campaign of 1984, poor Fritz Mondale charged around the country saying, "Let us *care* for one another, let us be a *community* again." The words were right, but the timing was wrong; to most people it sounded downbeat rather than compassionate. Fritz was out of sync.

If you want to see where we are in the cycle, turn to the business pages of the newspaper. In the 1920s business leaders were considered founts of wisdom, dispensing their opinions on the state of the world and the course of the markets. In the 1930s the public—ruined by the crash—exulted over the jail sentence given to Richard Whitney, president of the New York Stock Exchange. Stock manipulation did not come to an end in the 1920s, but in the 1930s bankers and brokers were villains to most of the country.

In the 1980s zealous federal officials watch over the banks and the brokerage houses, and television-watching Americans feel friendly toward Smith Barney and PaineWebber and Merrill Lynch. But there are still loopholes and passageways in the laws that can be exploited by the quick and the clever, and if and when the economic climate changes, public wrath could rise the way it did in the 1930s. In recent years, for example, we have seen some ingenious examples of what is called corporate greenmail. The recipe goes thus: Buy a block of stock in a company whose assets are undervalued in the marketplace. Then call up the management and say you've bought a big block of the stock and you'd like to come in and discuss some changes that ought to be made. If you've bought more than the management owns—and many managements have only salaries, not ownership—the management will be afraid of you. They will think, goodbye corporate jet, goodbye private limos, goodbye Lutèce and the Greenbriar. Tell the management you'll sell them your block at a *premium* to the market, that is, at a fat profit to you. The management will spend the company's money to buy your stock back and make you go away. Thus: greenmail—legal, unlike blackmail. It's legal because the rules say that a company's board of directors can use its best business judgment in determining whether buying a block of stock is in the best interest of the company.

So recently the oil-rich Bass brothers of Fort Worth, Texas, bought a block of Texaco in January and sold 25.6 million shares back to Texaco less than two months later, making more than $400 million. That's right, $400 million! Two months later! $400 million! Beats punching a time clock or teaching English. Texaco later was to have another battle with Carl Icahn, but I have not heard any great national outcry about the directors of Texaco paying the Bass brothers $400 million of the shareholders' money to go away, nor about the aggressive investment techniques that brought about such action. On the contrary, the money-gathering activities of the Bass brothers have brought fulsome praise. A newsmagazine crows that not only are they worth $4 billion, but they have "real sophistication, social conscience, and social ambition." The director of New York City Ballet says they are replacing the Morgans and the Rockefellers as America's premier dynasty.

Saul Steinberg played the game with Disney—his Reliance Group paid $132.5 million for 6.3 percent of Disney's stock one March, upped its share through the spring, and sold its share for $325.5 million in June, less than eighty days later. Big players, big profits. No profits for the ordinary shareholder, though. In fact, the shares of the ordinary shareholder are diminished in value, because usually the company has to go into debt to buy back the shares of the greenmailer.

We live in a time when business values are paramount, but even in an era like this, greenmail will surely inspire a fire-breathing reformer somewhere. Greenmail—and the reaction to greenmail—is a sign of the times.

The hungry young M.B.A.s are merely breathing in the values of the times with their morning coffee. The popular culture now addresses them—both men and women—all attired in suits and ties, with their portable computers, their running shoes, their willingness to limit their personal lives and to work long hours. This mode has become so popular that it can't help but be devalued. The M.B.A. degree is so widely sought by students that it has begun to lose its distinction. Some 63,000 M.B.A.s will be granted this year, against an average of only 9,600 in the 1960s, twenty years ago. There are going to be some disillusioned M.B.A.s, too. The baby-boom generation will find promotions hard to come by in corporate America, just because of intense competition from the sheer numbers that they are up against. One day, some younger people, perhaps the children of successful M.B.A.s, will don jeans and Army fatigues to show they are indifferent to brand names and designer styles. The M.B.A.s, as parents, will say that the kids do not understand the value of work, that they take things for granted, and have no respect. Then the rivers will all flow into the sea, but the sea will not be full.

John Marquand and Yesterday's Yuppies

He is self-confident. He believes in being in shape and completes an exercise program every morning. He believes appearances are important and pays careful attention to his clothes. He has always had a more expensive apartment or house than he could really afford, because he knew he would be moving up to the point at which he could afford it. He spends a lot of time "networking"; that is, he talks to people, has drinks with them, writes them notes—even when he does not have an immediate relationship with them. He works very hard—twelve-hour days are common—because that is what it takes to get ahead. He has an M.B.A. from Harvard, but he downplays it, knowing that many people who did not go to Harvard are put off by the name. He talks about loyalty and teamwork, but he has switched jobs whenever a better opportunity came along. His real loyalty is to himself—and to the bottom line. He knows the value of *things:* brand names, wines, antiques. He is a sophisticated consumer. Though he is in his early thirties, he is well on the way to running his own company.

That little summary is a profile of the prototypical hero of our age, the yuppie. The rising generation has now found an acronymic symbol, cartooned by Garry Trudeau and headlined by *Newsweek*.

"Barely looking up from the massed gray columns of the *Wall Street Journal* as they speed toward the airport, advancing on the 1980s in the backseat of a limousine," wrote *Newsweek* of its cover-story heroes.

I was mulling over how books reflect the business temper of the age as I was reading Lee Iacocca's autobiography, when I had a sudden sense of *déjà vu.* I hunted a book from the library. The description of the yuppie above—the exercised M.B.A., trim, hard-working, totally absorbed in success—is not contemporary. It is from a 1954 novel called *Sincerely, Willis Wayde,* by John P. Marquand. Like nearly all of Marquand's novels, this one was a best-seller. It is marvelously acute and quite funny; I hope the publisher keeps it in print.

I doubt that Marquand is widely read today. He won a Pulitzer Prize for *The Late George Apley,* and I suspect his commercial success cost him some critical acclaim. To my knowledge, Marquand is not taught in schools as Hemingway and Faulkner are, and he did not pioneer new forms for the novel, as they did. But you can learn more about the mainstream of American life from Marquand than from *The Sun Also Rises.* He wrote a novel about an investment counselor, *H. M. Pulham, Esquire,* and another about a banker, *Point of No Return.* As a young writer I was once so astonished by the cinematic ease with which Marquand moved the reader from present to past and back again that I sat down with a yellow pad and analyzed a chapter line by line. Not many novelists make the cover of *Time;* Marquand did.

Critics have said frequently that American writers do not write about business, or even about work. In the proletarian literature of the '30s, writers wrote about work, but they were expected to have been loggers, seamen, factory workers, to have been out among the people. Fiction as a career pays so little that most fiction writers are teaching in universities, and while teaching is certainly work, the raw experience of American life is not in the towers of learning. Consequently, the image of business is stereotypical, especially on television, where the black hats and white hats must be quickly established. Businessmen are J. R. Ewing in *Dallas,* or lesser villains. To a television writer, "business" means his producer and his agent. The images of business, then, are only a setting: boardrooms, company planes, expensive restaurants, jargon about mergers and megabucks.

John Marquand knew business because he was an astute social observer, because he played golf with businessmen at the Myopia Hunt Club near Boston, and because he made a lot of money and had married into a business family. Marquand's confidence in his craft can be seen in his choice of subject. He chose not the traditional glitzy business of TV-show fare (newspapers, advertising, fashion, a mythologized oil industry) but the *belting* industry—the making of webbing for machinery and conveyor lines—a business the public never thinks about, much less sees. Marquand's yuppie hero—not, of course, called a yuppie—is Willis Wayde, a rising executive. Like many of Marquand's heroes, he starts poor but not poverty-stricken; his father is an engineer in the Harcourt Mill, which makes belting. Willis works at the mill, moves to a New York management consulting firm, then to a New Jersey belting company, merges it with the Harcourt Mill, and is positioned to take over the biggest company in the belting industry. Even as a bachelor, he has a Persian carpet and a Morris chair. Married, he acquires a Chippendale mirror and a Kermanshah rug, and every house he owns he sells at a profit.

Willis pays attention to appearances. "You were judged," he thought, "by the way you handled yourself at the Stork or Twenty-one," and he wears tailored clothes. (Thirty years later, Lee Iacocca wrote of Henry Ford, "He was a sucker for appearances. If a guy wore the right clothes and used the right buzzwords, Henry was impressed.")

Willis's wife, Sylvia, has graduated from Radcliffe with honors, but not in an era when women could aspire to the Harvard Business School. Sylvia is working for a Columbia professor and is "tired of being poor and bright." Willis is happy to write out checks for her purchases.

Willis Wayde, the American businessman of the '30s and '40s, is not a sympathetic hero. He knows hundreds of people but has few real friends—and he never questions the bottom line as the arbiter of all good. He signs everything "Sincerely," but he lacks all sensitivity. His last action is to shut down the Harcourt Mill because it isn't contributing to the bottom line.

Yet the view of Marquand, the satirist, is positively benign compared to the nonfiction view of Iacocca, the automobile executive of the '80s. Here is Chrysler bringing out cars—the Aspen and the Volaré—that haven't been tested, the engines stalling dangerously, hoods flying open, fenders rusted. In 1978 the finances of the company were in a shambles—no one knew what was owed, to whom, or when.

Chrysler was chaotic, but Ford, according to Iacocca, who worked there for thirty-two years, was the domain of a malevolent despot. It was not merely that the Pintos blew up, or that automobiles designed for the market were capriciously canceled. Ford ordered Iacocca to fire an executive whose pants were too tight. ("He's a fag," Ford said, over Iacocca's objections.)

But Iacocca reveals more about the American automobile industry and its life-style than he perhaps intends. When he was feuding with Henry Ford, the word went around the company that it was unhealthy to be a friend of Iacocca's. So the company masseur, who came to Iacocca's house every Sunday, didn't show, and the chief stewardess of the company fleet got demoted because she was too friendly. Company masseur? Chief stewardess of the company fleet? *We taxpayers were supporting that style!* The company fleet was a deductible company expense. And Iacocca took the company plane to the Augusta Masters until a *Wall Street Journal* reporter spotted it. At the same time, the industry was so inept as to give the whole inexpensive end of the automobile spectrum to the Japanese. Reading Iacocca, you conclude that only self-restraint on the part of the Japanese and protectionist noises from Washington kept the Japanese from taking 80 percent of the American automobile market instead of 25 percent. And as for the taxpayer bailing out Chrysler in 1980, Iacocca writes: "[Government] loan guarantees were as American as apple pie." Didn't the shipbuilders and steel companies get them, too?

The executives in Marquand's belting industry slapped each other on the back, mouthed clichés, and sang silly songs at conventions— yet the belting industry of that era, as seen by the writer, seems more rational, and shows more devotion to customer service and quality, than the real-life automobile industry of the '70s.

As for the contemporary successor to Willis Wayde, the yuppie reading his *Wall Street Journal* on the way to the airport, I suspect we are not even halfway through his era. In 1963 Bob Dylan sang that the times they were a-changin'. But now they have changed *back* again: Willis Wayde, Lee Iacocca, and the yuppies all have more in common with one another than with the intervening generation. Willis Wayde seems familiar. The generation that called the police "pigs" and shocked parents with drugs and sex now seems exotic. We have a generation that doesn't want to overthrow the Establishment, it wants to *be* the Establishment, and as quickly as possible.

In their competitive world, fitness has replaced dope. Newspapers extol the women—not just the men—who can fly to Cleveland or Amarillo or Singapore and close the deal. And what's good for the *deal* is good for the country; the values of the business society are paramount. You can't argue with it, and it's not all bad. It's certainly better than mindlessly trashing the Bank of America and thinking of all the police as fascist pigs.

Cigar, Champagne, and Sermonette

Otto von Bismarck loved stock tips and hot deals. He also created the Germany we know today. His banker had all the prestige of J. P. Morgan in this country, but J. P. Morgan's bank is still here, and even his middle name is used on a group of funds frequently advertised in *The New Yorker*. The currents of history treated Bismarck's banker differently.

I have been reading with considerable pleasure a remarkable book about an era like ours in which the ideology of business was ascendant. *Gold and Iron,* by Fritz Stern, portrays the rise of ebullient business in another country, Germany. It is the story of which nineteenth-century novels are made, the rise and fall of a banking house, and more specifically the story of the relationship between Otto von Bismarck, the "Iron Duke" who unified Germany, and his German Jewish banker, Gerson Bleichröder. When Bismarck entered public life in 1859, there was no nation of Germany, only a string of independent dukedoms and petty kingdoms. When Bismarck was finally forced to resign in 1890, Germany was not only unified, it was the strongest power on the Continent and it was challenging Great Britain's industrial supremacy. Bismarck resisted the liberalism of the mid-nineteenth century; he called for "blood and iron." Bismarck and Bleichröder could not have come from more diverse backgrounds. Bismarck was a Junker, a Prussian aristocrat, born on an ancestral estate. I can recall no portrait of him laughing or smiling. Gerson Bleichröder was born in Berlin in 1822, only ten years after the king of Prussia had promised emancipation to the Jews. Bleichröder's father was a minor banker who later became an agent of the Rothschilds; Bleichröder exploited the connection.

By the time Bleichröder became Bismarck's banker, he was already prosperous, with banking clients from the court, the diplomatic service, and the arts. Bismarck had been appointed ambassador to St. Petersburg and had asked around for a reliable banker in Berlin—a Jewish banker, according to legend. "A Junker often boasted of a Jewish banker," writes his biographer. Bleichröder collected Bismarck's salary, paid his bills, and invested some of his capital. In 1862 Bismarck became the Prussian king's first minister. He had boundless energy, enormous self-confidence, an ability to improvise that exceeded that of Franklin Roosevelt, and an ability to create a mystique that was much like that of Charles de Gaulle. Just before he assumed office, he told Benjamin Disraeli: "I shall seize the first best pretext to declare war against Austria, dissolve the German Diet, subdue the minor states, and give the nation unity under Prussian leadership." And so he did. Bleichröder rose with Bismarck to become the leading banker of the new German state. Bleichröder not only became the leading banker of the nation, he became the banker *for* the nation, raising money for it in the capital markets of Europe. Later Bismarck wrote: "Bleichröder put at my disposal the necessary money for war. That was an undertaking which, under the circumstances of those days, when I was almost as close to the gallows as to the throne, compels gratitude."

And while the two men talked or wrote almost daily, Bleichröder continued to see that the accountants paid Bismarck's bills for champagne and cigars. For a contemporary market watcher, it is fun to eavesdrop on the chitchat of the day as conducted by two leading Germans. Railroad issues were the computers and electronics of the day; here is Bismarck getting options on the Berlin-Anhalter Railroad at 148 and the Rhenish Railway at 102. In an environment free of inflation, small profits were ample; 2 and 3 percent were accepted. Russia and America were the growth countries, risky but offering greater profits.

Bismarck defeated the Austrians in 1866 and the French in 1871. He called on Bleichröder to negotiate the reparations. Capital poured into Berlin, then a boom city, doubling its population in seventeen years. German chemistry and German metallurgy became the world leaders.

Bleichröder became a legendary figure, a man who moved in the innermost circles, who knew everything, who had a Midas touch. He had a handsome mansion, set the best table in Berlin, and grew perfect flowers at his country house. Yet this tall, formidable banker seems not to have had much fun; he worked eighteen-hour days and sat on a dozen boards. As soon as his riches became visible he faced outstretched hands, and he was always acting on behalf of his fellow Jews who were in dire straits in Russia and Romania. Junkers who invested in money-losing railroads begged him to step in and somehow get the enterprises turned around. What meant most to Bleichröder was to be accepted. He lobbied for each title and decoration from the emperor, and when he was granted nobility—hereditary nobility, to last forever, through his heirs—he was deeply pleased. He was the first Jew to be able to attach the noble *"von"* to his name.

Bleichröder was the J. P. Morgan of the era of business ascendancy in Germany. The Bleichröder bank financed ventures in Asia, Africa, and America, as well as in Europe. Bleichröder's philanthropies were, if anything, on an even greater scale than Morgan's. He befriended struggling writers and artists, endowed museums, and built Catholic hospitals, Protestant churches, synagogues, and a famous medical center. When Bleichröder died in 1893, the wealth of his family was rivaled only by that of the Krupps.

Bleichröder's success was not without its burdens and penalties. As all booms do, the German boom of the late nineteenth century left some people behind and displaced and brought new values in the wake of the old. Prussia had been a poor farming country, honoring feudal and military virtues; it became the leader of a rich Germany. The envious turned to anti-Semitism, and as the most visible Jew, Bleichröder was the focus of it.

Bleichröder's bank declined slowly after his death and was driven from Germany in 1938 by Hitler. A note of final and tragic irony is revealed by some correspondence in January 1942: A functionary at the Ministry of the Interior in Germany is writing a memo. One can picture a thin-lipped, rabbit-hearted clerk, still new to armbands and cavalry boots. Before him is the petition of *von* Bleichröder, a noble family, one of its members shot down in action in the First World War, another thrice wounded, so proud of their record as Germans— what is to be done about them? The query is answered by SS Obersturmbannführer Adolf Eichmann, who answers that there are no exceptions to the Führer's rules. Curt von Bleichröder, grandson of Bismarck's banker, made it to Switzerland, penniless. The Red Cross gave him a coat.

In an age when business values are triumphant, it is hard to imagine anything else. Like *The Treasure of the Sierra Madre*, *Gold and Iron* has mythic proportions. J. P. Morgan's bank is alive and well, though Bleichröder's is gone from Germany. But *Gold and Iron*, like Ecclesiastes, reminds us that wealth is not always forever.

Mr. Phillips and the Seven Laws of Money

Bankers, it is said, know their possessions. It's a way of thinking. Michael Phillips is an ex-banker, a former vice-president of the Bank of California, who is very much out of the mainstream, but certainly part of another, very consistent, way of thinking. He is unconventional, right off, in appearance: white shoes, white slacks, white sweater. He has gotten into the habit of wearing only white. "People know me around San Francisco that way," he says. Maybe at the bank they wore only black pinstripe suits and this is his reaction. Phillips is remembered in banking circles as one of the developers of Master Charge and of small consumer CDs (certificates of deposit). Then he went off with what I can best call the Whole Earth Catalog Alternate Life-Style, an agreeable mode drenched with the fogs and incense of San Francisco. Having spent a few formative years lending money, Phillips turned to giving it away, as the president of Point, then a small foundation. Somewhere along the way, he and a few collaborators devised the Seven Laws of Money, which grew into a little book of the same name. Recently I called him, and we had dinner in Washington, D.C. I had to lend him a tie to get him into the hotel dining room.

The only reason for coming up with precisely seven laws of money, I think, is that the phrase has a kind of mythic resonance, like the Seven Pillars of Wisdom. (Seven and three are the chief numbers of myth). The atmosphere of Phillips's book is enough to send me into a wonderful polymorphous nostalgia for the sweet reek of the late '60s. Take, for example, the acknowledged contributors to *Seven Laws*. There is Salli Rasberry, who "lived in a large teepee [amid] fog and rolling hills [with her] horse and an eleven-year-old daughter." There is a gentleman identified only as Jug 'n' Candle, who scored perfectly on a calculus examination after merely flipping through the text, who has two children, Brother and Sparrow, and "who once had a top secret cryptographic clearance, and became a wandering poet after dealing psychedelics at his top secret job in L.A." Ah, were we ever all so young? Brother and Sparrow indeed; once, in wandering through the counterculture, I met a woman who had named her children River and Ocean.

The flavor of the Seven Laws might thus be called Late '60s Bay Area Buddhist. Yet the Seven Laws, I think, hold up very well, and I would pass them along much more readily than I would the more materialistic prognostications of the financial evangelicals in our midst. I do not mean to repeat the Seven Laws and their Corollaries completely, but you will get the style if I tell you the Sixth Law: You Can Never Really Receive Money as a Gift. "A gift of money is really a contract . . . that is satisfactory to the giver." It seems obvious once you hear it; did money from home, for example, ever really come free? There Is No Such Thing as a Free Lunch could easily be one of the Seven Laws. Or take the First Law, which says Do It! Money Will Come When You Are Doing the Right Thing. That does not mean that money will come if you stay in bed late or smoke dope on the beach. It has to do with separating your worries about survival and your fantasies about money from how you mobilize your energy and time. It also has to do with defining your goals and perfecting your skills. Phillips's First Law is derived from the Buddhist notion of right livelihood—one that harms no one and provides satisfaction for the practitioner.

And what of the '80s?

"Very different from earlier decades," said Phillips. "For those of us raised in more bountiful times, this competitive era is depressing, and it leaves me feeling alone and vulnerable.

"First, inflation moves the average income into higher tax brackets.

"The second problem for younger people is that a couple borrowing for a home can expect to spend more than twice as much of its income for housing as the previous generation did. Even with both a husband and wife working, the pressures are still great because inflation has wiped out all the gains made since the middle '60s. The strategy that many young people are adopting is to fight their way into the newly crowded business schools, hoping to hone their competitive skills as they climb the corporate ladder. But the corporate ladder itself is wobbly. The industries in which the young people are trying to get ahead are themselves beset by high costs for money. Even more, they face competition from all over the world. Japanese products, for example, have come to dominate our electronic and high-tech markets with higher-quality design standards and better prices."

"So what should we do?" I asked.

"My response has been to lighten up on possessions, to spend more energy on my friends, and to try to look at the world as a home territory. After counseling private clients about their money, I began to see a pattern both in the young M.B.A.s starting work at Texas Instruments and in the retirees phoning from the docks of their vacation cruises. Their common drive is to collect objects: a house, a ski condo, a Cape Cod retreat. And cars: BMW sedans, Ford Mustangs, Toyotas, Porsches. And then all the stereos, furnishings, artwork, skis, apparel, scubas, and so on that fill those houses. The effect of all of the accumulation is to make people prisoners of their possessions. People have to spend a great deal of time on maintenance—remembering to call the plumber, replace light bulbs, fix the clocks, rent something out to someone, keep a record of the repair cost, and so on—nearly every day. Ordinary, hardworking people spend their lives like glorified bag ladies in our bigger cities, the ones who are carefully sorting out the trash in the trash cans, carrying their precious finds with them in bags."

"And so?" I said.

"So when you've seen enough of this, you take action yourself. What I did was, very consciously, to cut down the number of objects I own. I now own less than two hundred and fifty objects. That counts each dish, each fork, each knife, each screwdriver, and each pair of shoes as one item. Each house, each computer terminal, each book, and each towel is one item. I don't include objects at my office because those are the tools of the trade. Except for my house (which I rent out to someone else), my possessions all fit in and on one car. Traveling is easy, moving to a new apartment is easy. If I get a new possession, I give away some other possession.

"Now, this is not a new way to live. It is just a new way to live in this society, which focuses on acquiring objects. I just don't want to be the upper-middle-class equivalent of a bag lady.

"The value in the '80s of having few objects is to have a feeling of clearheadedness and lack of clutter, a wide-open range of choice for future life, and a living space in which my aesthetics are sharp, vigorous, and positive—instead of the cluttered, romantic, over-powering, and demanding atmosphere in the typical households around me. So the lack of possessions helps me to face a lonely era with a light, positive feeling."

"And you are doing this as a working householder?" I asked.

"I have a girlfriend, an ex-wife, three children, and my job as business manager of the Glide Memorial United Methodist Church. But I am not really doing this alone. The other part of the equation is friends. I am deliberately making less money and working fewer hours so that I can spend more time with friends. I use my money and resources to help my family and friends as much as possible. When I travel on speaking tours, especially overseas, I take friends with me, using my speaking fees to pay their way. In my community we share as much as possible and have created a 'friends' property trust. The trust is a secured room where a dozen of us store objects we use less than once a month, like gardening equipment, skis, camping gear, scuba equipment, special tools, and musical instruments. We all borrow from the trust as we would from a library. The concept is a combination of fewer personal objects and stronger friendship ties.

"Again, this is not such a new idea; it just seems radical in this society at this time. But I see a lot of social upheaval in the years ahead, and having strong friendships is a form of personal security."

Phillips and Salli Rasberry have just brought out a new book, *Honest Business,* which applies community values to business goals. Phillips's ideas seem un-American only if you forget some early American history. The center of the old New England towns—the green park—was called the common. A highway culture does not have a common. The social activities of those early Americans were based on the idea of mutual help: barn-raisings, husking bees, and sewing circles.

Perhaps these ideas will turn out to be as naive as the communes that the '60s children tried. Not many of us will live with fewer than 200 objects if each fork, each pair of socks, and each fountain pen counts as one. But there is something about Phillips's philosophy that is challenging to us. It makes us think, just for a moment.

Why Mort's Apartment Is Worth $8.5 Million

An acquantance of mine, Mort Zuckerman, just bought an apartment in Manhattan. It is a very nice apartment, on three floors—a triplex—with four bedrooms. Mort paid $8.5 million for the apartment. I'm not telling tales out of school here; there was a squib in the paper about it, since this was the highest price paid for a New York apartment, and real estate brokers like to talk. Mort is a

Boston-based real estate developer who has done very well, and who surfaced beyond the world of real estate when he bought *The Atlantic* magazine and, more recently, *U.S. News & World Report.*

The $8 million apartment is a social artifact, one of those little scraps of evidence that future historians may use to determine what the 1980s were like. At the turn of the century, the steel boys from Pittsburgh came to New York flush with cash, built themselves mansions on Fifth Avenue, and gave parties that recalled the days of Roman splendor. Today, spending on this scale has become fashionable again. We also have an increasingly divided society—students who go into business careers can make as much money in their first year as the professors who taught them, even though the professors may have been at it for a quarter of a century.

While I was still thinking about Manhattan real estate prices, I ran into Edward Lee Cave, a real estate broker who once headed the luxury residential division of Sotheby's auction house. Cave deals in big money and clearly likes being around it. I asked Cave whether $8.5 million for an apartment was a good investment. New York is full of stories about apartments that sold for $100,000 in 1970 and have been resold this year for $2 million, but an $8.5 million price tag makes everybody take another look at his digs.

"I know that apartment," Cave said. "There's no reason why it couldn't sell for ten or twelve million in a few years."

It seemed to me that $10 million—or even the income on $10 million—would buy not only cars, travel, and furniture, but possibly even a passel of houses or apartments somewhere else.

"Somewhere else is not the point," Cave said. "The fact is that New York is the place to be in the 1980s, the way London was in the 1960s, and Paris was in the 1970s."

Now, New York, as its residents know, is not the most agreeable city in the world to live in. The tiara'd women emerging from fashionable restaurants have to step past small mountains of garbage in plastic bags that stay on the sidewalks until ripe. Some innocent strollers near Bryant Park—right behind the Public Library—were gunned down by disputants in a drug transaction who simply had lousy aim. The citizens of Tokyo may be able to travel to any part of their city without thought for their own safety, but no one has

has ever held that to be true of New York, at least not for the past fifty years.

"New York certainly has its hazards," said Cave. "It has Harlem and all that, but there's always the possibility of making money. New York belongs to the world. It's the new money and the international money. In New York, you enjoy what you've done, what you've achieved so far. And you have to *work*, even women can't just drink at the Colony Club, they have to *do* something. But the best thing about New York is—*you don't have to apologize for being rich.*"

I said I wasn't aware that you had to apologize for being rich anywhere—at least anywhere where the government and the body politic permitted you to keep your wealth.

"In Europe, if you didn't go to the right school, you're out. In Britain, if you're successful, you're looked down upon. They don't want to see you spending money; it's all right to inherit it, but don't show it. The Europeans and the South Americans began to discover New York in the '70s. In New York, you can wear beautiful clothes. You can wear jewelry. You can entertain beautifully, the wives and children are well educated and attractive, and it doesn't matter who your grandfather was.

"In Paris or Rome, you can be targeted and in physical jeopardy if you're rich. I mean, they slash the tires of your Rolls, they scratch *'Salaud'* on your car. I was in Madrid, in my dinner jacket, and my chauffeur said, 'Turn up your coat collar, sir, it's dangerous.' He wouldn't take me until I did.

"On Fifth Avenue, all those doormen in white gloves aren't just there for show, they're security. In Paris there are no doormen, but there are often armed guards inside the buildings. The fact is, New York is the only great city in the world where you don't have to worry about being rich."

I asked Cave what it takes to live in New York, on his level of real estate.

"What we're talking about is the kind of apartments that aren't built anymore, with thick walls, parquet floors, high ceilings. I'd say for three bedrooms and three baths, you need a million. That's a lower floor with a lousy view on Park Avenue. On Fifth Avenue, three million. And that has to be cash—the good buildings don't let you finance. You have to have at least three times the purchase price in liquid assets, on a financial statement. And you have to pass the co-op board, which isn't easy.''

Couldn't this market go down? What about new buildings being built?

"There are new buildings being built that help meet the demand, but they have thin walls and boxlike rooms. That's all right for the fellow who doesn't have any real money but makes three or four hundred thousand a year. Those apartments could get overbuilt, but the real luxury market will always remain. If tax reform passes, that would hurt. Deductions for interest and taxes are very important to my people.

"And if the national economy turned down, that could affect it too. But I'd be surprised to see the market go down more than twenty percent.''

The unapologetic rich are not the only factor behind skyrocketing real estate in Manhattan. New York is a city where the municipal regulations have almost strangled the building of middle-class residential real estate. Rent control and rent stabilization permit people to stay in apartments far below the market rates, and building codes and union practices produce building costs that are very high.

Needless to say, New York is poor as well as rich. There is a large population on welfare, and there are people who have no apartments at all. Some of them sleep in large shelters, and some sleep on the sidewalks not far at all from the $1 million apartments with the poor views.

I think that the price of these New York apartments is telling us something—something even more than that rent restrictions aren't working, and that building costs are high. It is just one expression of the increasing velocity at which financial paper is changing hands. The raiders and the arbitrageurs and the rest of the financial community are changing the ownership of parts of American industry. The plants and the mills and the offices are still out there, but the ownership changes hands and the paper flies.

Even when there is no changing of hands, financial paper still moves at high velocity. For example: Ted Turner decided to make a move on CBS. To defend itself, CBS issued some debt and bought back some of its own stock (a "restructuring" to push the stock to a more "realistic" level, in the jargon—a price level that might deter a raider). Then, to service the new high level of debt, CBS had to fire or retire five hundred of its staffers. Some had been there a long time. Some were told in the morning to clean out their desks by the afternoon.

Just getting the defenses in order kept the lawyers working late. And getting that debt sold kept the investment bankers—and even the financial printers—up all night. They were well paid for their efforts, paid well enough to go looking for an apartment where the doorman wears white gloves, if that is their desire.

I'm not sure what happened to the apartments of the CBS staffers. Maybe they got other jobs and stayed put. Their problem was that they were at the wrong level of the company at this point in the company's—and America's—social history. Michel Bergerac, on the other hand, was the president of Revlon who defended Revlon against the attack of a raider. He lost and, like the CBS staff members, Bergerac was bounced. He was forced to give up his corporate Boeing 727 complete with a bedroom, kitchen, backgammon board, and gun rack, but he had a "golden parachute" of exit rewards totaling $35 million—enough to keep him safely in the territory of the doorman. No "golden parachutes" on the CBS staff level, though.

Takeovers are the big story in the stock market, and the raider likes to count on the target company's own cash. When he succeeds in his takeover, he can use the cash to help pay the debts he has piled up in the takeover process. Law firms count fees in the millions from this activity, investment bankers in the hundreds of millions. All good stuff for the real estate brokers.

But I wonder. In ten years, will the apartments on Fifth Avenue really sell for $10 million? Will the bag people still be sleeping on the sidewalk grates a block away? Will New York still be the great city where you don't apologize for being rich? Will the Rollses purr unslashed and unmarked? And will the white-gloved doormen still peer out vigilantly from their frontier posts?

Getting Noticed, the Metropolitan Way

There was once a man in New York who had a magnificent house and entertained lavishly. The house itself was a mansion on Gramercy Park originally built by one of the great families of New York. As a young man, I went to dinner a couple of times at this house. The interior suggested a fantasy of an English country house; everything was leather and brass and rich maroon carpets. There were so many antique clocks that a specialist came weekly to wind them, and the polishing of the brass was a major housekeeping effort. On the walls were hunting scenes and portraits, and the dining room was furnished with an imposing refectory table.

The house was owned by an enormously successful PR executive, Ben Sonnenberg, and its tone—from the brass knocker on the front door to the British butler who greeted you when you knocked—was designed to impress clients. "A fellow becomes head of a company," Ben would say, "and he's worked hard making ratchets or widgets or whatever, but nobody's ever heard of him. So we see that he gets heard of." To this end, Ben would invite writers and editors from news magazines and business magazines (hence my own presence) to meet the newcomer, who would be described as a dynamic genius in whatever he did, and soon *Time* and *Newsweek* and *Business Week* would have stories on J. J. Smedley, the dynamic ratchet maker. But J. J. Smedley—and Mrs. J. J. Smedley— also wanted to *arrive* on the New York scene, and to that end, Ben would stroke his white walrus mustache thoughtfully and then make a plan for what he would call "cleansing the money." It was not that the ratchet-industry money was illegal; it was simply not old and respectable enough. So Ben would chart a course through the institutions and charities of New York whereby, through the spending of their new wealth, the Smedleys would be considered to have arrived. The Morgan Library would receive a check, and Mrs. Smedley would go on the board; the tone-deaf J. J. would develop an interest in the Metropolitan Opera, and J. J. himself would follow his checks onto that board.

Ben died some years ago, and the magnificent house was sold to a perfume tycoon. The collection of clocks and the other carefully gathered antiques were auctioned off. But the process of "cleansing the money" is still very much extant—again, not with illegal connotations; it's just that making money, spending money, and wanting to be somebody with money have established the tone of the times. Those without any money at all can be made to feel positively guilty. A recent cover story in *U.S. News & World Report* tells "How Ordinary People Get Rich: Who They Are—How They Did It."

Ironically, while the United States has had trouble manufacturing products from clothes to compact-disk players competitively on the world market, we have seen an orgy of paper-shuffling with the existing assets: takeovers, "junk bonds," the "restructuring" of companies—exercises that push the prices of stocks up and have helped create a glittering new frontier.

Felix Rohatyn is an investment banker, a senior partner of Lazard Frères and the adviser to RCA in its merger with General Electric. He was given much of the credit for the financial program that brought New York City back from the lip of bankruptcy. No one has been more at the center of the merger-and-takeover exercises, and Rohatyn makes somewhere north of $2 million a year, perhaps considerably north. But Rohatyn maintains a skeptical and faintly gloomy air, perhaps because, having immigrated to the United States as a boy in the 1940s, he has an eye for the impermanence of glitz. "We used to have entrepreneurs making money by making things," he said to me recently. "Now we have money making money. Paper entrepreneurs are inheriting the U.S., and this unleashes values that are a bit gaudier than those of twenty or thirty years ago.

"I have never seen the kind of money being spent that people are spending today. It is conspicuous consumption without conscience. We have had other periods of this—after a good market in the 1960s we saw some of it—but the lavish amounts spent on co-op apartments and houses in the Hamptons exceed previous eras. Or maybe I'm just getting more sensitive to it. The Concorde is an expensive airplane ride—maybe twice the business-class fare—and I frequently see women who are flying to Paris for a fitting of their clothes, and flying back on the next Concorde."

Spending money is not new on the American metropolitan scene. At the turn of the century, the new steel-rich of Pittsburgh, the Fricks and Carnegies, built incredible mansions on New York's Fifth Avenue, almost all of which have become museums or other institutions. But the activities in "restructuring" and arbitrage are creating another tier of the rich. In Pantry Pride's takeover of Revlon, more than $100 million in fees was generated. No new jobs or products were created, but $2.7 billion in paper traded hands.

Ben Sonnenberg would have loved it—a whole new crowd to be led up the ladder of the "right" institutions in the quest for the bliss of social acceptance.

"If you really want to make yourself known," says a leading fundraiser, "you start with a check to the right board, and you get yourself on it. I'd say a million would be openers. You try to get in with the class acts—Brooke Astor, say—but after that, the older money, you know, Rockefellers and Dukes. And then the big rich who have just come to town, Ann Getty and the Texas Basses."

The caterers have names like the Upper Crust, Glorious Food, and the Silver Palate. They charge up to $200 a person for dinner at a charity bash, but the dinners can raise $1,000 a ticket. If you want to dine out on this circuit in New York, you can easily spend $500,000 a year.

This distressed Rohatyn and his wife, Elizabeth.

"We simply couldn't go out to any more of the golden galas," says Rohatyn. "Here we have a city with extremes of rich and poor, and everybody wants to go to the same places. You can go out three times a night in New York. The Metropolitan Museum parties in the Temple of Dendur, the Metropolitan Opera, the Public Library. And these are lavish parties. The Philharmonic gave a ball, a kind of evening in old Vienna, and there were actually rehearsals if you wanted them to teach you how to waltz. The most glamorous organizations—Lincoln Center, the Museum of Modern Art, the Memorial Sloan-Kettering Cancer Center—can raise almost any amount of money they want. But meanwhile, the community-based programs are starving. The settlement houses, the shelters for the homeless, even the Y, have trouble getting attention and raising money. If the subject is brought up, fundraisers say: 'That's the kind of party people will pay up for. There are no great private parties anymore. This is the way you get a million dollars from a party.' The corporate world goes for the top institutions. The CEOs want to turn out in black tie and have the other CEOs turn up. They want to make a splash that makes people notice them—and so that splash has to be for a prestige institution.''

Rohatyn's wife runs a settlement house that was having trouble raising money. A *New York Times* reporter wrote a story about how the Rohatyns thought the charity dollars should be spread to the less fashionable institutions.

"The response came from all over the country.'' said Rohatyn, "and it was heart-warming. But it didn't come from the people who like to build on these big parties.''

While there are cycles in American history, periods in which business values are more pervasive than in others, Washington does help set the tone. The view of our particular administration is that in the marketplace lies the ultimate truth. Even Paul Volcker, as chairman of the Federal Reserve, was criticized by the administration when he tried to impose limitations on some junk bonds.

The parties that flow from the money, and much of the money itself, now come from the same sources and the same attitudes—that all is well, that the marketplace rules benignly, that if people want junk bonds and takeovers, they should have them. Perhaps the key point is how our society views the corporation, its owners, and its responsibilities. A worker may work for the same company for twenty years. A manager may live in the community, support its schools, and work to integrate the company and the community. But the owner reigns supreme; it is up to him whether the plant is shut down, the worker laid off, the manager sent somewhere else. Yet the owner these days is seldom the founder with the big house up on the hill. Technically, the owner (or at least one of the owners) is probably a pension fund or mutual fund, represented by a young portfolio manager who shares neither history nor loyalty with the company and who will sell out in five minutes if that will improve his track record. Or the owner may even be a group of arbitrageurs seeking the fastest return possible on a very swift turnover—measured in hours, not in months or years.

The marketplace has served us very well, but on both the corporate and the social scenes it seems to me that the sense of community now missing is a basic element whose absence we've only just begun to feel.

The Closing of the American Mind

I have been rereading two of the best-selling books of 1987. Each was a sleeper whose success astonished both authors and publishers. One book is *The Closing of the American Mind* by Allan Bloom, a longtime professor of social thought, a teacher at the University of Chicago, and a translator of *Plato's Republic*. Bloom's book is an analysis of intellectual trends in the past half century, a lament that American universities no longer provide students with the great tradition of philosophy and literature in Western civilization, and a cry of alarm that most students aren't even aware of the basic core of our civilization and aren't hungry to learn about it in the way many students were a generation back. Such a lament may not be rare, but it is certainly rare to find it become a number-one national best-seller.

The other book is *The Great Depression of 1990*, by Dr. Ravi Batra, an economist of Indian origin at Southern Methodist University in Dallas, Texas. Batra's book is an economic treatise, offbeat in its reflection on the historical determinism of a little-known Indian thinker named Prabhat Ranjan Sarkar. Batra's book predicts "the worst economic turmoil in history . . . more cataclysmic than any mankind has yet seen." Our society is moving, says Batra, to a warrior age. "The acquisitors grow richer and richer at the expense of other classes," he writes. "Eventually, things become so wretched that angry warriors and intellectuals rise in rebellion and with the help of laborers bring an end to the age of acquisitors . . . . In the warrior age the army, headed by a dictator . . . controls the government as well as society. Political authority is centralized in the form of an absolute government, people are highly disciplined, family ties are morally binding, women well respected, and so on."

This cheerful prospect is only a couple of years away, according to Batra's pattern of business cycles. We have "a great depression every third or sixth decade," he says. Before the depression, the disparity in wealth grows greater between the rich and poor, and in fact the disparity is one cause of the turmoil. Excessive speculation precedes the depression; the rich get richer because stock prices go too high.

The success of Batra's book is a little easier to understand than the success of Bloom's book, and I know a bit about it because I watched it happen. Batra originally published the book himself with a vanity press in 1985, in three limited print runs. One night Dennis Sherva, a security analyst at the investment-banking firm of Morgan Stanley, was browsing in a bookstore in an airport. He spotted Batra's book, took it home, and read it.

"It was interesting," Sherva says. "You always have to look out for the odd ideas, because the conventional ideas are already out there, and here was this book—the title, of course, got me first—predicting radical changes based on long cycles and an Indian philosopher. So I sent it over to Barton Biggs."

Biggs is the chief investment strategist for Morgan Stanley and is also a thoughtful and skilled writer. He writes a weekly essay in Morgan Stanley's research bulletin, which goes out to about eighteen thousand investors. Biggs's daughter, Wende, did an eighteen-page summary of the Batra book, which Morgan Stanley made available to its customers on request. There were more than one thousand requests, and soon Batra was invited to the investment seminars where brokers trot out their ideas for institutional clients.

"Batra was not really impressive," said one analyst in attendance. "Everybody has agoraphobia after the market has climbed so steeply, so they are looking for any glimmer of wisdom, but here was this man calling for the stock of the largest corporations to be distributed to their employees and the profits to be distributed to the masses. That didn't fly."

I asked Sherva if he ever thought about what he had started. "There's nothing in that book I would act on, but the thought process is interesting," he said. "I guess doomsday books must sell well."

The success of Batra's book is due at least partly to the anxious seeking of money managers for ideas that will put them a step ahead of the game. Unlike many book buyers, they are not price-sensitive. They make a lot of money, and if a book will help give them a competitive advantage, they buy it quickly, even if in the end it turns out not to be directly relevant. Or maybe there are people concerned about the age of the acquisitor.

I've seen books about long business cycles before, and I doubt the immediate relevance of Prabhat Ranjan Sarkar, though I haven't read him in the original. We *do* now have extremes of wealth and a murky fear of depression, and I think *The Great Depression of 1990* mobilized these anxieties with its title, but serious readers will be disappointed.

The success of Bloom's book is more surprising. For one thing, it is a rather dense work. It assumes we know what Plato said about music ("the barbarous expression of the soul") and what Nietzsche said about Plato. Bloom rolls along like what he is, the classic liberal arts teacher—the kind I had and I hope many people had—who lectures in the basic freshman humanities courses. On a single page he can write, "Engels . . . said that the classless society would last, if not forever, a very long time. This reminds us of Dottore Dulcamare in *The Elixir of Love* . . ." and, a few sentences later, "The way we digest the European things is well illustrated by the influence of Thomas Mann's *Death in Venice* on American consciousness."

American liberal arts colleges are failing their students, Bloom writes, because they focus the students on careers or offer incoherent course selections. The student has a brief time to discover himself, to learn "there is a great world beyond the little one he knows, to experience the exhilaration of it and digest enough of it to sustain himself . . . if he is to have any hope of a higher life. The importance of these years for an American cannot be overestimated. They are civilization's only chance to get him." Bloom has a point. I once had a friend who sent me an ironic postcard signed "Tadzio," but references like that are lost on the MTV generation. Universities sold out in the '60s to special-interest groups, says Bloom, and they still do. They teach what sells, says Bloom.

We take for granted that they teach what sells; their costs are going up, and with the end of the baby boom, they are scrambling for customers. If you're scuttling around trying to find what sells, says Bloom, you don't teach eternal truths.

I asked Bloom, if Americans are so ignorant that they are confused by a comparison of Hobbes and Freud, and lack grounding in other common references, then who made his book a best-seller?

"I admit that is a surprise. I never had any thought this book would do what it has done," he said. "When I look at the best-seller list and see this book up there, I can't believe that it is me. There's probably a vulgar reason for its popularity—you know, all you need to know about the history of philosophy in one book—or maybe there really are a lot of people worried, as I am, about a crisis in literacy, not just literacy in the sense of reading and writing but in familiarity with things that open up the world.''

But Hegel and Nietzsche and Fichte all rolled together in a paragraph?

''That's a good liberal arts teaching technique. People get the point of what you're saying. But if you say, 'As Hegel said,' you hope they will get curious and look it up.''

Bloom's book began as an article in *National Review* called ''Our Listless Universities.''

''I don't really think of myself as a writer. I was writing the story of a teacher, of students today. It's a bleak picture with some sublime experiences.''

Why bleak?

''Because the material you feed to souls is going, is gone. The element of tradition is gone. We've been cutting three thousand years of tradition—Plato, Hegel, Aristotle, the Bible—both the knowledge of them and the taste for them are disappearing. We have a one-cylinder intellectual life.''

But hasn't this always been true—that each generation thinks the next one is going to the dogs?

''Yes, but sometimes these laments are true. There really were Dark Ages after Greece and Rome, when the Vandals burned the libraries and the barbarians were the conquerors. The problem of civilization always was going to be an American problem, it's always the problem of a pragmatic democracy rather than an aristocracy.''

Bloom laments not only the decline of classic readings, but of concern with what he calls higher moral principles. ''Students are less hungry,'' he says. ''People have to *believe* you can study good and bad, and what is happiness, the great moral themes, but if these are subjective givens, you can't. We've gotten used to thinking that what feels good is right.

''This was the first country with a youth culture complete in itself. Look at all the attention given to teenagers. Youth used to be a preparation for adulthood, but it is not now, and teenagers don't feel they're growing up into anything. Rock music is as deep as you get.''

What ought to be done?

''I'm not particularly prescriptive. A few people coming to their senses could make a great deal of difference. I'm talking about the top twenty or thirty institutions in this country—can they educate civilized men and women? Is there reflection on moral life? I think they're more worried about serving the masters of business and government.''

With the help of Saul Bellow, another Chicagoan who is a close friend, Bloom was encouraged to expand his article into a book.

''I had no inkling it would succeed like this—perhaps just one inkling. Just before the book came out I gave a talk at a major university, at which I presented a lot of the ideas, and I was worried about the response. The audience included many of the parents, I gathered many of them divorced parents, worried about their children, worried that they had lost the authority to deal with their children, and worried that there was no real authority the children would respect. So maybe parents worrying about education is part of my audience.

''I know that students today are obsessed with money and careers, but I think they will throw over money for the sense that their lives will be interesting. That's always been true of Americans. Students should take away some recognition that there are high, noble things to counter the egalitarian things they hear. Not all thoughts or ideas are equal. You have to look up to something splendid.''

In the mid-nineteenth century, the British general Sir Charles Napier, campaigning on the northwest frontier of India in the province of Sind, could send the one-word telegram ''Peccavi'' and know that Parliament, schooled in Latin, would appreciate both the news and the pun. (*Peccavi* translates as *''I have sinned.''*) A generation ago *The New Yorker* could run a parody of, say, a Hemingway novel, confident that its readers knew the original well enough to find the parody funny. Becky Sharp and Anna Karenina were women known well enough to my parents to be used as reference points, like cousins. My children and their friends say, ''Can you identify three heavy-metal bands?'' when asked about

Anna Karenina. Today if you want a common reference point, the only safe ground is television commercials. You can use "Don't leave home without it," but not much from a survey course on Western civilization.

The problem with Bloom's thesis is that it doesn't go nearly far enough. Compared with previous generations, the culture is fragmented. It isn't just that the leading universities don't coherently transmit the traditional values of the West. The more serious problem is that students learn from television and their peers, rather than from respected teachers and ministers and rabbis and parents. They are suffused in the ephemeral and the superficially exciting. It is astounding to me that 52 percent of high school seniors cannot identify the most important Amercian President of this century, Franklin D. Roosevelt. It is mind-boggling that a near majority cannot place the discovery of America by Columbus within 250 years. Irangate got thousands of hours on television, but I doubt that many Americans could find Iran on a map, name the language spoken there, or detail what the fuss is about. So the question is not only "What values do Americans value?" The larger question is "What is the future of the Republic if its citizens don't understand the context in which it operates?"

Serious Money

Once upon a time, I wrote a novel called *The Wheeler Dealers,* set on Wall Street. A handsome Texas oil promoter came to New York and met a pretty woman working as a security analyst. In the movie, James Garner played the Texan, and Lee Remick was the analyst. Women on Wall Street were so unusual that when Lee did a good job, her boss slapped her on the back and said, "That's my boy!" To court Remick, Garner got involved in the company she was researching, and together they planted rumors of mergers and takeovers and the stock of Universal Widget skyrocketed. The SEC got on to the case, but no one was hurt and Garner and Remick drove off into the sunset together. *The Wheeler Dealers* opened at Radio City Music Hall, was a modest success, and can occasionally be seen on

TV at three-thirty in the morning. It was made in the early '60s, but you couldn't do that movie today.

The Wheeler Dealers was a comedy. In later years, it was to seem like a good-humored feminist appeal. High jinks on Wall Street could be considered funny because the rest of America was solid, dependable, and middle-class. There were no X-rated movies and no drugs in the schools. The United States dominated the world economy and the Japanese had yet to send their cars to America. OPEC was a joke, a few Arabs in their kaffiyehs, passing resolutions that carried no weight. On the real Wall Street you had to love the game, because you didn't make money for many years. Lee Remick might have made $10,000 a year as an analyst, as would any young lawyer. The money on Wall Street was made by the partners— silver-haired patricians in their fifties who all belonged to the same clubs and left the office at four.

Great companies stood astride the American scene, GM, Alcoa, Gulf, Union Carbide. Companies like these were run by portly, whiskey-drinking WASPs who played golf with Eisenhower. It was unthinkable that any of these great companies could be taken over. And no one used Wall Street—or business—as a background for novels or movies. A Martian who watched American movies would scarcely know that Wall Street existed; my comedy was an anomaly. Otherwise, the money world slumbered as an artistic backwater.

But the world changed. In the '70s, OPEC choked the supply of oil, and when the West failed to respond, the price of oil went up fifteen times. Hundreds of billions went to the Middle East, came back to New York banks as deposits, and went out again as loans to Latin America. The money turners kept the change and began to prosper. Thatcher was reelected in Britain; Reagan was elected in the United States. Deregulation was the theme; the markets knew best. Junk bonds were invented, credit was easy to come by, and no government wanted to risk its tenure by limiting the supply of money too much. Money flowed. Suddenly it became possible to raid and take over quite large companies. Raiders like T. Boone Pickens became media heroes, and business magazines featured takeover artists who had never seen the Ivy League. Gulf Oil disappeared and Union Carbide defended itself to the point of anorexia. The M.B.A.s who did the scut work for Wall Street mergers could make bonuses in the hundreds of thousands. New hires at the prestigious New York law firm of Cravath, Swaine & Moore recently started at $72,000 fresh from law school; Cravath said they had to offer that much or lose bright new scholars to the investment banks. A generation grew up for which money was a way of life, and recently the artists—the playwrights and filmmakers—began to discover Wall Street and the business world.

Oliver Stone is the man who gave us *Platoon*, the wonderfully gripping story of one grunt in Vietnam. Stone's father once wrote a literate Wall Street newsletter, and not long ago Stone released his latest film, *Wall Street*. Charlie Sheen, who also starred in *Platoon*, plays a young salesman in a Wall Street firm, making cold calls on unknown prospects. But he's ambitious. He sends a box of cigars as a birthday present to the notorious corporate raider Gordon Gekko. That gets him an audience. To ingratiate himself, the young man gives some inside information to the raider about the airline for which his father works as a mechanic. The raider steps forward like Mephistopheles and offers the Faustian novice the material world— fast cars, sleek blondes, big bucks. "If you're not inside, you're outside," Gekko says. What does young Bud want? He wants to be a "player," he wants his own jet. And so he becomes not just a number cruncher but an industrial spy, dressing up as a maintenance man so he can open the files of a target company at night.

"Why wreck a company?" Bud asks at one point.

"Because it's wreckable!" says the raider. "That is *right*. I create nothing," he adds proudly, *"I own."*

Michael Douglas makes Gordon Gekko almost plausible—and almost likable. In one scene, he appears at the annual meeting of Teldar Paper—a company he is trying to take over—and points out, as Boone Pickens did with Phillips Petroleum, that there are thirty-three layers of vice presidents. But Gekko's speech itself is one that has been given in real life by that Gatsby of our age, Ivan Boesky: *"Greed works,* greed is right. . . . greed in all its forms, greed for life, money, love, knowledge . . ."* The raider gets a standing ovation, and Boesky's place in cultural history is assured.

So young Bud gets the sleek blonde and the East Side Manhattan apartment, and he learns to be as ruthless as his mentor, even to double-crossing the raider. The sleek blonde walks out, Bud's father has a heart attack, Bud learns that human values count and money is not everything.

Would a serious corporate raider really respond to the gift of cigars from an unknown youthful salesman with clichéd ideas? Would a young man really put his father's company in play?

I thought this a bit absurd, but what has happened in the Roaring '80s is even more absurd. A merger specialist in his thirties, Dennis Levine, not content with a $1 million annual salary, risks his career to make even more and ends up going to jail. Ivan Boesky rakes in hundreds of millions on inside information, and when the SEC moves in, tucks a microphone under his tie and walks around so he can implicate the people who gave it to him. And Ilan Reich, not content with a $500,000-a-year law partner's slot at the age of thirty-two, supplies the information on forthcoming mergers and goes to jail. *Wall Street* is absurd, but it is right out of the headlines.

London's financial district, the City, has followed Wall Street into the promised land of the takeover and the fast buck. London has a play, *Serious Money,* by Caryl Churchill, a talented playwright who in another play, *Cloud Nine,* had her characters change genders and eras. Like *Wall Street, Serious Money* is full of computers, shouted numbers, a takeover king, arbitrageurs, double crosses, venality, and megascale greed. It owes something to the irreverence of Restoration comedy, and something to Brecht, but it has its own manic, original tone. For one thing, it is in verse, mostly in rhymed couplets.

The sleek blonde in this play, Scilla, is no adornment. She is a trader on the floor at LIFFE, the London International Financial Futures Exchange.

> On the floor of LIFFE the commodity is money.
> You can buy and sell money, you can buy
> and sell absence of money, debt, which used
> to strike me as funny.

Scilla's well-to-do City father may have wanted her to be a proper lady, but she wants to play as hard as the men.

If we've a Porsche in the garage and champagne in the glass,
We don't notice there's a lot of power still held by men of
Daddy's class.

The takeover king, Corman, needs blocks of stock from the
arbitrageurs, and the top arb is Marylou Baines, a tough American.

Marylou Baines
Was originally a poor girl from the plains.
She set out to make whatever she wanted hers
And now she's one of America's top arbitrageurs

(second only to Boesky).
Marylou, in fact, admires Boesky, whose "greed" speech appears here, as it did in *Wall Street*. Marylou says:

He overstepped some regulations, sure, but
. . . the guy's no criminal.
Like he said about his own amazing wealth,
"Greed is all right. Greed is good. You can be
greedy and still feel good about
yourself."

All of this is done in a kind of cacophony, and in British accents
not always easy to understand. The chorus of traders chants:

Money-making money-making money-making caper
Do the fucking business . . . and bang it down on paper

Corman, the raider, wants to be respected. His PR lady, who
says, "Sexy greedy *is* the late '80s," advises him to have a girlfriend, and to sweeten his image by sponsoring the National Theater
to position himself for a knighthood. (Boesky served on theater
boards. Corman gets his knighthood.)

The floor traders on the LIFFE make dance of their hand signals
and turn their trading jargon into a rap number in which one trader
describes the process as "a cross between roulette and Space
Invaders."

The characters of *Serious Money* aren't rounded or real, any more than those of *Wall Street* are. But the rhythms of *Serious Money*, the sexy, slangy, raunchy verses, the shouted numbers, the million-a-year salaries, the flashing computers, all produce an experience that is a distillation of the late '80s.

In universities and boardrooms and government offices, savants are trying to figure out what has been going on. Why the boom? Why the crash? What will follow? It is fashionable to say that we now have one global market. We wake up in New York or Los Angeles and tune in to hear how the day started in Tokyo and London. Money is not green engraved paper, it is a blinking light in a computer, a shouted fraction between two traders on a phone who never had a day of Money and Banking, Economics 141. The money moves faster than the rules of any institution or any one government.

In the literature of the '80s, no one begins with the basic inno-cence which, in *The Wheeler Dealers,* allowed comic misunder-standings to play as counterpoint. The world is simply tough and moves fast, and the characters are tough—the Thatcher "top girls" in Britain, the partners slicing each other's throats, the raiders look-ing for prey. There are no heroes, and tragedy would be very difficult. You really can use the setting of frenzied money only for melodrama or savage satire. For decades, we saw businessmen only as occasional cardboard villains in Hollywood TV series; now they are still villains, but more interesting, and now we are paying attention to the scene itself, not just conjuring a villain for a soap opera. Someone once said that artists are like the canaries the miners used to hang in the mines to warn of noxious gases—and artists have now begun to look at the money frenzy of the '80s. That suggests to me that it is late in the era, for when the canaries start to sing, something is about to happen.

A Profound Change in World History

Einstein made no headlines with his original equation on which the atomic age is based. The technology that produced the Pill, and hence the sexual revolution, was reported only in technical journals when it was first developed. Sometimes the most important and influential events of our time do not appear on the front page or at the top of the TV news.

Now I see evidence of another revolution that will affect our lives, but that is reported only in fragments. Quite simply, in spite of the exploding population of the planet Earth, the production of food is increasing so rapidly that, at least statistically, there is more than enough food.

This is a radical change. Hunger and starvation and famine have been the story of humanity. Even in eighteenth-century France, as Lafayette set off for America, children were abandoned along the roadside because their parents couldn't feed them. Fairy tales tell the story of children ending up in the stewpots of giants because, as cultural historians such as Robert Darnton tell us, meat was so scarce that these thoughts lurked in the dark unconscious of starving populations.

More recently, in East Africa, the consequences of a severe drought were aggravated by parochial politics, by a Marxist colonel moving populations. Some of the major events in the world of music have been benefits for the hungry—Britain's Band Aid; USA for Africa, with the song "We Are the World"—just as sixteen years ago a well-publicized concert was organized for the benefit of the starving in Bangladesh.

We have gotten used to the idea of the starving masses in China— many excellent novels described it. When I was small, my mother told me to finish my dinner and said how many Chinese children would be glad to have it. Now China is not only self-sufficient in grain, it is exporting its excess corn to Japan more cheaply than can our midwestern farmers. The starving of India used to appear on the cover of *The New York Times Magazine,* but last year India had such a surplus of grain that much of it was left to rot; even the storage facilities were full. Bangladesh has become self-sufficient.

Western Europe was once a major importer of food. Now farm surpluses threaten to bankrupt the European Economic Community. The twelve member countries are storing a million and a half tons of excess butter, a million tons of powdered milk, and nearly three quarters of a million tons of beef. A reporter visiting a huge steel cold-storage warehouse found mountains of butter—eighteen hundred tons of it—packed in brown cardboard boxes and stacked all the way to the roof.

These tides of food and grain are appearing as *problems*. For example, two years ago Spain acted to keep out American grain— and the U.S. threatened tariffs and quotas on European wines and cheeses.

What happened? What happened to hunger and starvation? The vast surpluses of the food-producing countries are a function of political process, but even without farm subsidies we are seeing the result of three revolutions, the third of which is the most powerful and is just beginning. The three revolutions have all come within a century, after many centuries in which farming did not change from grandfather to grandson.

The first revolution was simply the substitution of the internal combustion engine for ox and horsepower. In the nineteenth century, Cyrus McCormick devised his mechanical reaper. In 1906, Benjamin Holt put treads on a primitive vehicle and demonstrated it in the mud near Stockton, California. His company became Caterpillar, which produced world-famous machines that could build dams and roads and move across rough country. From other companies came machines that plowed, combined, and harvested mechanically.

That revolution was mechanical; the second was largely chemical and came after World War II. Fertilizers such as ammonium nitrate and diamonium phosphate increased the yield per acre. Pesticides got rid of the beasts that used to eat the crops. The third revolution is going on right now. Francis Crick and James Watson, working at Cambridge University, determined the structure of DNA in 1953. It has taken thirty odd years, but now biotechnology is having an enormous impact. Plant scientists can introduce a gene with a desired trait into a plant cell, and the resulting plant resists diseases, insects, salt, or even bad weather.

Pioneer Hi-bred International is the world's largest developer of seed corn. Pioneer's researchers have introduced bacterial genes into tomatoes and other vegetables. These genes produce proteins toxic to insects. "You can select a one-in-a-million event and get a new plant back," says Dr. Nicholas Frey, its biotech director.

A couple of years ago, I got intrigued with biotechnology and did a show in my public television series about it. Would biotechnology produce cows twice the size of elephants? Would beef become so cheap that McDonald's would have a ten-cent hamburger? Not quite. But what we found was that *plants* were the first frontier. The public worries about the products of biotechnology that affect *people* directly, and some of the public worries about the monkeys and cats that undergo testing in the worldwide pharmaceutical industry. But nobody really worries about a sick tomato plant in a lab, and so the progress in agricultural biotechnology, unhindered by the intense scrutiny that greets substances to be tried on people, has been stupendous. And the profits have grown, too.

The American corn belt now stretches 250 miles farther north than it did just ten years ago—the new breeds of corn are so frost-resistant that corn can be grown where it couldn't be before. Midwestern farmers get *five times* the yield they got just fifty years ago. Seeds and techniques are easily transported, and the results can be seen all over the world. They are even more dramatic than those of the so-called Green Revolution a generation ago, which produced richer crops through cross-breeding that enabled plants to concentrate biological energies into producing, for example, wheat kernels, instead of growing tall.

More than half the world's rice is now planted in high-yielding varieties. China's agricultural production is up 50 percent in eight years. Indonesia, which used to be the world's biggest rice importer, now has millions of tons left over. The Bangladesh wheat crop is up tenfold since the introduction of modern hybrids in the mid-'60s. Governments around the world are searching for empty silos, barges, railroad cars, and airplane hangers in which to store 320 million tons of surplus grain, the most in world history.

In every revolution there are casualties. For my television show, I paid a visit to eastern Nebraska. I went to David City. To get to David City you rent a car in Omaha, drive west past Wahoo, and turn right. I had lunch with the editor of the local paper, I spent time at the diner, I talked to the store owners. David City was hurting; some stores were boarded up, the problems of the farm belt were really visible.

I spent a day with a typical Nebraska farmer, Don B. He is a hardworking, nice guy, with a Christmas-card-picture family. He's brought his sons up in the farming tradition, and they enjoy this way of life. But Don is in trouble. He grows corn and soybeans, and if it weren't for farm subsidies, he couldn't make the payments right now. The Brazilians had planted a million acres of soybeans on the central Cerrado Plateau. Don really didn't know what had hit him.

In any given year, of course, you can have a singular event like a drought. The drought of 1988 was particularly severe in the midwest and made the TV evening news night after night. In the areas of the country where there was ample rain, the farmers got a windfall, because the prices of grains had gone up sharply. Even with new seeds and new techniques in farming, it still has to rain. But the overall *world* production scene didn't change much with the American drought.

In what has become a world economy, the great American seed companies, Pioneer and DeKalb, sell their seeds everywhere. The techniques developed by the International Rice Research Institute in the Philippines are used everywhere. When Oklahoma State develops a new wheat hybrid, it doesn't take it long to get around. Our farm subsidies are $30 billion a year, and some experts think they're out of control. Meanwhile, the Brazilians can land excellent soybeans in New Orleans more cheaply than the Nebraska farmers can.

But does all this mean the end of world hunger? I asked John Hammock, the executive director of OXFAM, an international development and relief organization in Boston.

"Biotech has changed the focus," he said. "The *production* of food is being solved. Now politics and economic systems are the causes of hunger. Civil strife in the Third World is a major cause.

"Everybody knows about Ethiopia because there was a rock concert for Ethiopia and so many television pictures of the starving people. But Ethiopia has had good crops. The hunger in Ethiopia is a *political* problem." The realities of an ongoing civil war—and the absence of sophisticated storage and transportation—have made it difficult if not impossible to move food from Addis Ababa to the northeast. In addition, the rebels have shot down at least one civilian plane and have threatened to shoot down any others that they identify as supply planes.

"If you ship in massive amounts of grain, it can depress the *local* prices. Who will spend the effort to grow wheat if you can take it off a C-130 cargo plane? That puts pressure on the small farmers. Aid to Ethiopia has to be phased out so they will go back to growing their own grains."

One disturbing effect of the Green Revolution was that it led to the concentration of land on larger and larger farms. There are huge economies of scale in fertilizers and chemicals, so it's the bigger farmers who can afford them and are first to use them. Also, most countries subsidize *export* production. Costa Rica had enough grain to feed itself and was exporting beef, but as it lost its small farmers it began to import beans and grains.

"Many countries are dominated by their urban areas, which demand subsidized food," said Hammock. "There are riots if the price of tortillas or bread goes up. But small farmers can't afford to subsidize the city dwellers. I think the conglomeration of farms into giant units has political implications, even for our country.

"We still live in a world where crop failures are possible, and one in which food has become a *policy* problem. Can the people in the developing world afford to *buy* food? How will food be used politically? That's what needs study."

Less than sixty years ago, Herbert Hoover ran for President on the slogan "A chicken in every pot." He did not say *two* chickens in every pot. Chicken on *Sunday* was a luxury, and the thought of chicken once a week seemed bountiful, and a worthwhile goal. Hoover was elected.

Now chicken is a commonplace in our country, and the biotech revolution is still developing. For the entire history of mankind, men and women have had to devote most of their energies to the hunting, growing, tending, and gathering of food. The third revolution has begun, and our planet won't be the same from now on.

8 BAD NEWS, GOOD NEWS

"Do you know what these conferences produce?" said Karen House. "Pessimism!"

K aren is the foreign editor of the *Wall Street Journal,* and she goes to a lot of conferences. So do I. Sometimes we go to the same ones. These are issue-oriented conferences, put on by non-profit foundations, or institutes of universities. They are not sales meetings, the widget convention, designed to produce the sale and exchange of goods, and they are not academic conferences, designed to display papers and job opportunities. They focus on a problem, and some of the problems do make your eyes glaze over.

What can be done about Third World debt? What indeed? There's no doubt about the problem. The Third World owes a trillion dollars, much of it to American banks. (The number rolls off so easily, a trillion dollars. The conference goers file their expense accounts in the hundreds, and compare APEX discounted coach air fares.) If the Third World defaults, a large tube awaits our money center banks that so eagerly loaned the money. So the bankers are there, and so are the government people, because the Fed and the FDIC would have to make sure the crisis did not spread. If the Third World defaulted, would economic chaos follow? Would the Communists follow the chaos? That brings in the State Department. If the Third World has to spend its hard currency earnings for interest and amortization, then it

can't buy American farm machinery and American pharmaceuticals
and American aircraft and American linerboard and American telecommunications equipment. So industry comes too, it's ready to sell.
And the Third Worlders come too, the Mexicans and the Brazilians
and the Argentines have all been to school in the United States, and
the Nigerians and Egyptians in Britain, so they can deliver their papers
just the way they were taught at Stanford and Harvard and the London
School of Economics.

The Brazilians owe a hundred billion and the Mexicans owe a
hundred billion—give or take—and flight capital is two-thirds of the
debt. That is, Señor Delegate's friends, through the '80s, saw inflation coming, and wisely moved their money to Geneva and New
York. So the money is sitting as a *deposit* maybe in the very same
Yanqui bank that is stuck for the *loans* to the very same country!
What a puzzlement!

Somehow, some aircraft and pharmaceuticals and tractors do get
sold, and life goes on, but the conferencegoers can see things aren't
working like they should.

"The situation is grave," says the conference paper. There must
be another conference! So the conferencegoers say to each other:
have a good flight, I hope your boy gets into Stanford, I hope your
girl gets into Guadalajara Medical School, if they want a summer job
interning, let me know.

The conferences *seem* to produce pessimism because the problem
is still there, and the conference summary says, "The situation is
serious." It *is* serious. But what gets done doesn't always appear in
the minutes. What doesn't appear in the minutes happens in the
corridors, in the coffee breaks, and in the walks before dinner, and
can't always be quantified. The conferencegoers get to know each
other, and then when they go home they can pick up the phone, or
send a paper they have ready to a new friend and it gets the dialogue
out of the plastic binders.

I have already mentioned two representatives of automobile unions
at one conference on Japan. (Pursuit of corridor conversations has
taken me to more than thirty meetings on Japan, and I've been the
moderator of half a dozen.) The conferencegoers were thumbing
through their appendices and charts which delineated the flow of

cars in one direction and currency in the other. The Americans were for free trade, but couldn't seem to sell their cars in Japan, so what was wrong? The American union official slammed his binder shut and burst into an impromptu recitation of the problems of his members. Fifteen percent of them were unemployed and couldn't make the payments on their cars and trucks, even if they were *Japanese* cars . . .

"Fifteen percent?" said the Japanese union leader. He asked the translator to repeat the number. "I would get fired at *three* percent."

"Three?" said the American, and asked the translator to repeat the number. The Japanese union official was in vigorous conversation with the Japanese official from MITI, and of course it is MITI that helps determine the "guidelines" that voluntarily restrict the sales of Japanese cars to the United States. The statistics were all in the appendices, but not the *image* of a single automobile union man watching the repo man drive his car away. Perhaps it helped change the MITI position.

The dialogue goes on: how do we correct the imbalances? How do we sell to Japan? What about the non-tariff barriers, those customs and practices that aren't on the government schedules or the appendices of our conference books? How could we get the Japanese to loan some of that huge surplus to Latin America, so the Latins could buy again?

It takes a while to understand that understanding itself is only the first step. Then you have the consensus on each side, remember, it takes sixty-four *ringi* to get a Japanese decision, and the climate keeps changing. In dollar terms, the Japanese steelworkers get more than $20 an hour. Aiwa, the Japanese electronics company, is moving its production down the Rim to Singapore and closing one of its plants in Japan. Toshiba is setting up a plant to make VCRs in that faraway country on the Rim, the United States, back where it all began. If the Japanese wake up one morning and don't buy our Treasury bonds, how will the Post Office get the money to deliver the mail?

The statements of gravity—"the situation is serious"—and the accompanying hand-wringing in the press are not merely eruptions of pessimism. They are the tom-toms that summon the elders to the council fire. Sometimes what is produced really has a powerful impact. Take Social Security.

For example, a decade ago, there were full-page ads for the financial newsletters that warned of Great Cataclysm: Social Security was going bankrupt! The coffers would be bare! The newsletters assumed there was no solution, the clowns in Washington would simply let Social Security go bellyup. Many of these newsletters recommended buying gold and silver, and they even listed the phone numbers of friendly bullion dealers. That was the wrong time to buy gold and silver, but the retirees were n ade to feel like frightened primitives, subject to the random, unfathomable rages of the storm gods, like the Senoi of Malaysia, who peeled off their clothes and prostrated themselves in storms, back before they worked in the semiconductor plants.

The tom-toms went out about Social Security, the op ed pieces appeared, the future was dire. Alan Greenspan was appointed to head a Commission in 1981, and the Commission found, at first, rough waters politically. Then in January 1983, Senator Daniel Patrick Moynihan went up to Senator Robert Dole during a Senate recess— they were both on the Commission—and said they'd better meet informally and do something about Social Security. The Commission met for two weeks in Jim Baker's basement, and hammered out an agreement that passed the Congress in April 1983. Social Security was switched from pay-as-you-go to fully funded. That meant increased contributions from all of us, the equivalent of a tax increase. Social Security now has one of the largest revenue streams in the world. The impact is staggering, but you don't hear much about it.

Social Security funds are put into special issues of Treasury bonds. The Social Security funds are already $30 billion in surplus; without Social Security the Treasury would be borrowing $30 billion somewhere else. By 1995, the Social Security funds will have from $70 to $100 billion. Congress designed the buildup of surplus to accommodate the retirement of the baby boom generation, when there will be many more retirees than contributors to the funds.

With some fiscal prudence in Congress, the 1995 fiscal budget deficit would be less than $100 billion, and on a bookkeeping basis, at least, we would have a surplus for the first time since 1960! And as the funds built up—why, we could start to retire the national debt! Think of it!

No wonder the bond dealers began to salivate. No deficit? Why, there might be a *shortage* of long-term government bonds. Grab 'em now!

Don't hold your breath on that one. History suggests the trust funds will never wipe out the deficit, much less pay off the debt. Congress will raid it. Medicare, for example, is in surplus at the moment but will need constant increases in premiums to stay that way. The temptation will be to raid the Social Security trust funds. The assumptions about the buildup may turn out to be wrong. Recessions could diminish the flow of revenues.

Still, we had a crisis, and now we have a flow of savings in a country that has a very low savings rate. It doesn't relieve Congress of the need to keep the spending down, but with all the anxiety about the bad news, we should pause from time to time when things turn out right.

The tom-toms will go out again, you can be sure, and it will be said the situation is serious, and it will be. Here is something already on the horizon:

1992. This date has Europe giddy, but it still doesn't mean much to most Americans. In 1992, the European Economic Community will meld into one economic unit. British banks will take deposits in Italy, Danish banks will loan in Ireland. The diplomas of Dutch psychiatrists will be recognized in Spain, French lawyers will be able to argue in British courts. A truck that starts out in Britain today must carry thirty-five different customs forms to cross the Continent; in 1992, it will need only one, as easy as driving across the United States. There will be no residence requirements, the Portuguese can move to Germany, the Germans can move to Greece. The first venture-capital-sponsored Pan-European semiconductor firm is already launched, the banks and manufacturing firms are circling each other, and the mega-investment bankers are circling them both, preaching economies of scale.

For a thousand years, the nations of Europe have been at each other's throats. The British bowmen loosed their long arrows at the French horsemen at Agincourt, the Prussians met the British to turn back Napoleon in the farming countryside of Belgium, the Germans pounded Rotterdam into rubble. And now, Europassports! A market

100 million people larger than the United States! The Eurocrats say the growth rate will double, unemployment will drop. Of course, there are a lot of entrenched habits to overcome, a few hurdles left, but the European Community, we are told, will burst forth like another Japan . . .

. . . *another Japan! We're still dealing with the last one!*

Predictions are always risky. When the prestigious *Economist* magazine took a stab at the future in its book, *2025*, in 1984, looking back from 2025, it began its "history" with President Gary Hart! *Education* is already high on the tom-tom list.

In the 1990s, there will be more jobs in the United States than people to fill them. That's because, following the "baby boom," we had a "baby bust," with relatively few entrants into the work force. The economy will keep growing, result, more jobs than applicants.

That's the good news. The bad news is that the young people out there won't fill many of the jobs. They won't have the skills. So the jobs and the unemployed will exist side by side for a while, and then the jobs will be exported, unless we correct the situation. The openings in fiber-optic technology in Rochester don't help the minimum wage people in Buffalo.

From experience, I tread warily when commenting on higher education. Some years ago, my state produced a new Higher Education Act and a salty chancellor called Ralph Dungan. Dungan gave me one of those '60s speeches. "I have a job for you that pays nothing, is very hard work, won't get you any thanks, but you do something for the people." Weeks after I became a trustee, Dungan suggested that X college needed a new president, somebody dynamic who could turn it around. "Fire the guy there now and get a better one." *"Me?"* I said. "Fire the *president*?" "That's what trustees do," he said. "They fire presidents." As the head of a search committee I recruited a new president. Dungan was impressed. "How did you get *that* guy for *that* college?" he said. "I promised him he could have the next college we build from the ground up," I said, "with a lake in the middle, all the dorms on one side, and all the classrooms in a kind of galleria on the other side." (We did build the college with the lake, and my president is still there.)

It occurred to me that we did not really know how to build a state college system, so I went to California, which had an excellent system. I went with a notebook, asking naive questions. If you were starting today, what would be your priorities? What are the biggest potential problems, what grabs you that you don't expect? Who are the ten smartest people in this field, and what have they written? And so on. The California people were very nice and sent me all around the system. Then, at Dungan's request, I gave a little talk from my notebook at a major assembly of educators. I was not popular. Where was my Ph.D. in education? What did *I* know, anyway? They kicked me like a soccer ball from one end of the room to another. Even today, my ribs hurt in thunderstorms. Dungan whispered, like a manager whose fighter is on one knee after a nine count, "You're doin' good, buddy, you got 'em scared." But I learned that, like all establishments and monopolies, education resists change.

Educators can't do the job separately from the society as a whole, of course. California educators compared the school problems of the 1940s to those of the 1980s. The discipline problems of the 1940s were: talking, chewing gum, making noise, running in the halls, getting out of turn in line, wearing improper clothing, and not putting paper in the wastebaskets. The '80s problems were: drug abuse, alcohol, rape, robbery, assault, burglary, arson, murder, vandalism, extortion, gang warfare and venereal disease. But there was also a radical change in home life between those periods. As Harold Hodgkinson points out in a study of the Institute for Education Leadership, "In 1955, 60 percent of the households in the United States consisted of a working father, a housewife mother, and two or more school age children. In 1980, that family unit was only 11 percent of our homes, and in 1985, it was 7 percent, an astonishing change."

American public high schools graduate 700,000 functionally illiterate students every year, and nearly a million drop out. The dropout rates in many urban high schools is 50 percent; among Hispanic students, it can reach 75 percent. Four out of five young adults cannot summarize the main point of a newspaper article, and many of them never see newspapers anyway. They cannot read a bus schedule or figure the change from a restaurant bill. The Committee for Economic Development says that each year's dropouts cost the country more than $240 billion in lost earnings and foregone taxes. It will cost American industry $25 billion a year just for *remedial* training.

In New York City, only 23 percent of the sixteen- to nineteen-year-old age group is *in* the work force, or even looking for work. When New York Telephone sought to fill 2,000 *entry*-level jobs, it had to screen 90,000 applicants.

The problem isn't just at the entry level. The National Science Foundation says we are moving toward "virtual scientific and technological illiteracy."

The Foundation obviously means on a national level, taken as a whole, because there seems to be a new computer or software magazine every month. Taken as a whole, says Frank Press, the president of the National Academy of Sciences, it's a disaster. In order to be internationally competitive, American industry has to be capital intensive, it has to have the newest and most innovative machinery. But you can't operate numerically controlled machine tools if you don't understand fractions and scales. Aerospace and defense companies already use CADCAM and CADCAE techniques, computer-aided design and manufacturing, but as the demands of the jobs grow, the number of qualified blue-collar workers shrinks, and the companies resort to bidding workers away from each other. The aerospace companies in California formed a consortium with junior colleges to create an apprenticeship program with degrees in manufacturing technology. Ninety-five percent of Japanese students finish high school, and because they have been going to school 240 days a year rather than 180, they have completed the equivalent of two years of college.

Wait, it gets scarier. A majority of high school seniors can't identify Joseph Stalin, Winston Churchill, or who was on what side in World War II. They don't know what the war was about. They don't know *Brown vs. the Board of Education,* the 1954 Supreme Court decision affirming racial equality in education, so they don't have a clear idea of how democracies *reform.* They don't understand the First and Fifth Amendments, and they don't understand jury trials and the obligation to serve on a jury.

Left alone, you could extrapolate a population that could be sold anything by a television commercial that plucked at emotions, or a demagogue who distorted facts, ignored history, and played to prejudices.

If you *don't* hear a lot about this in the years to come, then something is really wrong. Democracies do have the capacity to repair themselves, but first the bad news has to get out. If a master teacher of thirty years can't make as much as a new lawyer one day out of law school, something is still wrong. The bad news is good news, and television won't take a picture of the good news anyway. I'm not prescriptive. My ribs still hurt.

Scientific illiteracy goes on side by side with the biggest explosion of scientific knowledge in history For example:

* Between six and seven thousand scientific articles are written every *day*.
* Scientific and technical information increases by 13 percent a year, which means it doubles every five and a half years.
* This rate will soon jump to 40 percent a year because of new and more powerful information systems.
* The above numbers are all probably obsolete already.

Cray has sold a supercomputer it will not build for three years, which will be able to do sixteen billion calculations a second. Tell the truth, I'm not sure what you do with a machine that can do sixteen billion calculations a second.

That wasn't on the evening news, because you can't take a picture of a computer that doesn't exist. Frequently, the real news is not on the news, because the perspective is wrong or because the real news is not visual. The real news is that the grain belt has moved north 200 miles. A picture of a seed, though, doesn't play like a fire or an automobile crash or a train wreck. A researcher splicing a plant gene could—down the road—turn the Soviet Union into a grain exporter, because new seeds travel everywhere. That could change the course of history.

A lot of things have gone *right* that don't always get noticed. We have built up the biggest debts in our history, but we do start new businesses at the rate of 700,000 a year. We created 16 million new jobs in the '80s. The personal tax rates went down, but the tax revenues went *up*, from $517 billion a year in 1980 to $909 billion in 1988.

When we talk about stock markets, we generally measure them in Averages, like the Dow Jones, which is made up of mature companies. But the Averages do not "see" or take in new companies, startups like Sun and Compaq that go from nothing to a billion dollars in sales in less than a decade, and create billions of dollars of market value. We will have more of this.

The four-letter word of the 1980s is *debt*. Bad news, and we haven't heard nearly enough about it. We've issued a lot of claim checks on the country, and we have to get some of them back. It can be done, but it will be work, and you can't let your congressman speak cotton. In 1980, the external pluses and minuses looked very roughly like this:

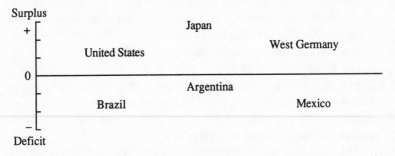

Eight years later, it looked like this:

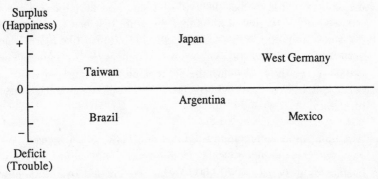

We are the world's largest debtor, and we passed Brazil and Mexico as if they were standing still. When this happens to countries like Brazil and Mexico, the creditors blow the whistle. Tighten your belts, say the creditors. Increase your savings, stop your spending, earn your way.

Why didn't this happen to us? Well, we do get some gentle clucking from, say, the finance ministers of the European Community. They say, we'd better fix it, but gently, slowly—because their companies have been selling into this market, American deficits have meant prosperity for European and Japanese exporters. The whistle is late.

First, we have a large reservoir of moral credit from our position as a world military leader and from our past as an investor and lender. Second, the dollar is *the key currency*. Dollars are what the world banks in, insures in, denominates. Before the dollar, it was the pound sterling, and the British got an extension on the tenure of their empire because the world hadn't found another currency in which to denominate. If you operate in the key currency, it takes longer for the whistle to blow.

The trouble with debts is that you have to pay them back, and the interest compounds against you. That does sound like third-grade arithmetic, but it isn't news and we pay no attention to it. If we owe $400 billion today to foreigners, at 10 percent, in seven years we will owe $800 billion without borrowing another penny—and we *will* be borrowing another penny tomorrow. The financial threat is obvious. Someday the creditors fatigue, and the key currency becomes less key. Markets are bigger than governments, and it doesn't even have to be debated in a parliament. Eight Japanese insurance company portfolio managers having lunch decide the *gaijin* are never going to get their act together, and they go back upstairs, hit the computer keys, and bring the funds back to Dai Nippon. Interest rates spike up in the United States, and we remember what recession was like. Or a depreciating dollar accelerates inflation, and the foreigners cash in their chits for farms and buildings and companies, tangible assets. They can't cash the chits for Waikiki because they already own it.

If you think the $400 billion of debt is a Marshall Plan from the kind-spirited Japanese, then everything is wonderful. If it isn't, the next generation will have to work hard to get some of the claim checks back, and they won't especially see the fruits of their labors; the house is still the house but they're paying the second mortgage. That could cost something in social mobility and a dynamic sense of progress. We've been the country where the foreign physicists come to study and then stay to work on superconductors.

The worst development of all would be if we lost the faith that we can fix what isn't right. So we had better hear a lot of bad news about debt. That would be good news.

It takes only a moment of stepping back to realize that we could be entering a brilliant period of history. For perspective, go back fifty years. A quarter of our work force was unemployed, and capitalism was being pronounced dead. Democracy itself was considered weak, indecisive, decadent, no match, said some, for the might of the militaristic states. The Soviet Union and Nazi Germany were murdering their own citizens, preaching the holiness of terror, and no one knew where they could be stopped. It makes the '80s look lucky and benign.

Japan was a military state, fighting across East Asia, with plans to subdue the rest of Asia. Spain was a Fascist country. So was Italy. Today Spain is in the takeoff stage, Italy is booming, and both are democracies. The Latin American dictatorships are becoming democracies, albeit fragile and indebted. Japan and Germany are engines of economic prosperity, like the United States. Communist China, eyeing the "Tigers" around it, is moving toward a market economy. The Soviet Union is calculating the cost of the arms race and trying to figure how to open up. This is the real news. It is our system the whole world is moving toward, not religiously, but pragmatically.

Closed societies don't generate bad news. Kim Il Sung doesn't want to hear it. The strength of a great society is the spirit and capacity to change.

The British visitor is watching television. He is staring at the Verrazano Bridge over New York harbor, a long, graceful span packed with runners. It is the New York marathon.

"Unbelievable," he says. "Let me understand this. Twenty *thousand* ordinary people are going to run twenty-six straight miles. Bank clerks, secretaries, dentists, the lot."

"Surely that happens in Britain," I said.

"Not like this. Twenty thousand *Greeks* don't run from Marathon to Athens, and a marathon is the distance from Marathon to Athens. As I recall, the Greek who ran it was bringing the news of victory over the Persians—Pheidippides, was it? He was a soldier, and I think he dropped dead. These are ordinary people, working adults, people with jobs."

"A lot of people just watch on television," I said.

"Things do bubble up in America," said the British visitor. "You never know what it's going to be. When did everyone decide to go running? Suddenly, millions of people, tens of millions of people, are running, and then the French discover *le jogging,* and so does the rest of the world. Then the Americans decide to stop smoking. It's not healthy. The Europeans are still smoking, but the rest of the world will soon start to pay attention. Why does it happen here first? What makes it happen? Where is the place it starts?"

ABOUT THE AUTHOR

Adam Smith is the host of "Adam Smith's Money World," the Emmy Award-winning TV show now in its fifth year on public television. He is the author of four previous books: *Supermoney, Powers of Mind, Paper Money,* and *The Money Game,* which Nobel Prize recipient Paul Samuelson called "a modern-day classic." Adam Smith first appeared in print in 1966 when a lively, irreverent column appeared in *New York* magazine under the name "Adam Smith," a pseudonym which for a short time masked the identity of George J. W. Goodman. Mr. Goodman has had a double career in finance and letters. Born in St. Louis, he was graduated from Harvard *magna cum laude.* While a Rhodes Scholar at Oxford, he wrote a novel instead of a Ph.D. thesis, which was published as *The Bubble Makers.* He went to work on Wall Street first as a magazine editor, then as a securities analyst and fund manager. At the same time, writing evenings and weekends, he published three more novels, one of which, *The Wheeler Dealers,* also became a successful film.

The Adam Smith columns brought together his unique combination of financial and literary talent and won an international audience of investment professionals. Mr. Goodman became a co-founder of *New York,* of two more regional magazines, and of the financial journal *Institutional Investor.* He has been a member of the Editorial Board of *The New York Times,* and among his corporate directorships have been those of a worldwide hotel chain, a major airline, an international mutual fund, and a producer of specialty chemicals.